When the Cubs Won It All

When the Cubs Won It All

The 1908 Championship Season

GEORGE R. MATTHEWS

McFarland & Company, Inc., Publishers
Jefferson, North Carolina, and London

LIBRARY OF CONGRESS CATALOGUING-IN-PUBLICATION DATA

Matthews, George R., 1950–
    When the Cubs won it all : the 1908 championship season /
George R. Matthews
       p.   cm.
    Includes bibliographical references and index.

    ISBN 978-0-7864-3495-4
    softcover : 50# alkaline paper ∞

    1. Chicago Cubs (Baseball team)   I. Title.
GV875.C6M38 2009
796.357'640977311—dc22
                                                                   2009006863

British Library cataloguing data are available

©2009 George R. Matthews. All rights reserved

*No part of this book may be reproduced or transmitted in any form
or by any means, electronic or mechanical, including photocopying
or recording, or by any information storage and retrieval system,
without permission in writing from the publisher.*

On the cover: West Side Grounds in Chicago, New York Giants vs.
the Chicago Cubs, August 30, 1908 (Library of Congress)

Manufactured in the United States of America

*McFarland & Company, Inc., Publishers
   Box 611, Jefferson, North Carolina 28640
   www.mcfarlandpub.com*

To the memory of
Reet and Max Howell
for their kindness, guidance,
and inspiration

Acknowledgments

Members of the Society for American Baseball Research (SABR) graciously responded to my many requests for specific information concerning the West Side Grounds, World Series medallions, photographs, and more. Mark Fimoff, Marc Okkonen, and Mike Reischl deserve special recognition and my sincere appreciation. Mark Fimoff, an expert on Cubs photographs, made an extra effort to find several obscure photographs, including Del Howard's World Series medallion of 1907. Author Marc Okkonen provided several photographs and schematic drawings along with his letter regarding the appearance of the entrance to the West Side Grounds. Mike Reischl, president of a special group of Cub baseball fans called The Way Out In Left Field Society, provided the information that solved one of my childhood riddles. As a kid I often heard, "You're way out in left field." Since I played second base, I knew my teammates were not referring to my position. I quickly figured out the phrase meant to be crazy or nuts, but I never did understand why left field; center field was always further out. After all these years, Mike and The Way Out In Left Field Society came to my rescue. The phrase originated in Chicago. Behind the left field wall of the West Side Grounds ballpark, the home of the Chicago Cubs from 1893 to 1914, stood a hospital for mentally impaired patients. Fans and players inside the park could often hear boisterous hospital patients. Over the years, the phrase spread throughout the country, eventually reaching me in Baltimore County, Maryland.

My heartfelt expression of gratitude goes to Sandra Marshall, my partner in life. An accomplished writer and award-winning photographer, she unselfishly devoted many hours to reading and making editing suggestions for the manuscript. Also, a member of the American Society of Indexers (ASI), Sandra, to my great relief and appreciation, provided the index.

Most of all, my thanks to *Chicago Tribune* reporters Charles Dryden and I.E. Sanborn.

Contents

Acknowledgments vii
Preface 1
Introduction 3

1. Spring Training 7
2. Fast Start 30
3. Caught in the Rain 46
4. The Brawl 68
5. Backs, Legs, and Thumbs 91
6. Bottomed Out 116
7. Touching Second, Twice 141
8. Triumphs and Scandal 173

Chapter Notes 203
Bibliography 211
Index 213

Preface

This is the story of a single team for a single season. In 1908, the Chicago Cubs ruled baseball. The names Tinker, Evers, and Chance, Three-Finger Brown, and Jack "The Giant Killer" Pfiester still echo through the years.

From spring training to the World Series, *Chicago Tribune* reporter Charlie Dryden witnessed the players' every move, on and off the field. On the sport pages of the *Tribune*, Dryden provided a daily account of Cub baseball heroics and miscues. He also wrote a daily column called "Cub Notes" describing the team gossip and providing spicier player anecdotes. Cartoons, drawn by Claire Briggs, provided visual highlights for Dryden's stories. This is the first time most of Briggs' cartoons have been published since 1908.

The *Chicago Tribune* and *New York Times* on microfilm, from February through October 1908, served as my primary resources. The bibliography lists the secondary sources consulted. Three excellent books (Fleming's *The Unforgettable Season*, Anderson's *More Than Merkle*, and Murphy's *Crazy '08*) have been published on the 1908 baseball season, but this book is the first to place the emphasis squarely on Chicago and the Cubs.

The inspiration for this book came during research for an earlier book, *America's First Olympics*. As I scanned the sports pages of Chicago and St. Louis newspapers (the 1904 Olympics was originally awarded to Chicago, then transferred to St. Louis), I often found myself distracted by baseball stories about the Cubs or Cardinals while searching for articles on the Olympics. Reading game accounts and stories about the players, I felt transported to a bygone era and struck upon the idea of writing a book about one great team's greatest season as experienced by their fans. I knew the 1908 season to be the most exciting in baseball history, as three outstanding clubs — Wagner's Pirates, Mathewson's Giants, and the Cubs of Tinker, Evers, and Chance — battled it out for the NL pennant. It also happened to be the last year the Cubs won the World Series.

Introduction

Once there was a time before television or radio, before Babe Ruth, even before Wrigley Field, when the Chicago Cubs ruled baseball. After two consecutive National League pennants and a World Series championship, the Cubs reached the pinnacle of their greatness in 1908. Their names echo through the years: Tinker, Evers, and Chance; Three-Finger Brown; Wildfire Schulte and Circus Solly Hofman; Johnny Kling and Big Ed; Orvie and The Giant Killer; Chick and Lundy; Sheck, Steiny, and the Rabbit. The best team in baseball history, they thrilled Chicago with their heroics.

"Baseball Stories by Dryden and Sy in *The Tribune* This Year" greeted Chicago fans at every home game as they took their seats in West Side Park. The huge letters on the wall behind the outfield bleachers extended from center field to the right-field corner. No other advertising appeared in the ballpark. Charles Dryden and Irving Ellis (I.E.) Sanborn, popularly known as Sy, were the two sportswriters for the *Chicago Tribune*. Dryden chiefly covered the Cubs, while Sanborn concentrated on the American League White Sox.

The "Mark Twain of sportswriters,"[1] Charley Dryden wrapped the game results around a humorous incident giving readers an entertaining narrative. Dryden is considered "one of the first, most popular and most influential baseball writers who ever lived."[2] Ring Lardner, complimented on his own humor-filled sportswriting, retorted, "Me, a humorist? Have you ... read any of Charley Dryden's stuff lately? He makes me look like a novice."[3] Dryden coined many player nicknames and aphorisms: "Peerless Leader" for Frank Chance, "The Old Roman" for Charles Comisky, "Bonehead" for Fred Merkle, "The Hitless Wonders" for the 1906 World Champion Chicago White Sox, and, most famously, "Washington—first in war, first in peace, and last in the American League."[4] In 1908, Dryden became a charter member of the Baseball Writers' Association of America and, in 1965, posthumously received the J.G. Taylor Spink Award for excellence in baseball writing, the equivalent of membership in the National Baseball Hall of Fame.

Despite little formal education, Dryden was a natural-born writer. Working as an iron-molder at a foundry in Monmouth, Illinois, his hometown, Dryden wrote stories about his work environment to amuse his friends. One friend said he was wasting his talent and told him to quit the foundry and become a newspaper writer. The thirty-two-year-old Dryden took his friend's advice, moved to Chicago, and joined the *Chicago Sunday Times* in 1889. The next year, Dryden became one of the nation's first sportswriters with the *San Francisco Examiner*. In 1898, he moved to New York to join the *Evening Herald*. Dryden's description of a game at the Polo Grounds offended the Giants' owner, who barred Dryden from the press box. One story claims that Dryden climbed a telegraph pole outside the ballpark and, perched on a cross-bar, continued to report the games day after day.[5] The telegraph pole may be legend, but Dryden was barred from the Polo Grounds and did continue to report each day's game perched, not on a telegraph pole, but atop Coogan's Bluff, which overlooked the Polo Grounds. But according to Dryden, "the team looked no better from there."[6]

Incompatible with the New York Giants, Dryden moved to Philadelphia in 1899 to cover the Athletics for the *Philadelphia North American*. He remained in Philadelphia for six years and in 1905 wrote a book, *The Champion Athletics*. Philadelphia won the American League championship in that year, but lost the World Series to the Giants. Dryden ignored the Series in his book, calling the 1905 postseason a waste of time and saying he preferred to go fishing.

In 1906, Dryden accepted a position with the *Chicago Tribune*, and he spent the rest of his career in Chicago. Tragically, his career came to an end when he suffered a stroke in 1921 at the age of 64. He lived his final years with his sister in Biloxi, Mississippi, dying February 11, 1931, a month short of his seventy-fourth birthday. The *Chicago Tribune* headline read, "Charles Dryden, Humorist and Baseball Writer, Dies at 74."

In 1908, Dryden was in his prime. His arrival in Chicago two years earlier was perfect baseball timing. The Cubs established a record single-season winning percentage of .763, 116 wins against only 36 losses, and, most satisfying to Dryden, ended the two-year championship reign of the New York Giants. And, 1906 was an all–Chicago World Series. The powerful Cubs were heavy favorites to win, but lost to their cross-town rivals four games to two. Dryden tagged the light-hitting White Sox team that somehow managed to squeeze out just enough runs to win four games, "The Hitless Wonders." The Cubs repeated as National League champions in 1907 and won their first World Series, dominating Ty Cobb and the Detroit Tigers, four games to none.

The most memorable and dramatic baseball season in history? Without doubt, 1908. Pennant winners in both leagues were decided on the last day of the season with three teams in each league vying for honors. In the National League, the Cubs, Pirates, and Giants battled all season for the crown. Pittsburgh needed one more win in their last game of the season against the Cubs to win the pennant, but the Cubs victory sent the Pirates home empty-handed and created a first-place tie between the Cubs and Giants. It all came down to the first postseason playoff game, a replay of the infamous "Merkle Game," to decide the National League champion.

Charley Dryden told the Cubs 1908 story every day in the *Chicago Tribune*. With original and entertaining style, he gave Chicago readers the baseball results and, in a special "Cub Notes" column, provided spicy player anecdotes and human-interest stories. Graphic humorist Clare A. Briggs complimented Dryden's writing with comic illustrations on the juiciest Cub stories. All season, from spring training to the World Series, Dryden rode the train with the players, ate meals with them, gambled and drank with them, watched them on and off the field, and wrote their story.

Chapter 1

Spring Training

Frank Chance, thirty-year-old Cubs manager and first baseman, plunged through the Polk street station doors just in time to see his train inch away from the depot. Looking about frantically, he threw his suitcase to Charlie Williams, Cubs secretary and treasurer, and sprinted furiously down the platform. Teammates pulled him on board at the last instant. Catching his breath, the Cubs manager realized that in his haste to fling his body aboard the train, he had not only sacrificed his suitcase, but also failed to get his ticket from Williams. But Williams wired the conductor, and Chance was allowed to remain aboard for the trip to West Baden, Indiana.[1]

The reigning champions of baseball, the Chicago Cubs, to a player, expected to win again in 1908. Most had been together since 1906 when they won 116 regular-season games, setting a record. They repeated as National League champions in 1907 and won their first World Series, sweeping four straight games from the Detroit Tigers of the American League. Eleven-year veteran pitcher Chick Fraser and utility men Henry "Heinie" Zimmerman, Del Howard and Blaine Durbin were the only exceptions. Fraser joined the Cubs in 1907, replacing Jack Taylor, who retired after that season. Zimmerman played five games with the Cubs in 1907, his rookie season. Third-year big leaguer Del Howard had also come to the Cubs in 1907, from Boston. Pitcher and outfielder Blaine "Kid" Durbin, another 1907 rookie, split his time by pitching in five games and playing five games in the outfield. The "Sigma Outfield" (three S's) of Jimmy Sheckard in left, Jimmy Slagle, a Cub since 1902, in center, and Frank "Wildfire" Schulte in right, formed when Brooklyn traded nine-year veteran Sheckard to Chicago in 1906. Schulte joined the Cubs as a rookie in 1904. Johnny Kling joined the Cubs in 1900 as a rookie and became the regular catcher in 1902. Pat Moran played five years in Boston before joining the Cubs in 1906 as the backup catcher. Utility man Artie Hofman played his rookie year with Pittsburgh before joining the Cubs in 1904 at the age of twenty-one. Traded from Cincinnati, eight-year veteran third baseman Harry Steinfeldt joined the team in 1906, rounding out the infield with shortstop Joe Tinker, second baseman Johnny Evers, and first baseman and manager Frank Chance. Tinker and Evers both arrived in Chicago as rookies in 1902. Chance also began his career as a Cub, but in 1898 as a twenty-year-old catcher. He converted to a full-time first baseman in 1903 and became the player-manager in 1905 when manager Frank Selee's ill health forced his retirement sixty-five games into the season. Of the eight position players, five (Tinker, Evers, Chance, Kling, and Schulte) had played only for the Cubs. Besides Fraser, the six-man pitching staff consisted of Jack Pfiester, Carl Lundgren, Orval Overall, Ed Reulbach, and the ace of the staff, Mordecai "Three-Finger" Brown. Chicago planned to carry a twenty-man roster, and with nineteen Cubs returning only five rookies were invited to spring training.[2]

It was a ragged departure from Chicago for Chance and his team. The scheduled evening departure had been moved up to 8:30 A.M. The bats had not been loaded, and groundskeeper Charlie Kuhn, remaining behind, still had the key to the uniform trunk in his pocket. Evers did not get word of the time change and arrived in Chicago at noon. Unperturbed, he spent the afternoon with Cubs President Charles Murphy and other friends, then collected Chance's suitcase and one bat bag, and settled aboard the evening train. President Murphy did not accompany the team. He remained in Chicago to supervise improvements to the Cubs home field, West Side Park, especially the grandstand extension, and to establish new ticket prices.[3]

The Cubs scheduled six weeks of spring training in preparation for their April 14 opening day. The first week, in West Baden Mineral Springs Resort, was strictly for conditioning; no games were scheduled. After West Baden, the Cotton States League team in Vicksburg, Mississippi, hosted the Cubs for two weeks and provided the competition for the first two exhibition games. After another exhibition game in Meridian, Mississippi, the Cubs embarked on a three-week barnstorming tour, winding their way north in time for the season opening game in Cincinnati.[4]

On Wednesday, March 4, Chance and his party arrived in West Baden just before 6:00 P.M. after a nine-and-a-half-hour train ride. The players included Chick Fraser, Joe Tinker, Carl Lundgren, Jimmy Slagle, Pat Moran, Artie Hofman, Heinie Zimmerman, and a rookie, Joe Donahue. Also along were A. Bert Semmens, the new Cubs trainer for 1908, and the wives of Fraser and Tinker. Expecting several players to be waiting, Chance was surprised that only pitcher Orval Overall and his wife were on hand to greet the Cub contingent. The evening train brought three more Cubs to town.

1. Spring Training

CUBS SPRING TRAINING SCHEDULE

March 5 to 12	at West Baden, IN
March 13 to 24	at Vicksburg, MS
March 25	at Meridian, MS
March 26, 27	at Montgomery, AL
March 28 to 30	at Atlanta, GA
March 31	at Chattanooga, TN
April 1 to 3	at Birmingham, AL
April 4, 5	at Memphis, TN
April 6, 7	at Nashville, TN
April 8	at Evansville, IN
April 9	at Terre Haute, IN
April 10	at Fort Wayne, IN
April 11	at Indianapolis, IN
April 12, 13	at Dayton, IN

Mordecai "Three-Finger" Brown came from his home in Rosedale, Indiana, about 100 miles northwest of West Baden. Brown lost the index finger of his right hand in a childhood farming accident to gain the "Three-Finger" title. The press also gave Brown the nickname "Miner," referring to his young days working for a mining company in Indiana. But Brown, good at arithmetic, worked as a bookkeeper, not a miner. The press ignored this detail. His teammates used neither term. They called him "Brownie." Along with Brown, pitcher "Big Ed" Reulbach and recently signed rookie catcher Vincent Campbell both arrived from St. Louis. At 6'1", 190 lbs., Reulbach was not the largest Cub pitcher, that distinction belonged to Overall (6'2", 214 lbs.), but the Chicago press tagged him "Big Ed." Southpaw pitcher Jack Pfiester and third baseman Harry Steinfeldt were expected from Cincinnati, and right fielder Frank Schulte was on his way from Syracuse, New York. Catcher Johnny Kling would come later; he had been granted an extended leave of absence to compete in a professional billiards tournament in St. Louis. The rest of the Cub's 24 players were scheduled to arrive within the week. Players, manager, trainer and wives already in town settled into the hotel, their home for the next week.[5]

A robust thunderstorm also arrived late Wednesday evening. By morning, the local stream flooded its banks, depositing a layer of mucky yellow mud on the grounds of the hotel and the baseball diamond. Chance and center fielder Jimmy Slagle, at 5'7" the smallest of the Cubs, set out on an early-morning reconnaissance. Struggling through the mud from the hotel, Chance took a look at the baseball field, which, according to *Chicago Tribune* reporter Charles Dryden, who traveled with the team, "resembled a large German pancake full of gravy." The mud was so thick and heavy in places that short-legged Jimmy Slagle needed help pulling his legs out.[6]

Unable to conquer the mud, Chance hit upon a new idea for conditioning his players. Shortly after noon, Chance assembled his athletes and led them on a hike along the railroad tracks to the nearby town of French Lick, a few miles from West Baden. Johnny Evers had arrived on the morning train, but without the key to the uniform trunk, so the players trudged the rails in street shoes, pants, shirts and hats. Chance left instructions with a porter to hire a locksmith to burglar the uniform trunk. Evers, nicknamed the "Crab" both for his manner of patrolling the ground around second base and his cranky disposition, did not accompany his dutiful teammates. Characteristically, he remained in his room writing letters. Neither did affable pitcher Jack Pfiester trudge the rails. For the past two weeks, Jack had walked the floor day and night, bottle-feeding his new baby. Chance ordered the new father to take time to recuperate; he needed rest more than exercise.[7]

The weather improved on Friday, but mud still prevented use of the baseball field. In the morning, Chance made the squad repeat the previous day's hike to French Lick. But when the sun broke through in the afternoon, a few high spots of dry land were found for the Cubs, now in uniform, to throw and bat for a couple of hours. A promising rookie pitcher had arrived the previous day and joined his teammates for a light workout. He was Martin Walsh, the younger brother of "Big Ed" Walsh of the cross-town White Sox. Four years younger than "Big Ed," Martin was almost as big as his famous brother and was said to be a sure bet to make the club. Good-natured and full of spirit, Walsh came to the Cubs from the Danville team in the Virginia League. He told the press that he hoped for a Cubs versus White Sox World Series in October, in which the Walsh brothers would oppose each other on the mound.[8] Brother Ed had won twenty-four games the year before and beaten the Cubs twice in the 1906 World Series, leading his White Sox to an unexpected victory over the favored Cubs.

The weather was perfect and the ground dry for Saturday's practice. The players, happy to abandon their daily hike along the rails, had full sessions of throwing and batting in both the morning and afternoon. Ed Reulbach impressed his teammates with both his velocity and lack of control by heaving several fast balls into the adjacent stream. At the end of the marathon training sessions, most players complained of soreness. Shortstop Joe Tinker developed a charley horse. Even Martin Walsh, iron-armed rookie pitcher, complained of arm soreness. The exertion, however, did not pre-

1. Spring Training

vent the young hurler from impressing an audience with his singing in the hotel dining room after dinner. After a booming rendition of several Irish tunes and other sentimental ballads, the lingering diners expressed their pleasure with both the fine quality of his voice and the impressive strength of his vocal cords.[9]

Another pitcher, Jack Pfiester, provided entertainment of a different sort later in the evening when a small group of Cubs decided to try out the local bowling alley. Pfiester liked to bowl but had a hard time finding a ball to fit his large hand, especially his enormous thumb. During a roll, his thumb stuck, and the ball dragged him half the length of the wooden alley. According to journalist Dryden, "In transit Mr. Pfiester resembled the tail of a comet all spraddled out." It took several anxious moments of gentle wiggling before he was able to carefully extricate his thumb from the bowling ball, greatly relieved that his pitching hand survived intact. Back-up catcher Pat Moran won the Cubs bowling tournament, but the chagrined Pfiester won the entertainment award and the sympathy of his teammates. Arriving Saturday evening, right fielder Frank Schulte was too late for practice but not for the evening's entertainment, enjoying both Walsh's voice and Pfiester's bowling. Schulte explained that he was late because he needed extra time to sell his racehorse back in Syracuse. He confirmed his story by producing a roll of 650 one-dollar bills from the pocket of his trousers.[10]

Sunday was a scheduled day of rest, which was just as well since it rained all day. Players still straggled in; utility outfielder Del Howard reported for duty from his home in Kenney, Illinois. Reporter Dryden used the lull to interview Bert Semmens, the new team trainer. Dryden asked Semmens if he had been a boxer like his predecessor, Jack McCormick. Semmens replied that he did not care for the ring and mat, and that the only fighting he did was for his country. He was a veteran of the Spanish-American War and served in the Philippines. Dryden immediately tagged the trainer with a new moniker, "Soldier" Semmens, and informed Cub fans that their patriotic new trainer used an eight-pound cannon ball, a souvenir from the late war, to roll on the aching muscles of their baseball heroes.[11] But unconventional medical equipment should be handled carefully. The day before, utility infielder Heinie Zimmerman came to the trainer for treatment of a soft corn on his left foot. While inspecting the corn, "Soldier" Semmens dropped the cannon ball on Zimmerman's right foot.[12]

Another storm hit West Baden Sunday night. On Monday morning, Chance and the rest of the Cubs awoke to three inches of snow. Despite this, training began promptly at 8:00 A.M., but after a few laps around the paved and covered bicycle track, the team retreated indoors to wait for the snow to melt. During the day, Chance received word from Chicago that Secretary-Treasurer Charlie Williams was on his way to West Baden and that players Sheckard, Durbin, rookie Evans, and possibly Kling, would join the team in Vicksburg, Mississippi. Chance took advantage of the slow day to correct a Chicago newspaper story that claimed he had won $2,900 in two days playing the horses in California the past winter. Chance corrected the figure to $2,890.[13]

Sunshine melted the snow on Tuesday, but too late for the Cubs to do anything but repeat the exercise of the previous day and circle the paved bicycle track a few times. In the afternoon, three bored and restless athletes, pitchers Ed Reulbach, Joe Donohue, and catcher Vincent Campbell, donned uniforms, and found a knoll high and dry enough for a game of toss. The rest of the Cubs killed time hanging around the hotel, wearily playing cards, writing postcards, and anticipating Thursday's departure for Vicksburg in the sunny south.[14]

Wednesday in West Baden was another disappointment as the poor weather continued. Treasurer Williams arrived in time to watch the morning practice. After a dreary workout in the mud, a light drizzling rain arrived around noon, forcing the bored Cubs indoors again. Third baseman Harry Steinfeldt joined the team in the afternoon. He had spent the winter pleasure hunting in the hills of Kentucky.[15]

The sun and warm temperatures returned on Thursday, but rain from the previous night had added liquid to the mud soup on the playing field. Everyone spent the final day in West Baden packing, bowling, eating, and impatiently awaiting the early evening departure for the southern base training camp. After a dinner stop in Louisville, Kentucky, the Cubs' train continued south via Memphis, Tennessee. The landscape revealed spring by degrees as the train sped southward. Blossoming peach trees greeted weary eyes just after daybreak, and in the final miles the blooming dogwood signaled proper baseball weather. Twenty-four hours after leaving West Baden, the Cubs' train arrived in Vicksburg. The team was delivered safely, despite being on train number thirteen, consisting of thirteen cars, and arriving on Friday the thirteenth. A brilliant sunset and a large proportion of the Vicksburg populace welcomed them. George Blackburn, manager of the Vicksburg Hill Billies, offered official welcome. Smiling citizens lined Main Street for a glimpse of the players as they rode in two open-faced tallyho coaches, each drawn by four-horse teams, to the Hotel Carroll just in time for dinner. Cub players Jimmy Sheckard, Blaine "Kid" Durbin, and Arthur Evans, a rookie catcher, arrived earlier in the day and practiced with the Hill Billies before meeting their teammates for dinner. The only disruption occurred when Jack Pfiester was suddenly called home to Cincinnati by the serious illness of his wife.[16]

The baseball diamond, located high on a bluff above Vicksburg, afforded a grand view of the Mississippi River to the west, and to the east the battle monuments marking the site of the Confederate fort that surrendered to General Grant in 1863, only 45 years before. Although the citizens of Vicksburg warmly hosted the northern baseball team, they still stubbornly refused to celebrate July Fourth, the date of surrender, as a holiday. Vicksburg merchants offered the Cubs products and services gratis, including the two horse-drawn carriages, admission to the Majestic Theater, and free use of the street car system for daily transport to the ball field at Suburban Park, about a mile from town. Vicksburg manager, "Smiling George" Blackburn, promised an excellent playing surface for his guests. Before the pleased Cubs began their three-hour morning practice, Blackburn leased a steamroller from the city and had the field pressed. The 36-year-old Blackburn appreciated the needs of ballplayers. He had been one himself, pitching eleven years earlier with the 1897 National League Baltimore Orioles. Smiling George appeared in 5 games, started 4, pitched 3 complete games, and posted a record of 2 wins and 2 losses. Two of his 1897 Oriole teammates, third baseman John McGraw and shortstop Hughie Jennings, were now the managers of the New York Giants and Detroit Tigers.[17]

Big, good-natured, and the life of the party, Martin Walsh was literally "pepped up" at the first practice in Vicksburg. During breakfast, Walsh mistook Tabasco sauce for ketchup and doused his fried eggs. One bite inflamed his mouth and throat, dilated his pupils, and caused the tears to flow. Some players later commented that the Walsh fastball, already lively, seemed to have a little extra "pepper" during practice. Heinie Zimmerman did not practice. The corn on his left foot was joined by a second, this time on his already sore right foot. Twenty-year-old rookie catcher Arthur Evans, from the Virginia League, displayed a strong throwing arm and hit the ball hard, impressing Chance and his teammates during Saturday morning practice. Evans' black hair, worn unfashionably long, stuck out under his cap, and he wore two magnificent diamond rings on his left hand, concealed by his mitt while catching, but otherwise, impressively visible.[18]

Veteran shortstop Joe Tinker rose the next morning and, for reasons known only to himself, started a phantom boxing match in his hotel room, landing a solid left uppercut to the chandelier and gashing his hand. Unable to play that day, Joe joined Vicksburg manager Blackburn as impartial umpires for the first exhibition game of the year. That morning, grounds-keeper "Sham" Myers had painted "Welcome Chicago" with whitewash in the dirt behind home plate. Before the game began, the Vicksburg team, shy one first baseman, borrowed Cubs utility man Del Howard. Nine innings later, the Cubs had failed to score a single run. Vicksburg scored a lone run in the bottom of the third inning to defeat the major leaguers 1–0. Walsh, Donohue, and Durbin shared the pitching duties for the Cubs, toiling three innings apiece. The one run was scored off Walsh when Vicksburg pitcher Al Klawitter singled after one out. Vicksburg second baseman Bebeau laced a long double to left over the head of Sheckard, scoring Klawitter with the game's only run. Walsh and Donohue pitched well, but "Kid" Durbin was especially effective, striking out six batters in his three innings of work. While the Cub pitching trio allowed a paltry three hits, the Chicago hitters managed only three hits of their own. Singles by Schulte and Walsh were harmless, but a one-out double by Chance in the ninth inning gave the Cubs a chance to tie the score, before Steinfeldt grounded to second and Schulte, unable to gather his second hit, fouled out to third. While all three local pitchers held the Cubs scoreless, Al Klawitter was especially effective in his three innings of work, allowing only one hit. Klawitter joined the New York Giants the next year for two seasons and finished his three-year major-league career with the Detroit Tigers.[19]

Frank Chance had a bum foot and was in pain. An injury to his left foot the year before, which sidelined the first baseman for 43 games, flared up again during this first exhibition game and nearly crippled him when he ran to second after his ninth-inning double. At noon on Monday, March 16, Chance left Vicksburg for Chicago to consult with a foot specialist, expecting to have surgery and hopefully rejoin the Cubs in about two weeks. Left fielder Jimmy Sheckard assumed the managerial duties.

High temperatures and miserable humidity limited Monday morning practice to a few hours. That evening, the Cubs were the guests of the beautiful actress and singer Lillian Russell, touring the south in the comedy stage production *Wildfire*. Almost all the players attended and enjoyed the show, especially Frank Schulte. Afterwards, the twenty-five-year-old Schulte, obviously infatuated with the still-beautiful forty-seven-year-old actress, hit up his teammates for donations and sent a bouquet to her dressing room. This earned him the nickname he carried for the rest of his career, "Wildfire" Schulte.[20]

Tuesday was St. Patrick's Day. The players divided into two teams, one "Irish" and one "German," and played an intra-squad game. The Irish squad, led by Johnny Evers, had tentative claims at best to Irish ancestry. Brown, Fraser, and Howard all claimed Irish blood. Pitcher Orval Overall put forth the theory that the correct spelling of his name was O'Verall. Ethnically, the

German team was more legitimate, being led by acting manager Sheckard, with players Slagle, Hofman, Zimmerman, and Reulbach. Art Evans agreed to be German for the day. The Germans had their way most of the game, scoring three runs in the second inning and adding another in the sixth against a lone run scored in the third at bat for the Irish squad. Trailing 4–1, the Irish came to bat for the last time. When the dust had settled, three runs had crossed the plate, knotting the score at four. Umpires Charley "Treasurer" Williams and Joe "Injured Hand" Tinker saw their chance and, to the satisfaction of both countries, declared a tie and called the game on account of supper. The two warring nations happily reunited over dinner, hosted by the local Knights of Columbus, and once again became a family of Cubs, joking and teasing. Catcher Art Evans was a favorite target. Evans played a fine game behind the plate for the Germans, but every time a fastball hit his mitt a shower of white feathers puffed out. Evans had padded the inside of his glove with a pillow, but the players insisted that Arthur was beginning to molt. The rookie catcher had been the proud owner of a meerschaum pipe until it was stolen from the Cubs bench during the Sunday game against Vicksburg. Dryden claimed this was a handicap for Evans, since, "while he is catching Arthur wears the pipe in his face with the bowl outside the mask, and he flashes smoke signals to the pitcher. One puff means the straight ball and two puffs, the curve. When Arthur expectorates the pitcher throws the spitball. The Virginia backstop is a wonder." Evans's habit of scratching his matches against the side of trainer Semmen's imported Russian leather medicine case might have had something to do with the pipe's disappearance.[21] After dinner, the Knights of Columbus invited the Cubs to the local roller-skating rink. During his initial lap around the wooden floor, the ever-dexterous trainer Semmens collided with a stranger and was knocked to the ground. Fortunately, neither party needed first aid.[22]

The Cubs hitters found their batting eyes on Wednesday afternoon, easily defeating Vicksburg 7–2. Donohue and Durbin shared the pitching duties, and both performed well. The team collected ten hits, three each by first baseman Del Howard and shortstop Artie Hoffman. Blackburn again served as umpire, joined by the previous game's pitcher, Martin Walsh.[23]

Later in the evening, veteran catcher Johnny Kling arrived from Kansas City. A member of the Cubs since 1900, this was the first time Kling made it south for spring training. Kling yearly became embroiled in salary negotiations with President Murphy and routinely remained in Kansas City until the start of each season. More good news for the Cubs came from Chicago. After an examination and tests of Frank Chance's left foot, foot specialist Dr. Archibald Church diagnosed "Morton's Neurasthenia." Surgery was not necessary. The doctor prescribed a special shoe fitting tightly across the instep and loosely across the toes, preventing pressure on the troublesome nerve, allowing Chance to play without pain and giving the nerve time to heal.[24]

After another solid day of practice under a brilliant warm sun and blue skies, Blackburn invited the northern tourists on a river cruise. The boatload of Cubs departed at 5:00 P.M., relaxing and enjoying the breeze and scenery along the fifteen-mile course. A gracious host, Blackburn served his guests refreshments and told funny stories. His new friends were glad for a break from the monotony of hotel living and hotel food.[25] The next day turned cold and wet, forcing the athletes indoors. Most of the Cubs spent the day at the local country club, playing pool and bowling. Howard remained back in the hotel bravely allowing trainer Semmens to put his injured finger in a plaster cast. At lunch, Howard could not cut his meat or get his food safely to his mouth, and asked that the heavy cast be replaced with a lighter splint.[26]

On Saturday, the Cubs boarded the 7:00 A.M. train bound for Jackson, Mississippi, a short one-hour train ride from Vicksburg, to play one game with the Senators, the capital city's team in the Cotton States League. The host team provided a live mascot for the Cubs, a young cinnamon bear chained to the Cubs bench to remind the visiting ballplayers which team they were on. Playing their first game of the season against the world champions of 1907, the Senators did their best but were no match for the Cubs, scoring only one run when Reulbach walked four men in a row in the fourth inning. Meanwhile, the Cubs gathered twelve hits, scoring eight runs for an easy victory even without the injured Chance and Tinker.[27]

After the game, the Cubs returned to Vicksburg. A storm blew in during the night, and it rained incessantly the next day. Unable to play their scheduled game against the Hill Billies, the players had to fill another wet Sunday with little to do. But they had time to review the new Cubs Program Guide sent to each player from President Murphy, featuring the 1908 schedule and cover portraits of Frank Chance and Uncle Sam. Pitcher Chick Fraser spent the day tracking down and returning catcher Evans's meerschaum pipe, incurring his gratitude.[28]

The wet weather continued on Monday. Pitching practice took place indoors at the roller-skating rink and country club. In the dim light of the skating rink, Evans misjudged a pitch, suffering a blow to his finger that required a plaster cast. Later that evening, the skating rink was transformed to honor the team at a grand farewell reception, with music and dancing followed by a splendid spaghetti dinner at a local Italian restaurant. Several Cubs spoke of their gratitude to the citizens of Vicksburg, manager Blackburn, and his gallant ballplayers, for the royal treatment they had received. Frank Schulte gave his speech attired in a vertically-stripped black-and-white suit, producing a vivid window-awning effect.[29]

On Tuesday, the sun warmed the Cubs' last day in Vicksburg, but the playing field was still a sea of red mud. Unable to play the scheduled game, the Hill Billies manager saved the day by securing permission from the police department for the Cubs to practice in the streets of the city. Reporter Dryden described the scene: "With a brick church on one side of them, a sanitarium on the other, the Louisiana monument in the middle, and trolley cars shooting the chutes down a steep hill to southward, the athletes toiled morning and afternoon in full view of an admiring populace.... An entire block was filled with Cubs in gay baseball attire, while little boys and girls sat on the curb and discussed the big league doings in learned accents."[30]

Three weeks remained before the regular season began. A special three-car train carried the Cubs eastward 135 miles from Vicksburg to Meridian, the largest city in Mississippi in 1908. The Meridian White Ribbons, defending champions of the Cotton States League, were managed by Frederick Schmit. Now forty-two years of age, the Meridian manager was better known as "Germany" or "Crazy" Schmit.[31] He had had an erratic and losing major-league pitching career; over an eleven-year period, from 1890 to 1901, he played a total of five years for five different teams, recording 7 wins against 36 losses.[32]

A native Chicagoan, Schmit immediately incited a controversy by beginning the game as the sole umpire. The Ribboners batted first, and Schmit called every pitch, regardless of location, a ball, allowing the first two hitters to reach base. Cubs pitcher Carl Lundgren was not pleased, but on the next play, Schmit went too far. The Meridian runners attempted a double steal, and catcher Pat Moran rifled a throw to third base. Heinie Zimmerman caught the ball and waited for the runner. Tagging the late-sliding runner, Zimmerman tossed the ball back to Lundgren. But Schmit, to the surprise and delight of the crowd, declared the runner safe. Interim manager and current left fielder Jimmy Sheckard raced to the infield and confronted Schmit, heatedly challenging both his judgment and sanity. Crazy Schmit wilted under the attack and relinquished his umpiring responsibilities. Injured Cubs outfielder Del Howard, sitting out in his street clothes with his bandaged finger, traded his derby for a baseball cap and replaced Schmit.[33]

In the bottom half of the first inning, Howard returned the favor. The Cubs had runners on second and third with two outs. Zimmerman was playing for the regular third baseman Harry Steinfeldt, who remained in his hotel room nursing a severe cold. Zimmerman grounded to third, but instead of throwing to first for the third out, the Meridian third baseman tried to tag Johnny Kling coming toward third from second base. Kling avoided the tag but ran several yards out of the baseline to do so. Umpire Howard refused to call Kling out. The rattled Meridian infielder frantically and erratically threw toward first base. The ball sailed into foul territory, into a carriage enclosure, striking a family horse on the left eyelid. By the time the horse and the Meridian players recovered, Zimmerman had rounded the bases and the Cubs were given three runs. The Cubs then tallied six more times, scoring an easy 9–3 victory.[34]

Jack Pfiester, still in Cincinnati with his ailing wife, received a contract offer from President Murphy, but refused to sign. After helping to win two pennants and one world's championship with a two-year record of 35 wins and 17 losses, Pfiester wanted more money. "I have not signed a Chicago contract for the simple reason I believe I am worth more money to the Chicago club. I was sent a contract, but it did not suit me in the least and I returned it. I have had some correspondence with Manager Chance, and I believe we will come to an agreement. This is not the reason, however, that I am not training in the south. My wife is seriously ill and I am here only on her account. Otherwise I would have remained with the club, as I feel sure of a satisfactory arrangement."[35]

After a single game in Meridian, the Cubs left for the depot to catch the midnight train to Montgomery, Alabama. There, aggressive questioning by a Meridian newspaperman led Joe Tinker to pick up an orange and hurl it at the reporter's head. The orange missed the intended target, hitting, perhaps symbolically, a nearby newsstand. Called to restore order, police allowed Tinker to depart with his teammates. It was quite a ride. The 150-mile trip in cramped sleeping quarters, with only twenty-six berths for thirty-one bodies, and continual pre-dawn train whistles clearing Alabama cows from the tracks, left the defending champions sleep famished.[36]

Manager Frank Chance was a welcomed sight as he greeted the bleary-eyed team in Montgomery. Chance brought a trunk full of his new scientifically designed baseball shoes from Chicago and was anxious to test them against the Montgomery Climbers. A few hours later, the weary Cub hitters managed only five hits and one run, but it was enough to win a 1–0 squeaker as Fraser and Overall threw a combined seven-hit shutout. Chance collected one hit, two stolen bases and, most importantly, played pain-free in his new shoes.[37]

Jimmy Ryan, the forty-five-year-old player-manager of the Mont-

1. Spring Training

gomery Climbers, knew the Chicago team well. Ryan played for the Cubs before they were the Cubs, joining the team in 1885. The legendary Cap Anson was his manager, and the Cubs were then known as the White Stockings, the name taken by the new Chicago American League team in 1901 after the National League team abandoned the name. For two seasons, Ryan and Chance, who joined the Cubs in 1898, were teammates. As an outfielder, Ryan had a long and distinguished major-league career. For sixteen years, Ryan played in Chicago, finally finishing his major-league career by playing two years with the new American League Washington Nationals. After eighteen seasons, Ryan's career statistics were impressive: lifetime batting average .306; 2,500 hits; 803 walks; only 361 strikeouts; 408 stolen bases; and 3,808 putouts.[38] Ryan could still play in 1908. He was the lead-off hitter and played center field for Montgomery against the Cubs, displaying his defensive talent by throwing out a Cubs runner at the plate in the first inning.[39]

Ryan and his Montgomery Climbers played well the next day, losing another close game 4–3. Montgomery took the lead, scoring single runs in the first and second innings. The Cubs tied it with two runs in the third inning and took a 3–2 lead when Zimmerman stroked a home run to left in the fourth inning. Another Montgomery run in the eight inning knotted the score at 3, but a walk, sacrifice bunt, and a solid single by Johnny Evers plated the winning run for the Cubs in the ninth. Martin Walsh was impressive on the mound, pitching the last four innings, giving up only two hits, one walk, and an unearned run, while striking out four.[40]

The Cubs' express train left Montgomery that evening for two games in three days against the defending champions of the Southern League, unselfconsciously named the Atlanta Crackers. The Cubs continued their winning ways, scoring their sixth consecutive victory against the minor-league champs, 7–4, on Saturday afternoon. Members of the American League's New York Highlanders, training in Atlanta, were in the stands. So was Ty Cobb, who was passing through Atlanta on his way to Arkansas to join his Detroit Tigers teammates. Cobb and the Tigers were the defending American League champions, but they had lost the 1907 World Series to the Cubs in four straight games (after an opening game tie).[41]

The press, referring to the New York American League team, used the names "Highlanders" and "Yankees" interchangeably. As Sunday baseball was illegal in Georgia, Cub and Yankee/Highlander players spent the next day socializing and dining together in the parlors and lobbies of the luxurious five-year-old Piedmont Hotel, a ten-story Flat Iron-esque building on Luckie Street. During this lull, the *Chicago Tribune* paused to assess the Cubs rookies and their chances of making the team. Pitcher Joe Donohue "is good enough for any team. The semi-pro lad acts like a veteran under fire. He can hit and field and never loses his head in a pinch." Heinie Zimmerman, the utility infielder, had only played five games with the Cubs in 1907, so he was still considered a rookie. Zimmerman could play all four infield positions, "and is hitting the ball hard and often." Pitcher and Irish ballad singer Martin Walsh, popular with his teammates and members of the Chicago press, "made a favorable impression with his spikes in a game against the fast Montgomery team, and will have another try soon." Vincent Campbell and Arthur Evans battled for the third catching spot behind Johnny Kling and Pat Moran. Campbell "is a more finished backstop and stronger at the bat and on the bases, but Evans has it on him in throwing." Outfielder Curt Elston "is improving daily and falling into his stride. Little Rock has put in a bid for the speedy outfielder, but he probably will go to Montgomery if not retained by the Cubs."[42]

After the Yankees took the field for a Monday morning practice, the Cubs and Crackers followed with their second contest. This time, Atlanta prevailed 2–1, ending the Cubs' six-game winning streak. But most of the action proved incidental to the actual game. Just as the Cubs came to bat in the ninth, New York sports reporter Sam Crane turned loose a fire alarm — a grandstand awning near the ground was ablaze. Del Howard, injured finger and all, jumped to the rescue, dousing the flames with one splash from the Cubs' drinking water bucket.[43]

Fireworks continued into the ninth inning, however, with Frank Chance the lightning rod. The Atlanta pitcher unleashed a fast ball that hit Chance squarely above his left ear. The crowd heard "a loud and reverberating thump. The bean ball knocked Chance flat and a hush

Tough and fair, manager and first baseman Frank Chance was respected by his players. Refusing to dodge errant pitches, Chance was frequently hit by the pitch, often in the head.

fell upon the multitude when the warring factions gathered about the writhing form in the dirt." There were no batting helmets in 1908, and Chance had been leaning his head into pitches since high school. Dryden cavalierly described the incident, claiming, "The only damage to the managerial ear was a slight inflammation where the ball landed. Luckily the blow fell on the ear already out of commission from repeated thumpings in the past."[44]

The series in Atlanta completed, the Cubs traveled to Chattanooga, Tennessee, to play, oddly enough, the Toledo Mud Hens. The Ohio team had accepted an invitation from Charlie Williams to meet in a city along the Cubs' southern spring training route. Reulbach was the master on the mound for the Cubs, throwing six shutout innings, while the Chicago hitters scored five runs in six times at bat. His team leading five to nothing, Walsh came on to pitch the final three innings. Walsh gave up a run in the seventh before retiring the side. Then disaster struck. Walsh lost his control in the eighth. He walked five men and hit another, and when the ball did cross the plate, the Mud Hens hit it hard. Before the third out was recorded, five Mud Hens scored, giving the Toledo team a 6–5 lead. Walsh did not get another chance. The game ended in the top of the ninth when the Cubs failed to score.[45]

The affable Walsh was miserable, his self-assurance shaken, and his boyish enthusiasm muted. He no longer talked of pitching against the White Stockings and his brother Ed in the 1908 World Series. Failure and doubt lead him to think the unthinkable. He was no longer sure that he would be a Cub when the regular season began in two weeks. It was a bad day all the way around for the Cubs: Johnny Evers with a migraine headache; Joe Tinker with his injured hand; and Frank Chance with a serious blow to the head in the previous game, were all unable to play. The sour mood of the day infected *Chicago Tribune* reporter Dryden's account of the events. After a series of dour comments on the game, Dryden turned his spleen on the uncomfortable accommodations and poor food experienced in the southern states, specifically lamenting the new hotel being built in Chattanooga. "The Cubs made a touch and go stop at the new hotel here in the course of completion. Nothing but the sleeping rooms are ready, the office floor and eat works being in a state of chaos. For the most part the athletes looked at Lookout Mountain during their twelve hour stay here and foraged for meals...." Voicing the ugly racism prevalent in baseball and America generally at the turn of the last century, he continued: "The lower floor was full of busy white artisans and scores of coon helpers, who are adept at the art of not being busy."[46]

The 8:00 P.M. train to Birmingham left the station an hour late. With several delays in route, it was nearly 3:00 A.M. on April 1 before the Cubs put heads to pillows. Sleeping through breakfast, the ravenous Chicago athletes gorged themselves at their hotel lunch on turkey patties, pork and beans, and everyone's favorite, according to Dryden, strawberry salad. In the afternoon, the Cubs ended their two-game losing streak, beating the Birmingham Coal Barons 6–3. Fraser was adequate on the mound, giving up the three Baron runs in six innings. Rookie Donahue again pitched well, allowing four hits but no runs, in his three innings. Chance was hit again, this time on the kneecap.[47]

The next afternoon, with temperatures hovering around freezing, the Cubs and Coal Barons engaged in a bizarre, nearly riotous contest. The trouble started in the third inning. A local gentleman named Charles Harris umpired. Molesworth, the center fielder for the Coal Barons, attempted a bunt, but missed for the third strike. Assuming himself out, he headed for the dugout, but Umpire Harris called the pitch a ball. Returning to bat, Molesworth then reached first base safely on a Cub error and managed to work his way to third. The next pitch got away from catcher Kling. Molesworth and pitcher Lundgren raced each other toward the plate. Lundgren successfully blocked the plate, but he did not tag Molesworth with the ball. Without touching the plate, Molesworth trotted to his bench, but Umpire Harris still allowed the run. Several Cubs ran up, surrounded Harris, and aggressively protested the call. Harris, intimidated, reversed himself and called Molesworth out. Hearing this, Molesworth trotted back out and touched the plate. Since Molesworth still had not been tagged with the ball, Harris again reversed himself and called him safe, awarding the run to Birmingham. Enraged Cubs descended upon the waffling umpire, spewing verbal abuse. A couple of players lost control, pushing Harris and spiking him on the foot. Police arrived. Dryden noted, "At this point a burly officer of the law wearing a grim look of determination and a large red mustache with a good five-cent cigar in the middle of his face" forcibly removed Cub third baseman Harry Steinfeldt from the crowd surrounding the umpire and escorted him to the Cubs' bench. Birmingham manager Vaughn replaced the rattled and slightly injured Harris with one of his players to umpire the rest of the game. Order restored, the game resumed. The Cubs scored four runs in the seventh inning to tie the score at five; at that point, the game was called on account of cold and darkness.[48]

Chance had removed himself from the game the previous day when he was hit in the kneecap. The Birmingham newspaper reported that many fans were disappointed that Chance did not tough it out and continue to play.

Dryden leaped to Chance's defense, describing his history of injuries and attesting to his courage.

> The idea of his going to the bench ... just because his knee pan was shot off makes us peevish and we herewith submit some vital statistics to show how lightly Mr. Chance regards the wild pitch in its burning flight. In eleven years of active service he has been stung on an average of once per game, making a total of 1,694 punctures. While Mr. Chance himself does not flinch under fire, his floating ribs are trained to dive when they sense the ball approaching. The bean ball—i.e. to the head—has done him more dirt than anything else. Let the following incident suffice to place Mr. Chance right in the eyes of the southern fanatics: During his school days he went ... to Visalia ... to catch the game of his life in a wheat field. On the slab for Visalia was a butcher seven feet high and with an arm like a water main. He stung the future peerless leader behind the left ear. He bled a couple of hours ... while friends subpoenaed a special train to convey the remains to Fresno. There he lay unconscious for two months with an ice wagon standing in front of the ancestral home.... His vocal cords were paralyzed and he did not speak for one year. Knowing these facts as we now do, it rolls us to have the people of Birmingham think Mr. Chance would back up in response to a mere hole shot through his knee pan. O, piffle![49]

The Cubs played a third and final game against Birmingham the next day. A new umpire, Mike O'Brien, called the game without incident. O'Brien was a local ballplayer, a catcher, who was slated to play for the Dubuque, Iowa, team later in the summer. Donohue starred for the Cubs in this game, pitching all nine innings and collecting two hits, including a double, in the Cubs' 3–2 victory. Charles Harris, the starting umpire from the previous day, was in attendance along with two deputy sheriffs. Before the game, the two officers had loitered around the Cubs bench. Fearing police action against his players, Chance called a meeting with the opposing manager and the two deputies, who assured Chance they were only there to maintain order. Ex-umpire Harris maintained a menacing presence all afternoon, conferred frequently with the lawmen, and threatened repeatedly to "get the Cubs."[50]

At 9:00 P.M. that night, the two deputy sheriffs arrived at the Cubs' hotel and served Del Howard with a $5,000 lawsuit summons. The deputies intended to serve Harry Steinfeldt as well, but the third baseman dodged them at the hotel, took a circuitous route to the depot, and hid on the train preparing to depart for Memphis. One determined deputy arrived at the depot and proceeded to serve the Steinfeldt summons on a graying, middle-aged, cigar businessman from Tampa, Mr. T. B. Parker. Parker denied being a ballplayer and refused to accept the summons. Undeterred, the deputy found a younger man to serve, trainer Bert Semmens. At first, Semmens denied he was Steinfeldt, but when the deputy insisted, Semmens accepted the summons just to please him. At this point, a lawyer retained by Howard arrived at the station and took affidavits from Treasurer Charlie Williams and a half dozen players, to prove in Birmingham courts that trainer Semmens was not Harry Steinfeldt.[51]

The next morning, President Murphy met the team as they arrived in Memphis. Told of the $5,000 damage suit against Howard, Murphy wrote President Baum of the Birmingham team, asking his assistance in settling the incident. That afternoon, their legal problems in the hands of their President, the Cubs returned to the diamond. Overall, in mid-season form, allowed only three singles and struck out eight, in a 9–1 Cub victory. The lone run scored by the Memphis Turtles was unearned. Chance and Slagle were the whirlwind brothers on the bases, stealing five and scoring four of the runs.[52]

Memphis bats were silenced again the next day. Reulbach pitched a complete-game shutout, striking out eight, and giving up only four singles. And shortstop Joe Tinker was in the lineup for the first time, as the Cubs won 4–0. But, the real excitement blazed across *Chicago Tribune* headlines the next day.

MAD DOG SCARE NO BAR TO CUB VICTORY
Chased to Roof of Coop by Canine, Chance's Men Retain Their Nerve
Trainer Semmens Becomes Hero, Subduing "Fido"

At the end of the sixth inning, a sadistic fan poked a black-and-white pointer in the behind with the lighted end of a cigar. The dog howled, leaped from the stands, and started running wildly around the field. Passing behind home plate, he snapped at the Memphis catcher. As he headed toward left field, the panicked Memphis bench players climbed to the top of their dugout. Spectators confined to "Jim Crow" seating on a grassy slope in left field hopped a fence to escape the rampaging dog, a few hurling pop bottles before retreating. The unhappy dog continued his flight, sending the Memphis right fielder, screaming for help, to the top of the outfield fence. The *Tribune* described the scene as the dog approached the Cubs' dugout: "On the homestretch Fido neared the Cub bench and scattered those bold athletes to beat the band. There wasn't room on the roof of their coop for all, but the fence was close by. Artie Hofman cleared the space from the ground to the roof in one standing jump of seven feet.... On the next lap Howard and Zimmerman tried to stop the dog, which snapped at them and passed on for a fresh shower of pop bottles from the coon sharpshooters perched on the left field fence." At this point, the police were dispatched to shoot the innocent dog, but trainer Semmens rescued him by running to the flag pole in deep center field where the pointer had taken refuge, and grabbing him around the neck. Howard assisted, holding the dog's rump. Together, they carried the exhausted canine to a gate in the fence behind first base, past the pistol-drawn police, and released him to the streets of Memphis. The mad-dog panic subsided, and the game continued.[53]

In the stands, petite Mrs. Kling, wife of Cubs' catcher John (a married woman's first name was never used by the press), witnessed the dog episode. The unfortunate patron sitting behind her did not see much of anything that day, for she was wearing the champion "Merry Widow" hat of the season. This style of enormous cartwheel hat was named for the vivacious character in Franz Leher's operetta of the same name. The show opened in the U.S. in October 1907, and by the following spring, anything labeled "Merry Widow" was a fashion sensation. Understandably, most spectators at the ballpark did not appreciate these amazing hats. Mrs. Kling's multi-colored creation, with a palisade of white feathers in the front, measured three-and-a-half feet in diameter, which was only a "little less than the wearer's altitude above sea level." Her husband claimed the hat was so large that if he could place it on the ground behind him when catching, he would not have a passed ball all season.[54]

On April 6, only eight days before the regular season began, President Murphy met with manager Chance in Memphis to decide which players would not make the cut. Three rookies, outfielder Curt Elston, catcher Arthur Evans, and pitcher Martin Walsh, received the bad news in individual meetings with Murphy. Elston received the news stoically; he expected it. The left-handed outfielder was solid defensively, playing right and left field, and collecting six hits in eight games, including a triple against the Birmingham Barons. But the Cubs outfield corps was deep, with veterans Slagle in center, Sheckard in left, and Schulte in right, with Howard and Hofman providing strong backup. Rookie Elston had performed well, but he could not match the talent of the veteran outfielders. Elston still hoped to play for a team near his hometown of Marietta, Ohio.[55]

Arthur Evans was not as sanguine as Elston when given the bad news. Evans was competing against another rookie, Vincent Campbell, for the third catching spot behind Johnny Kling and Pat Moran. Evans had a strong arm and was better defensively than Campbell. He had even cut his long hair in a effort to fit in. But he had only one hit all spring, a double, playing for the pretend Germans against the faux Irish in the Cubs' intra-squad game. Still, Evans felt slighted. Campbell admittedly had less skill behind the plate, and had only three hits all spring, with two of those in the German-Irish game. But Campbell had played both first base and right field. So, while Evans had a case for being the better catcher, Campbell was viewed as the more versatile player and perhaps a slightly better hitter. With two veteran catchers already on the roster, Evans was the man to go. He wanted to return to his former team in Lynchburg, Virginia, but was further disappointed when he was released to the Wichita, Kansas, team.[56]

Martin Walsh had expected to join the 1908 Cubs and dreamed about pitching against his older brother, Ed. But his dismal performance against the Toledo Mud Hens in Chattanooga sealed his fate with manager Chance. The jovial, ballad singing youngster was well-liked by his teammates, and all were sad to see him go.[57] Walsh returned to his former team in Danville, Virginia, but never joined his famous brother in the major leagues.

President Murphy returned to Chicago while his team boarded an evening Illinois Central train for a two-game series against the Nashville Volunteers. The train slowly wound its way through the southern countryside of Kentucky, before turning south to Nashville. Players trying to doze on the bench seats of the lurching train were tired and cranky. Dryden wrote, "Most of them were in a humor to burn a warehouse and scrape the tobacco beds and the train stopped often enough to permit of these popular pastimes. Only the fear of the law restrained the desperate athletes."[58]

Fraser pitched a two-hit complete game shutout against the Volunteers, while the Cubs crossed the plate seven times to score an easy victory. Playing on the Volunteer's field was unnerving. Dryden described the scene, "Where the Cubs cavorted today looks ... like a dry reservoir sown to bluegrass. All four sides rise at an angle of 90 degrees, and right field is close to the diamond. Mr. Wiseman, who works that patch of upended ground, has been on the job eight years. That is why they keep him. He runs up the steep slope like a goat and kills all kinds of doubles and triples. When the ball does get by him on the lower level it hits a bluff and squirts straight up like a geyser in the park."[59]

Students of Nashville University, where Campbell had played college football, hailed him as a conquering hero. Old teammates greeted him at the hotel in the morning, hung around him during practice, and shook hands with him over the grandstand railing during the game. The next day, the Cubs, behind a four-hit complete game by Carl Lundgren, scored a 7–2 victory over Nashville. Campbell's admirers filled the stands and were thrilled when he came in to relieve Johnny Kling in the seventh inning. Campbell dropped the third strike of the first hitter, but was able to recover and throw the batter out at first. In the eighth, Campbell came to bat, sending his college pals into a frenzy. Campbell struck out, but his fans gave him a round of applause anyway.[60]

After two weeks of dry weather, rain greeted the Cubs in Evansville, Indiana, canceling the scheduled game against the local nine. The players spent the gloomy day getting haircuts, writing postcards, and shopping. Slagle bought a new briarroot pipe. That evening, the Evansville Elks hosted a sumptuous dinner for the team. At midnight, still sated, the Cubs trooped to their train sleeping berths and departed Evansville without ever touching ball and bat, only knife and fork.[61]

Mordecai "Three-Finger" Brown, the ace of the Cubs pitching staff, had not yet pitched during spring training due to a sore arm developed in early March. But Indiana was his home state, and Terre Haute, the next stop, was only twelve miles from his hometown of Rosedale. Brown was ready to try his arm and perform for his hometown fans. Rosedale became a ghost town for a day as three hundred Brown enthusiasts boarded an early special train for the short ride. The Rosedale party included a 52-piece marching band resplendent in brilliant green uniforms. Arriving the same hour as the Cubs, they organized an impromptu parade, escorting their hero and the rest of the team to the hotel. In front of the hotel, the band broke into "Down in the Coal Mine," saluting Brown's previous occupation as a coal miner. Every Rosedale bug (baseball fans in 1908 were called bugs) wore a brown ribbon inscribed, "Brown of Rosedale." Above the ribbon, on the lapel, they pinned a typewritten cheer for their hero and town.

> Brown, Brown, Brown,
> He's from our old town,
> Rah! Rah! Rah!
> It's Rosedale[62]

They were not disappointed. Brown started the game and pitched four shutout innings against the Terre Haute Hottentots. Overall pitched the final five innings, allowing only one run as the Cubs easily dispatched the locals 10–1. The wet weather had kept the Hottentots from practicing for two weeks, and their play proved it. They committed eight errors, gave up fourteen hits, and allowed ten runs. Lew Drill, the Hottentots' manager and catcher, had played in the American League between 1902 and 1905, primarily with the Washington Nationals. The performance of his Hottentots on this day must have reminded him of his 1903 season with the hapless Nationals, who finished last with a dismal record of 94 losses and only 43 wins.[63]

Two announcements were made before the Cubs departed Terre Haute. The contract of rookie outfielder Curt Elston had been sold to the Fort Wayne, Indiana, Central League team. Elston, relieved that he had not been sold to a Southern League team, could now play close to his hometown of Marietta, Ohio. Veteran left-handed pitcher Jack Pfiester had finally come to terms, undisclosed, and signed his contract with the Cubs. He planned to leave his home in Cincinnati and join his teammates as soon as possible. Only four days remained before opening day.[64]

Leaving Terre Haute, the Cubs traveled northeastward across Indiana to Ft. Wayne, arriving at noon for their next game. But the Indiana skies did not cooperate, and the heavy rain precluded playing. Treasurer Williams, in charge of transportation and logistics, decided not to waste time in town. Within three hours, the team was back on a train, speeding at fifty miles per hour back across Indiana to the state capital, Indianapolis, arriving at six o'clock for a hearty dinner at their hotel.[65]

On Saturday, April 11, the Cubs defeated the Indianapolis Indians 8–4. Immediately afterward, they headed east again, across the state line into Ohio to play the final two games of spring training against the Dayton Veterans on Sunday and Monday, April 12 and 13. Although Sunday baseball was legal in Ohio, it was against the law to make loud noise on the Sabbath. Baseball bugs could applaud only with their hands; no stamping or shouting allowed. Warnings to this effect were posted conspicuously around the ballpark, and special police were hired to preserve the legal decorum. In the fourth inning of Sunday's game, Kling swatted a home run, compelling the police to hold up warning fingers to subdue the more than 5,000 spectators. The Cubs scored an easy 8–1 victory.[66]

Monday dawned a beautiful spring day in Dayton for the last practice game. Inspired by the delightful weather, Chance called a special morning practice, and the Cubs, feeling frisky after so many rainy days in hotel rooms, frolicked around the diamond for a few hours prior to their afternoon contest. Francois Earl de Montmorency Yingling, a talented nineteen-year-old southpaw for the Veterans, pitched a complete game against the Cubs. He allowed only five hits, striking out three and walking none. Unfortunately for Yingling, his team collected only three hits and could not score against Lundgren and Brown. The Cubs scored two unearned runs in the fifth inning to win a hard-earned victory.[67] Three years later, at the age of twenty-two, Yingling began his five-year major-league career, pitching for Cleveland, Brooklyn, Cincinnati, and finally, Washington.[68]

After this last game, the Cubs were returning to their hotel for dinner in a horse-drawn bus. Rowdy Dayton fans in a passing trolley heckled the players, frightening the horses, who jumped the street curb. The bus overturned, spilling players onto the grass. No one was hurt, but the horses galloped away with what remained of the bus, chased by outfielder Artie Hofman trying to retrieve his glove and spikes.[69]

The Cubs' spring training record totaled 16 wins, 3 losses, and 1 tie.

Rain canceled four games. Now it was on to Cincinnati to start the season against the Reds. Having won National League pennants in 1906 and 1907, dominating the American League Detroit Tigers in the 1907 World Series by winning four straight games, the Cubs were looking forward to the regular season. They claimed to be the best team in baseball and were eager to prove it.

Spring Training Game Results[70]

March 15	Vicksburg Hill Billies 1; Cubs 0
March 18	Cubs 7; Vicksburg Hill Billies 2
March 21	Cubs 8; Jackson Senators 1
March 22	No game at Vicksburg, rain
March 24	No game at Vicksburg, mud
March 25	Cubs 9; Meridian Ribboners 3
March 26	Cubs 1; Montgomery Climbers 0
March 27	Cubs 4; Montgomery Climbers 3
March 28	Cubs 7; Atlanta Crackers 4
March 30	Atlanta Crackers 2; Cubs 1
March 31	Toledo Mud Hens 6; Cubs 5
April 1	Cubs 6; Birmingham Coal Barons 3
April 2	Cubs 5; Birmingham Coal Barons 5 (seven innings)
April 3	Cubs 3; Birmingham Coal Barons 2
April 4	Cubs 9; Memphis Turtles 1
April 5	Cubs 4; Memphis Turtles 0
April 6	Cubs 7; Nashville Volunteers 0
April 7	Cubs7; Nashville Volunteers 2
April 8	No game at Evansville, rain
April 9	Cubs 10; Terre Haute Hottentots 1
April 10	No game at Fort Wayne, rain
April 11	Cubs 8; Indianapolis Indians 4
April 12	Cubs 8; Dayton Veterans 1
April 13	Cubs 2; Dayton Veterans 0

Chapter 2

Fast Start

On Tuesday morning, 14 April, opening day of the season, Charlie Williams rolled out of his Cincinnati hotel bed early. Williams needed time to organize the new uniforms for distribution. The gray wool, black-pinstriped outfits featured a small brown bear cub standing upright in a black letter C on the breast, but no names or numbers. (Uniform numbers first appeared in the 1920s; player names took another forty-plus years to appear.) The black warm-up jacket had a large white bear on each sleeve. After some initial preparation, Williams joined the players in the hotel dining room for breakfast, then returned to his task. By noon, Williams had laid out twenty sets of uniforms, organized by size; they quickly disappeared as each player arrived at his door. But, there was either one too many players or Williams was one uniform short. There were twenty-one Cubs and only twenty uniforms. Arriving late, Danny "Kid" Durbin missed out.[1]

Cincinnati's Palace of the Fans opened its gates at noon for the three o'clock game. A brass band serenaded the fans as they arrived in overloaded trolley cars, and by 2:30, the Palace overflowed with 19,257 bugs and bugines (female bugs).[2] A clothing company gave multi-colored paper megaphones printed with the company name to spectators entering the ballpark. Red-hatted vendors skipped among the bugs hawking beer and German sausages in bright purple wrappers. Patrons with hearty appetites could buy pig's knuckles. The more squeamish could get ice cream.[3] As the players concluded their pre-game practice, a woman photographer wearing a blue skirt and a hat with pink roses appeared on the field. She herded the Cincinnati players together, assembled her equipment, quickly composed the 1908 Cincinnati Reds Baseball Team photograph, and promptly disappeared.[4]

Charles W. Murphy, Cubs' owner and president, joined National League President Harry Pulliam in his box. Murphy brought along the twenty-five-year-old Chicago sculptor, Osborne T. Olsen, who had crafted a life-size

2. Fast Start

concrete figure of Frank Chance for the West Side Park entrance in Chicago. Murphy also wanted Olsen to visit the $1,000,000 art collection of Charles P. Taft, a close friend of Murphy and publisher of the *Cincinnati Times-Star*.[5] Taft was also the older brother of the current Secretary of War and soon-to-be 1908 Republican candidate for President of the United Sates, William Howard Taft. Charles Murphy knew Cincinnati well. He had served as the sports editor of the *Cincinnati Enquirer* and assistant city editor for the *Cincinnati Times-Star* under Taft. In 1903, when John T. Brush, president of the Cincinnati Reds, left his post to assume the same duties with the New York Giants, Brush hired Murphy to serve as the press agent for his new team. Two years later, in 1905, Murphy accepted an offer from James Hart, owner of the Cubs, to serve as press agent in Chicago. But before he could even arrive on the scene, Hart decided to sell the team. On his way to Chicago, Murphy stopped in Cincinnati, borrowed $100,000 from his good friend Charles Taft, and bought the Cubs for $105,000.[6]

The Cubs started the season with the championship lineup from the year before, all pronounced healthy by trainer Semmens. Lead-off hitter Jimmy Slagle patrolled center field. Left fielder Jimmy Sheckard batted second with Frank Schulte, playing right field, in the third spot. Slugger Frank Chance, manager and first baseman, was the clean-up hitter. Third baseman Harry Steinfeldt hit fifth, followed by second baseman Johnny Evers. Shortstop Joe Tinker hit seventh. Catcher Johnny Kling hit in the eighth slot, and opening-day pitcher Orval Overall batted ninth.[7] Twenty-seven-year-old Overall led the team the previous season with 23 wins, only 8 losses, and an earned run average (ERA) of 1.70 per nine innings.[8] "Orvie" began his major-league career with Cincinnati in 1905 with 17 wins against 22 losses. In the middle of the next season, after only 3 wins and 5 losses, the Reds traded Overall to the Cubs; he performed magnificently for the rest of the season with a record of 12 victories and only 3 losses.[9] Overall wanted to do well on opening day against his former team for another reason; his father had come all the way from their hometown of Farmersville, California, to watch his son.[10]

Players of both teams, heads uncovered, assembled at home plate facing the crowd. Mayor Markbreit delivered a short address, received polite applause, then made an errant pitch of the ceremonial first ball. Dressed in dark blue, Hank O'Day, "king of the umpires," and the sole umpire for the season opener, retrieved the ball from the dirt, massaged it clean, and in a crisp authoritarian voice announced to the crowd the starting pitcher and catcher for both teams. O'Day tossed the ball to Reds pitcher Bob Ewing and shouted, "play ball."[11]

The game started badly for the Cubs. In the first inning, the Reds collected four hits, the Cubs committed three errors, including one by Overall, and before three outs were registered the Reds scored five times. But after the Cubs plated two runs in their next at bat, Overall found his rhythm and held the Reds scoreless for the next seven innings. The Cubs tied the game, scoring single runs in the fourth, fifth, and sixth innings.[12]

In their last at bat, Johnny Evers drew a walk to lead off. Joe Tinker followed with a perfectly executed sacrifice bunt, moving Evers to second. Johnny Kling lofted a high fly ball to left for the second out, with Evers holding at second. Twenty-one-year-old utility infielder Heinie Zimmerman, pinch hitting for Overall, laced a line drive over second base, scoring Evers with the go-ahead run. Adrenalin flowing, Zimmerman rounded first and tried to stretch his hit into a double, but he was tagged out at second base to end the inning. Manager Chance called on Mordecai Brown to pitch the bottom of the ninth. Brown promptly retired the side in order, running the Reds' scoreless streak to eight consecutive innings. After one hour and fifty-five minutes, the reigning champions of baseball had begun the new season in style with a gutsy comeback performance.[13]

The next day, ominous clouds gathered over the ballpark as the Cubs and Reds concluded their pre-game warm-ups. Only three thousand fans were in the stands as "Tornado Jake" Weimer took the mound for the Reds. Before Weimer could deliver the first pitch, the heavens opened up, and fans scampered for cover. The downpour lasted only five minutes, but the field had already been soaked the previous night. Umpire O'Day declared "wet grounds," giving the players a day off.[14] Almost immediately, the sun returned and Reds manager John Hackenschmidt Ganzel put on a show for the departing Cincinnati fans, galloping in the mud around the edge of the field. Like Chance, Ganzel was a player-manager, and, like Chance, he played first base and batted fourth.[15]

The Cubs retreated to their hotel. President Murphy and his guest, Osborne Olsen the sculptor, sat in the lobby, plugging nickels into the automatic harp all afternoon, listening to music until they caught the early evening train for Chicago.[16] The Cubs incurred an injury that day even without playing a game. Before leaving for the park, Artie Hofman relaxed in his room reading the sports section of the *Chicago Tribune*. In a snide passage, the paper claimed the Cubs had won the first game through sheer luck. Hofman exploded, punched his right hand in the air in disgust, and gashed it open on the reading lamp.[17] Another self-inflicted lamp injury.

Dry but chilly weather greeted the athletes as they prepared for their game on Thursday. Jake Weimer again took the mound for Cincinnati. Carl

Lundgren pitched for the Cubs. This time, the Cubs took the early lead, scoring three runs in the first inning, then scoring three more in the seventh. Lundgren held the Reds scoreless for three innings, extending their two-game scoreless-inning streak to eleven. Finally, the Reds pushed across a solo run in the fourth inning, but the Cubs matched it in the top of the eighth. Lundgren entered the bottom of the ninth ahead, 7 to 1, and promptly threw eleven balls in a row wide of the plate, walking the first two Cincinnati hitters. With the count three balls and no strikes, Miller Huggins, the Reds diminutive second baseman, sent a sacrifice fly to center, scoring a run. The next hitter, left fielder Hans Lobert, flied out to Jimmy Sheckard in center field, but Lundgren walked the next man to load the bases. Manager and first baseman Ganzel strode to the plate and walloped a drive down the third-base line, past a diving Steinfeldt, to score two more Cincinnati runs. The score stood 7 to 4 with runners on second and third. Reds catcher Larry McLean represented the tying run, but he hit a weak pop-up to Evers at second to end the game.[18]

On their way down to dinner that evening, Lundgren, Tinker, Reulbach, Steinfeldt, Donahue, Moran, and Williams all entered the elevator cage together from their rooms on the fifth floor. As soon as the gate closed, the elevator plunged two-and-a-half floors before the safety clutch caught with a jolt halfway between the second and third floors. It took hotel personnel fifteen minutes to restore elevator service and release the players.[19]

The Reds Andy Coakley pitched superbly on Friday, holding the Cubs to a single sixth-inning run, but Cincinnati bats were cold. After loading the bases with none out in the first inning, it appeared the Reds might duplicate their productive first inning (five runs scored) of the first game of the series. But it was not to be. The Cubs starting pitcher, Reulbach, walked the first two Cincy batters and delivered two more balls to right fielder Mike Mitchell before manager Chance yanked Reulbach and inserted Fraser. Mitchell received two more balls to walk, loading the bases. Loud applause greeted clean-up hitter Ganzel as he strode to the plate, but Cincinnati bugs fell silent when their hero meekly rolled a grounder to third baseman Steinfeldt, who threw home to force Huggins, and catcher Kling threw to Chance at first for a double play. Catcher George "Admiral" Schlei then lofted a fly ball to left fielder Jimmy Sheckard to complete the Reds' first-inning frustration.[20]

Coakley and Fraser matched each other pitch for pitch for the next five innings. Neither team came close to scoring. The sixth inning began with Sheckard driving a ball deep into center field, but George "Dode" Paskert made an excellent running catch. The next hitter, Schulte, also drove a ball to center, but this time Paskert misjudged the line drive and allowed the ball to sail over his head. Schulte raced to third and tried to score, but Paskert retrieved the ball quickly and made a good throw to the relay man, second baseman Miller Huggins. Catching the ball, Huggins whirled around to throw a strike to catcher George Schlei. Blocking the plate with his body, Schlei tagged Schulte for the second out. It looked like another scoreless inning for the Cubs, but Chance followed Schulte with a triple and stayed at third. With two out, Steinfeldt rapped a sharp single to left, scoring Chance with the first and only run of the game.[21]

The Reds left fielder, Hans Lobert, badly misplayed a ball in the Cubs' seventh. While Cincinnati was batting in the bottom of the seventh inning, a disgruntled bug, seated behind a low railing in back of the Reds' bench, began heckling Lobert for his poor play. The two exchanged heated words, with Lobert throwing threats and insults over his shoulder but keeping his eye on the game. After two Cincinnati outs, the heckler, afraid Lobert might attack him, left his spot. A visitor from Nashville, looking for a seat, spotted the vacant chair, and, congratulating himself, glided into the empty space. As soon as the third out was recorded, the enraged Lobert, not realizing his tormentor had fled, whirled on the man in the seat. He landed several quick punches to the man's face, breaking teeth and drawing blood, before yelling spectators could intervene. Composing himself as best he could, the southern gentleman excused himself to attend to his wounds. He left, muttering in a barely audible voice about assault and battery charges. Indifferent, Lobert trotted out to his position in left field for the eighth inning.[22]

Sheckard singled to begin the inning. Schulte, the next hitter, bunted in front of the plate. Coakley and Schlei surrounded the ball, but their indecision caused third baseman Mike Mowrey to field the ball and make a quick throw to first. The ball and Schulte arrived at first at about the same time; O'Day, the only umpire, called Schulte safe. Manager Ganzel bolted from the Reds' bench to voice his disagreement. The "king of umpires" listened briefly but then, hearing something he considered disrespectful, informed the Reds' manager of his displeasure and promptly bounced Ganzel from the game and the ballpark. The Cubs subsequently loaded the bases with a walk to Chance, but Coakley recovered his composure and retired the side without a run.[23]

Larry McLean replaced Ganzel at first base and lead off for the Reds in the bottom of the eighth inning, smacking a double. The next hitter, catcher Schlei, bunted down the first-base line. Fraser raced toward the line, fielded the ball bare-handed, whirled, and fired a strike to third where Steinfeldt, with the ball, fell on McLean as he slid hard into the bag. Fraser retired the next two hitters to end the Reds' threat. The ninth inning proved routine, allowing the Cubs to prevail 1–0.[24] Off to a good start, the Cubs had three consecutive victories against Cincinnati.

All but three of the Cubs boarded their train at 9:00 P.M. that night and headed to St. Louis for a three-game series against the Cardinals. The others, Joe Donohue, Kid Durbin, and the injured Artie Hofman, not in the lineup for this series, went on ahead to Chicago. Players not scheduled for an away game were usually sent home so the team could avoid paying extra traveling expenses. The rest of the team would join them the following Wednesday for the home opener at the West Side Grounds. President Murphy announced that tickets for the home opener, on sale beginning Saturday, were available at the new ticket office downtown at Spalding's store. In fact, all ticket reservations would be taken at Spalding's instead of the Cubs' office.[25]

Pitcher Jack Pfiester joined the team in St. Louis. Umpire Hank O'Day also materialized. He never traveled with a team (that could attract accusations of cronyism) but always appeared just prior to the game he was scheduled to call.

After his short stint the previous day, Reulbach took the mound again for the first game against the Cardinals. But Chance was worried about Reulbach's control problems. As a precaution, Chance stationed Pfiester and rookie catcher Vin Campbell in a fenced area behind third base, telling Pfiester to keep his arm warm. Reulbach walked the first two hitters and, after a sacrifice bunt, issued another free pass to load the bases. Reulbach struck out the next hitter for the second out, but then shortstop Patsy O'Rourke singled to right, scoring one run. Schulte's strong throw to the plate nipped the second Cardinal trying to score, ending the inning. In the second inning, Reulbach walked two more hitters and surrendered another run. The erratic Reulbach began the third inning by hitting the first batter in the leg and throwing two pitches off the mark to the next hitter. Chance had seen enough. He summoned Pfiester to the mound, and for the next six innings the left hander pitched brilliantly, holding the Cardinals scoreless. Tinker doubled home two runs in the seventh inning to tie the score. Schulte threw out another runner at the plate in the bottom half of the seventh, keeping the score tied. In the bottom of the ninth, after one out, Cardinal catcher Art Hoelskoetter and second baseman Billy Gilbert each singled, placing runners on first and third. Pitcher Art Fromme then hit a hard grounder to Evers, who fielded the ball cleanly, moved to the base path, and tagged Gilbert for the second out. But then, instead of tossing the ball to

Chance, Evers decided to race Fromme to first base. At the last instant, he dove, ball in glove, hitting the bag. Hank O'Day called the runner safe. Meanwhile, the Cardinal runner, Hoelskoetter, coming from third base, crossed the plate, winning the game for St. Louis. The Cubs, certain that Evers had touched the bag ahead of Fromme, "swarmed around O'Day in loud and angry protest, but what Hank says goes and that settled the matter."[26] The first loss of the season for the Cubs was also the first win for the Cardinals, and the irascible Evers left the park bearing a grudge.

That evening, some of the players attended a touring production of *A Knight For A Day*, a musical featuring a chorus of pretty girls and songs such as "Life is a See-Saw" and "Little Girl in Blue." Vin Campbell's champagne-colored suit, not seen since Nashville, received mention in the newspapers. But Chance, down with a bad head cold and frustrated by his poor hitting (Cardinal pitcher Fromme struck him out twice), remained miserable at the hotel.[27]

St. Louis citizens could not purchase alcohol on Sundays, but they could watch baseball. Over 15,000 bugs and bugines, many in Merry Widow hats, came to Robison Field (named after Cardinals owner Stanley Robison) hoping the Cardinals would win two in a row against the Cubs. Just before the game started, umpire Hank O'Day assembled all players on the field and presented Cub rookie Vincent Campbell with a silver loving cup as a gift from his former college classmates. Cardinal fans overflowed onto the field and were held back by rope barriers and policemen patrolling on horseback.[28]

Overall made his second start of the young season, pitching well enough to go the distance, giving up nine hits but only one free pass. Chance felt better, especially after his two hits, including a double in the first inning that scored Schulte. Evers, however, continued to nurse his grudge from the day before. The Cubs second sacker still seethed because O'Day had called Fromme safe at first, allowing the Cardinals to win Saturday's game. But everyone knew that O'Day did not tolerate players or managers arguing his calls, so Evers managed to contain himself until the eighth inning. Then, when O'Day called a ball that Evers knew was a strike, self-control failed. From his position at second, he yelled his opinion of O'Day and his calls in words deemed unfit to print by the press. O'Day left his position behind the plate, stalked toward Evers, stopped, and struck the earth with his open palm. Reporter Dryden wrote, "When Hank smites the United States that way the blow means one of two things, viz.: shut up or go over the fence."[29] Evers fell silent. In the ninth inning, Chance, feeling better, made a stellar defensive play by diving to his right, knocking down a hard grounder, and tossing the ball to Overall at first to record the out. The Cubs won the close contest 4 to 3.[30]

The Cardinals hoped to win their second game of the season on Monday, April 20, with pitcher Arthur "Bugs" Raymond. Raymond turned in a fine performance, allowing only one hit, a single to Steinfeldt in the second inning. Unfortunately for St. Louis, the Cubs scored two runs in the sixth inning without a hit (two walks, sacrifice bunt, double steal, fielder's choice, and an error), and Lundgren held the Cards scoreless, giving the Cubs a 2–0 victory and two of the three games in St. Louis. Win or lose, the Cubs played most games in slightly less than two hours, but Monday's game was especially fast-paced and concluded in one hour and thirty-five minutes.[31] Frank Schulte played well in St. Louis, but still he could not help feeling a little depressed. On the train ride from Cincinnati to St. Louis, his watch and 1907 World Series medal had disappeared.[32]

The team had been on the road for forty-nine days, since spring training began. Tired of living in strange hotels and trying to sleep in bouncing railroad cars, the players were anxious for Wednesday's first home game in Chicago. The train finally rolled north, but stopped short in Springfield to let out twelve Cubs, scheduled to play an exhibition game against the Springfield Senators. Chance wanted Reulbach to pitch once more, hoping he could regain his control. Most of the other players were the regular starters, except Zimmerman in left field instead of Sheckard, Moran who caught in Kling's usual position, and Howard who replaced Chance at first base.[33] Reulbach pitch a complete game, giving up only four hits, but his control remained erratic; he made two wild pitches and allowed eleven Senators to reach first without swinging a bat. Still, the Cubs scored eight runs and won the game 8 to 4.[34]

While the Cubs played an exhibition game, newspapers noted a larger baseball milestone. On April 21, 1908, the *Chicago Tribune* reported that Henry Chadwick, the "Father of Baseball" had died at his home in Brooklyn, New York, at the age of 83. Chadwick came to the United States from England in 1837 at the age of thirteen and played both cricket and baseball in the 1840s, playing shortstop in 1847 on the Elysian Fields of Hoboken, New Jersey. In 1854, Chadwick began his sport journalism career, reporting on cricket matches for the *Spirit of the Times* and other newspapers. Two years later, he became the baseball editor for the *New York Times* and spent the rest of his life reporting, promoting, and contributing to the establishment of baseball as the "National Pastime." Chadwick was the leading adviser in formulating the rules for the National League in 1894 and for twenty years served as editor for Spalding's *Official Baseball Guide*. Henry Chadwick died from heart failure after falling ill with pneumonia. He was buried in Brooklyn's Greenwood Cemetery in a plot presented to him some years earlier by Albert G. Spalding, the sporting goods magnate and publisher of the annual baseball guide, who was a former owner of the Cubs, co-founder of the National League, and former star pitcher for the Chicago White Stockings.[35]

On Wednesday, the West Side Park, home to the Cubs since 1893, sparkled. Improvements for the 1908 season included a grandstand extension down the third-base side, new bleachers in front of and extending above the clubhouse in left center field, new dressing rooms with showers for the men in blue, new concrete "coops" (dugouts) for the home and visiting players, and a new office for President Murphy upstairs behind the grandstand. Reporter Dryden rhapsodized:

> That new playground on the west side is a poem of beauty and comfort and Mr. Murphy has reached far and wide for artistic effect. As yet he has not issued a catalogue directing special attention to the many works of art and lumps of bric-a-brac. Among the rare creations are 1,200 regulation Spalding bats worked into balustrades guarding the stairways. The upper boxes are railed off with iron piping ornamented with 460 gilded cast iron baseballs, facsimile reproductions of the playing article. At various places about the pavilion entrance cement Cubs may be seen climbing huge cement bats. This section of the zoo contains fourteen bears done in Sculptor Olsen's best zoological vein. But the Olsen masterpieces greet the bulging eye from the outside. As the bug approaches the park he beholds two heroic cement athletes facing the street from the roof of the office. One of the figures is Manager Chance in batting position and the features depict the well known lineaments of the Peerless Leader. Until wind and rain and sun have warped the legs a bit the rank and file of bugs will experience some difficulty in recognizing their hero. The opposite statue is a right handed composite of the Cubs' eight pitchers in the pose following the delivery of the ball. The statues weigh 800 pounds each and are clothed in cement baseball uniforms.[36]

Groundskeeper C. Kuhn suggested the idea for the cast iron baseballs in the upper pavilion, while Secretary Williams suggested the idea of bats for the staircase.[37]

Fair weather and mild temperatures prevailed for the opening ceremonies. A band concert greeted arriving bugs when the gates opened at 2:00 P.M. At 2:30, the band assembled in foul territory between home plate and third base. Players from both teams fell in behind, and all marched down the left-field line and then swung across the outfield to the flag pole in left center field for the raising of the 1907 championship banner. Cincinnati players watched without enthusiasm as Kuhn supervised the banner hoisting. After two attempts, the dark blue pennant with a large white bear cradling a baseball bat and a white baseball proclaiming in red lettering,

"National League Champions 1907" fluttered from atop the mast.[38] Players and band returned to their respective benches, but the festivities continued. Trainer Semmens and a helper suddenly dashed in from the clubhouse behind center field with a huge horseshoe-shaped floral arrangement carried flat over their heads. At the pitcher's mound, the horseshoe was placed on end, revealing the inscription, "Our Cubs." After a flurry of photographs, Semmens and his helper trotted the good-luck piece back to the clubhouse.[39]

Cubs pitcher Chick Fraser stood near the mound, and the Reds' lead-off hitter, second baseman Miller Huggins, approached home plate. The game appeared to be getting underway when suddenly and dramatically umpire O'Day, standing behind home plate, turned and pointed to the Cubs' bench. Adrian "Cap" Anson bolted out to the pitcher's mound to thunderous and sustained applause. Anson, a Chicago legend, dressed in coat and tie and sporting a derby hat, unleashed the ceremonial first pitch. It went a little wide of the mark, but catcher Johnny Kling lunged to his right to spear the ball as applause again erupted.[40]

Mordecai Brown, the ace of the Cubs' pitching staff, had a sore shoulder and was unable to pitch the home opener. Chance decided to give the ball to Fraser. After losing three straight to the Cubs to begin their season, the Reds had won three in a row from the Pittsburgh Pirates and hoped to continue their winning ways. But Cub bats pounded out ten hits and scored seven runs while Fraser allowed seven hits and three runs. The Cubs scored a run in the first inning and never trailed, securing a 7 to 3 victory to the delight of over 15,000 Chicago rooters. The box score recorded the sixth-inning double play: Tinker-Evers-Chance.[41]

Rookie pitcher Joe Donohue performed well during spring training, survived the player cuts, and was in uniform for the Cubs' home opening game on Wednesday. But, after seven games, Donohue still had not been given an opportunity to pitch. After this game, Chance decided to send his promising rookie to Montreal where he would pitch in the Eastern League and be retrieved to Chicago when needed.[42]

After all the opening day hoopla, the game itself, although a Cub victory, was a hum-drum affair. But, the next game against the Reds, on Thursday, thrilled the attending bugs. In a well-played game, both teams exhibited outstanding defense and pitching, the Cubs managing to squeak by the Reds, 2 to 1. The fast-paced thriller concluded in one hour and twenty-five minutes. Both pitchers, Bob Ewing for the Reds and Orval Overall for the Cubs, pitched well. The Reds scored their only run in the first inning after Miller Huggins walked, was sacrificed to second, advanced to third on a sacrifice fly, and scored on a sharp single to right by John Ganzel. The Cubs knotted the score with a run of their own in the bottom of the first. Slagle singled and was sacrificed to second. With two outs and Chance at bat, Ewing uncorked a wild pitch. Slagle raced to third and without hesitation headed for home. Catcher Schlei fired a strike to Ewing covering the plate; Slagle slid hard, throwing dirt over the plate, but umpire O'Day immediately rendered his call, safe. The Cubs scored the game's last run in the second inning when Steinfeldt smashed a ball to left which hit the foul line for a double. He advanced to third on Evers's ground out and scored on a single by Tinker. Neither team scored another run, but there were opportunities for both teams. Each time either team threatened to score, Ewing and Overall rose to the occasion or were saved by stellar defensive plays. The Reds were especially frustrated, stranding eight runners on base, including loading the bases in the fourth, gathering seven hits to the Cubs' six, and playing error-free defense.[43] All in vain, the Reds remained winless against the Cubs.

Introduced in October 1907, the "Merry Widow" hat craze swept across America. Ladies wore the monstrous headgear everywhere, including baseball games. The hat almost completely obstructed the view of any spectator unfortunate enough to be seated behind the latest fashion expression. Baseball writers across the country sounded the alarm, requesting that something be done. In Chicago, *Tribune* baseball writer Dryden described the "Merry Widow" hat: "Briefly, the hat resembles a manhole cover with an exploded ox liver scattered around on top."[44] While baseball owners wanted to increase attendance by attracting women as paying customers, the "Hat" was rapidly becoming a problem. Another fashion issue for a number of Cubs' spectators and reporter Dryden was the black-and-white horizontal-striped socks worn by the players. Most fans suggested the socks be all black. Referring to their socks, reporter Dryden stated, "the black and white barred legs of idle Cubs roosting in the concrete carpeted coop suggest a den of zebras at the zoo."[45]

After losing five straight to the Cubs, Cincinnati's frustration finally ended on Friday, April 24. Pitcher Billy Campbell used his spitter to perfection, blanking the Cubs for the first eight innings while his teammates scored four times. The Cubs did rally in the ninth, scoring two runs, but it was too little too late, and the Cubs lost for only the second time against their seven victories. Lundgren suffered the loss, giving up eight hits including two doubles and a triple and two walks in six innings. Reulbach, however, provided a silver lining for the Cubs. He relieved Lundgren, regained his control, and pitched three solid innings (one hit, two strikeouts, and only one walk).[46]

Although the rest of West Side Park gleamed, the clubhouse where vis-

April 22 — A female Cub in a Merry Widow hat comes onstage for the 1908 home opener. Nineteen players' faces adorn the hat like roses. "Husk," front and center, is Frank Chance.

iting players changed and showered was a mess. Defective shower heads produced only a trickle of water, but that was nothing compared to the thick layer of duck droppings in the shower area. Groundskeeper Charlie Kuhn kept a flock of ducks at the ballpark during the winter months, and the animals made their deposits in the visiting clubhouse. The Cincinnati players found the odor offensive. Reds manager John Ganzel lodged a complaint with President Murphy the day his team arrived. The next day, after no action was taken, Ganzel complained to the Reds President, Garry Herrmann, who had made the trip to Chicago. Herrmann inspected the clubhouse and immediately pronounced it unfit and unsanitary. He ordered his players to change and shower at their hotel until the situation was corrected. The following day, with the problems persisting, Herrmann filed a formal complaint, sending a telegraph to National League President Harry Pulliam. League rules required a fine of twenty-five dollars per day against the host team if the complaint was judged valid.[47]

The weather turned wet Saturday producing the first rain-out of the season, preventing the Reds and Cubs from playing the last game of their scheduled four-game series. Holding a press conference at his new downtown office at the Corn Exchange Building, Charles Murphy pronounced the visiting clubhouse sanitary, and as fine, excepting the luxury baths in St. Louis and Cincinnati, as any visiting clubhouse in the National League. He also claimed that Cincinnati players, led by pitcher Jake Weimer, had vandalized the clubhouse, twisting off locker doors and throwing them outside, and placing the ground roller inside the clubhouse. Murphy confessed that other ballpark improvements had consumed his energy and he had not had time to pay attention to "outlying details."[48] He promised the visiting clubhouse would be painted and put in shape as soon as possible. Still, he placed a call to Pittsburgh, warning the Pirates, due in Chicago on Sunday, that they might want to change in their hotel rooms until the clubhouse was ready.[49]

Cincinnati players were not the first to complain about the condition of Chicago's visitors clubhouse. The previous summer, the Cardinals publicly chided the Cubs for inadequate facilities, and the New York Giants more actively protested their accommodations. On two separate occasions, Giant players had tried to start fires inside the clubhouse to register their displeasure.[50] Dryden, reporter turned poet, wrote:

> You may scrub, you may paint the coop if you will,
> But the odor of ducklings will cling to it still.[51]

The clubhouse controversy aside, the Cubs were off to a fast start, winning seven of their first nine games to lead the National League. Two Cubs were hitting better than .300; center fielder Sheckard at .321 and third baseman Steinfeldt at .355. Steinfeldt lead the team and was sixth in the National League. Catcher Kling was next at .267, followed by right fielder Schulte .258, second baseman Evers .217, first baseman Chance .208, shortstop Tinker .160 and the anemic .118 average of left fielder Slagle. As a team, the Cubs' batting average of .231 was third behind Cincinnati and Pittsburgh.[52]

April showers continued as the Pirates arrived in Chicago. The Pittsburgh players changed into their uniforms at their hotel, as instructed, and rode in open, horse-drawn carriages to the ballpark as a light drizzle fell from the gloomy, gray sky. A few hopeful spectators, most with umbrellas, purchased tickets. Inside, the Cubs players, still in street clothes, milled about the field by the stands chatting with their fans. At 2:30, players and spectators, still socializing, were informed the game was canceled. Hardly anyone departed; players and fans alike enjoyed the personal interaction. Finally, uniformed policemen politely asked the reluctant fans to leave.[53]

The weather turned worse. Cold temperatures joined the rain; sleet, slush, and mud made a mess of the field. Pirate players spent the next two days huddled about the steam radiators in their rooms.[54] Winter had returned to Chicago, and baseball waited.

The lull gave Murphy, always scheming to increase attendance, time to think up a new attraction. "Father of Baseball" Henry Chadwick had admonished Albert Spalding in his will to fulfill a pledge: "I remind Albert G. Spalding of his promise to see that a monument shall be erected over my grave in Greenwood cemetery." Spalding had asked for donations. Murphy decided to place donation boxes in the stands and asked Chicago baseball bugs to contribute to the memory of Henry Chadwick by dropping their Indian-head pennies in a box: the Father Chadwick Penny Memorial Fund. Miss Lenora Kuhn, four-year-old daughter of groundskeeper Charlie Kuhn, unofficial Cubs' mascot, and a favorite with fans and players alike, would make the first penny donation.[55]

On Tuesday night, April 28, after four straight days without baseball, the West Side Rooters Club hosted a ball for the Cub and Pirate players. Over a thousand people attended the dance and voted for the Most Popular Cub and Pirate player. Chance (318 votes), Tinker (207 votes) and Evers (167 votes) received top honors for the Cubs. Honus Wagner, the great shortstop, followed by Fred Clarke and Tommy Leach, received the most votes for the visiting Pirates.[56]

The weather improved just enough to allow the Cubs and Pirates to finally play a game on Wednesday. Temperatures were still chilly, and from the third inning on a light drizzle fell, but players, spectators, and umpires (Cy Rigler and John Rudderham) willingly braved the elements. Before the soggy contest began, Pittsburgh's manager and left fielder Fred Clarke upstaged little Lenora Kuhn, by dropping the first penny in one of the two Chadwick Fund boxes set up at the foot of the double stairway leading into the stands.[57] President Murphy, anxious to resolve the clubhouse incident with Cincinnati, sent a photograph of the visiting clubhouse, sans ducks and droppings, to National League President Pulliam to counter the complaint filed by Herrmann.[58]

Usually, only one umpire worked a game. He stood behind home plate to call balls and strikes until a runner reached base. Then, the umpire moved to the infield behind the pitcher to call balls and strikes and to be in a better position to make calls at the bases. Occasionally, for an important game or to break in a rookie, two men in blue took the field. Such was the case for the Cubs-Pirates series. Charles "Cy" Rigler, a three-year veteran, and rookie John E. Rudderham made the calls. Since opening day, until the Cubs-Pirates series, Hank O'Day had been the sole umpire for every Cubs game.[59]

Both Pfiester and the Pirates Howie Camnitz pitched superbly. The first four innings were scoreless. The Cubs managed to push across a single run in the fifth, and neither team scored again until the ninth inning. Pfiester retired the first two hitters before right fielder Beals Becker, a left-handed lead-off hitter with excellent speed, grounded toward the hole between first and second. Chance ranged wide to his right to spear the ball. Becker and Chance raced toward first. Chance thought he won the sprint, but rookie umpire Rudderham called Becker safe. Chance slammed the ball to the ground in disgust, added a verbal comment, and was promptly ejected by Rudderham. Artie Hofman replaced Chance at first base. Tommy Leach drew a walk, the first allowed by Pfiester, to place runners on first and second. Pfiester thought he had struck Leach out, but plate umpire Rigler call two of the close pitches balls and awarded Leach first base. Pirate manager and left fielder Clarke took himself out of the game and sent Patrick O'Connor to pinch hit. O'Connor sent a sharp single to left. Sheckard charged the hard-hit ball and threw to the plate. Becker beat the throw to tie the score. On the play at the plate, Leach moved to third and O'Connor to second. Then Honus Wagner stepped to the plate and delivered a single to center, scoring Leach with Pittsburgh's second run. Wagner and O'Connor attempted a double steal, but Kling's quick throw to Evers and the return to Kling nailed O'Connor at the plate for the third out. The Cubs had one more chance in their half of the ninth, but Lefty Leifield replaced Camnitz and struck out Steinfeldt, retired Evers on a grounder to second, and ended the game by striking out Tinker. Gloomy weather, a heartbreaking loss, and a dismal yield of only $1.33 for the Father Chadwick Penny Memorial Fund made for a disappointing day in Chicago.[60]

On the last day of April, the St. Louis Cardinals arrived in Chicago, and Hank O'Day returned as the sole baseball arbiter. Cardinals President Stanley Robison and Manager John McCloskey inspected the visitor clubhouse facilities and gave their approval.⁶¹ Chick Fraser, dubbed the "Trusted Twirler" by Dryden, proved to be just that as he allowed only four Cardinal hits in a 3 to 1 Cubs victory. In the sixth inning, utility player Del Howard served as third-base coach. Steinfeldt occupied second base and attempted to steal third. Umpire O'Day called Steiny out. Coach Howard objected, or, in the words of reporter Dryden, "he ... airy persiflaged a bit." O'Day banished Howard to the clubhouse. The Chadwick collection improved to $1.92 for the day.⁶²

Chapter 3

Caught in the Rain

April showers did not bring May flowers, only more rain to cancel the second game of the Cardinal series on Friday, May 1. Frank Chance seized the opportunity to make several announcements. First, he proclaimed the nerve of his injured foot healed, giving credit to the specially designed street shoes he wore off the field. On the field, he wore the normal cleated shoe. Second, although Cardinal Manager McCloskey had expressed interest in possible player trades, the Cubs planned to go through the season with their current players. And third, he had been impressed by a pitching-machine demonstration earlier that morning and might recommend the Cubs make a purchase.[1]

Charles Dryden gave a full account of the pitching-machine demonstration in the *Tribune*.

> An agent of the pitching machine in use at Yale and Harvard for several seasons took his brass howitzer to the park yesterday morning and fired off its repertoire for the Cubs to hit at. The thing resembles a cannon mounted on a wooden frame, and it does everything but chew tobacco, soil new balls, and kick at the umpire. Compressed air shoots the ball at the batsman fast or slow, high or low, and applies the in and out curve, the fadeaway, and the raise curve, the gravity drop, smoke ball, grape vine sinker, and fooler. The addition of a metal gland at the breech containing a wad of loose chewing gum would enable the machine to throw the spitball, it is said.
>
> The maximum speed of the best meat and bone pitchers of the present era is equal to about nine pounds pressure in the machine. The tank can be pumped up to twenty-five pounds at which gauge the howitzer shot a ball from home plate over the clubhouse and into Wood Street. To show the Cubs how the machine works the agent placed it on the pitching slab and had the sluggers blaze away. There is a wire shield to protect the operator and framework from liners batted back at the gunner. As the batsman doesn't know what is coming, he gains excellent practice picking out the good ones.
>
> Fearing the machine might explode a five ounce projectile among his personality the peerless leader sent up a couple of fall guys in Howard and

3. Caught in the Rain   47

Zimmerman to take the first whacks at the strange twirler. With Secretary Williams firing from behind the shield, Zim poled a liner that dented the double thickness of hen wire. If the brass barrel is set true there is no danger of puncturing the batsman unless he steps into a curve. Chance is considering the installation of a machine to tune up batting eyes without arousing the jealousy of his all star pitching staff. Pfiester thinks the howitzer has a bigger jump on its fast ball than anything he can chuck, and Reulbach hates the dodgasted thing for its control alone. The compressed air exhaust, following the discharge of the ball, simulates the grunt of our best pitchers. After practicing the exhaust a few times, Fraser said the machine had nothing on him. Brown examined the wooden frame, which is similar to the structure surrounding a high grade Indiana feed chopper. Then he looked at the mangled mitt that brought him fame and $$, stroked the machine gun, and turned away without a word.[2]

President Murphy used the off day to follow up the photo he sent to the National League president the previous day with a wire inviting Pulliam to visit Chicago and inspect the visitor clubhouse for himself.[3]

The wet weather impacted the team in other ways. Johnny Evers and Johnny Kling both suffered from intense colds. Cloudy and chilly conditions persisted, but the rain ceased to allow the Cubs and Cardinals to continue their series on Saturday and Sunday. On Saturday, Artie Hofman played second base and Pat Moran caught, while the two regulars, Evers and Kling, recuperated.[4]

Orval Overall allowed six walks, but only two hits with seven strikeouts against the Cardinals on Saturday. In the first inning, the Cardinals scored two runs on a walk and a home run by right fielder John "Red" Murray. Murray's hit found a small hole in the wire screen and, to the obvious disgust of Overall, allowed the Cardinals outfielder to circle the bases.[5] After that, Overall held St. Louis scoreless, while the Cubs scored single runs in the first, third, and seventh innings to win the game 3 to 2, giving "Orvie" his fifth-straight 1908 win. The previous season Overall won his last nine starts for an impressive fourteen consecutive victories.[6]

The Cubs played their first doubleheader of the season on Sunday. Unscheduled, the doubleheader made up for Friday's rained-out game. The Cubs won both games. Mordecai Brown allowed one hit and no walks with only three balls hit out of the infield during the first seven innings. Leading four to nothing, Brown, in his first outing of the regular season, tired in the eighth and ninth innings. The Cardinals collected five hits, including a double and triple in the last two innings, and scored single runs in both innings, but it was too little, too late; Brown and the Cubs held on to win 4 to 2.[7]

In the second game, Ed Reulbach and Fred Beebe locked up in a fast-paced (one hour, twenty-three minute) pitcher's duel. Beebe held the Cubs scoreless for seven innings while his teammates scored single runs in the first and sixth innings to lead 2 to 0. But in the eighth, Joe Tinker walked. Moran popped out to second baseman Gilbert for the first out. Reulbach singled to right center field, and Tinker raced to third, just beating the throw. Reulbach went to second on the play at third. With one out, the Cardinals moved their infielders in on the grass to prevent Tinker from scoring on a ground ball. The strategy almost worked. Slagle hit a smash right at Gilbert, but it was too hot for the second baseman to handle. Slagle reached first, and Tinker scored. While Jimmy Sheckard struck out, Slagle stole second. With runners on second and third, Frank Schulte came to bat and beat a slow grounder to deep shortstop. O'Rourke easily fielded the ball and made a strong and accurate throw to first, but Schulte was safe while Reulbach scored the second run, tying the game as Slagle moved up to third on the throw to first. First baseman Del Howard (Chance, still nursing a cold, did not play the second game) came to the plate. Beebe's first pitch landed in the dirt at Howard's feet; catcher Hoelskoetter could not block the ball as it scooted back to the stands. Slagle scored standing up with the third run of the inning. Howard proceeded to foul out to end the inning. The Cardinals could not score against Reulbach in the ninth, giving the 3 to 2 victory to the Cubs.[8]

Trainer Semmens watched the action from the stands until a lady wearing a Merry Widow hat with long black plumes arrived and cast the entire section in shade. Able to view only the sky and the expanse of hat in front of him, Semmens returned to the Cubs' bench. It was a good day for Murphy: the Chadwick Fund reached a new high with $3.95 donated, and the Cubs' president received a letter from the Cincinnati Reds' Garry Herrmann complimenting him on the improved condition of the visitor dressing room and adding that Stanley Robison, president of the Cardinals, commended the quarters to all visiting teams.[9]

Wet weather returned Monday and washed out the last game against the Cardinals. Cub players spent the day packing for Pittsburgh. In between purchasing tickets and checking baggage, Secretary Williams spent the day in the rain searching for his bull terrier, which had strayed from his home that morning. Although the terrier was handicapped by a cut in the right hind foot and a charleyhorsed tail, Williams did not find his dog and sadly boarded the 8:00 P.M. train for Pittsburgh without his companion.[10] Meanwhile, Murphy received word that Arthur Evans, the rookie catcher released to the Wichita, Kansas, team for $500, was being returned to the Cubs. Wichita manager Frank Isbell offered no explanation, nor had Murphy received the money.[11]

Morning sunshine greeted the Cubs in Pittsburgh, but by noon the storm had followed the team to the Monongahela Valley and soaked the city. For the eighth time, rain postponed Cubs' baseball. This fourth postponement with the Pirates meant that, twenty-two games into their schedule, the Cubs had played only thirteen. That evening, most of the Cubs attended the theater performance of comedian Willie Collier in his aptly-titled routine "Caught in the Rain."[12]

The soggy weather continued. It rained two of the next three days, allowing the Cubs and Pirates to play only one game, on Wednesday, May 6. The Pirates halted the Cubs four-game winning streak, 5 to 2, behind pitcher Lefty Leifield. Leifield pitched well, but he received a little extra support from the Pirates' groundskeeping crew. In the third inning, Slagle attempted to bunt his way on base, but the ball landed in foul territory, rolling away from the third-base line. Slagle remained at the plate preparing for the next pitch. Suddenly, the ball changed directions and began rolling toward the base line. Pirates third baseman Tommy Leach let the ball continue to roll. Slagle watched in amazement as the ball regained speed and rolled into fair territory. Leach grabbed the ball and threw to first, retiring a befuddled Slagle. After the Cubs complained, umpire O'Day inspected the landscape and informed the Pirates an artificial slope had been created slanting toward fair territory. The Pirates admitted the slope, but insisted there was nothing sinister in the design, claiming it was done for drainage purposes. O'Day pointed out the slope would drain water onto the playing surface, not away from it, and ordered the slope removed before the next game or the Pirates would forfeit.[13]

Tinker, Evers, and Chance turned a double play in the fifth inning, or so the Cubs thought. O'Day ruled that the runner had beaten the throw to second base. Chance challenged O'Day's judgment. Shortly thereafter, Hofman stationed himself at first base as O'Day expelled Chance to the clubhouse.[14] Pirate pitcher Homer Hillebrand announced his retirement from baseball.[15] Only twenty-eight years old, Hillebrand began his major-league career in 1905 as a Pirate. He injured his arm that year against the Cubs and only pitched in ten games during his rookie season. His arm failed to heal during the winter, but Hillebrand tried to pitch in 1906; he appeared in seven games and posted 3 wins against 2 losses, but his arm never recovered. Hillebrand tried again in 1908, but after only one poor performance and a negative medical prognosis, Hillebrand made his announcement.[16]

As the game ended, the storm clouds returned. Barney Dreyfuss, the Pirates' president, decided the time had arrived to introduce his new concept to the baseball world, a canvas cover to keep the infield dry. The players watched as the Pirate ground crew rolled out the first baseball tarp across

A strong-armed defensive catcher, Johnny Kling compiled a .978 fielding average in 1908. A solid hitter, he had a .276 batting average and ranked second on the club in home runs (4) and third in runs batted in (59).

the infield, nicknaming it the "rain coat."[17] Cubs' chief executive Murphy, in a typically dour mood, said he was not impressed and believed it benefited the manufacturer more than the ball club. As the rain fell that evening, Murphy, disgusted with the weather, returned to Chicago.[18] Late that night, the rain came down with a vengeance. Torrents swelled the Ohio River, threatening to flood Pittsburgh and the ballpark and even to render the Dreyfuss "rain coat" useless.

From St. Louis to New York, the monsoon-like rains covered the entire eastern half of the United States. On May 7, rain canceled every game in the major leagues.[19] The Ohio River crested just below flood level, and the outfield of Exposition Park stood submerged in six inches of water. But the "rain coat" worked. The infield and baselines remained dry.[20]

Many of the Cubs players spent the day playing pool in the billiards parlor at their hotel. Players occupied every table, playing eight or nine games simultaneously. Suddenly, late in the afternoon, everyone began making miscues with exasperating regularity. A piece of soap discovered on the parlor floor gave the clue to the mystery. Every piece of billiard chalk in the room had been coated with soap, producing miscues after the players chalked their cue sticks. Circumstantial evidence all pointed to Johnny Kling, catcher and professional billiards player. "Just before the miscues started he was earnestly engaged in showing a player at each table in succession how to make a difficult shot."[21]

The days off gave management the time to ponder the question, who owned Arthur Evans? The answer: either the minor-league Wichita, Kansas, team or the Chicago Cubs. Murphy sold Evans for $500 to Wichita and had a signed document to prove it. Wichita owner and manager Frank Isbell had not made payment and had informed Murphy that Evans was being returned. Meanwhile, Evans, with a contract but no income, met with Murphy in Chicago. The Cub boss assured the young catcher that someone would be responsible for his salary while the case awaited settlement by baseball's three-member National Commission.[22]

The Cubs were involved in another case before the National Commission. Released by the Cubs to Lynchburg, Virginia, prior to the regular season, pitcher Martin Walsh filed a complaint stating that $86 was inappropriately deducted from his salary. Lynchburg sent the money to Chicago for funds advanced to Walsh during spring training. Walsh claimed no advance had been made and that he earned the money for services rendered in good faith as a member of the Cubs.[23] The National Commission expected to decide both cases quickly.

After the Thursday and Friday wash-outs, sunshine and several inches of water in the outfield greeted the players for the start of Saturday's game. The grounds crew formed a bucket brigade to remove as much standing water as possible. But by the second inning, clouds and a fine drizzle had returned. While the sun shined in the first inning, Chance, still nursing a cold, stroked a two-out double over the head of left fielder Fred Clarke, scoring Schulte. Kling picked off two runners in the bottom of the first to preserve the one-run lead. Second-inning lead-off hitter Becker walked, and Leach followed with a single. With Clarke at the plate, Becker wandered a little too far from second base. Kling rifled a throw to Evers, who tagged an embarrassed Becker. Clarke reached on an error by Evers, putting runners on first and second. But then Wagner forced Clarke at second for the second out. Leach, on third, and Wagner attempted a double steal. Kling bluffed a throw to second and pegged the throw to Steinfeldt at third instead, catching Leach for the third out. Chick Fraser allowed only one more hit, a double by Wagner in the seventh inning. As the Pirates came to bat in the last of the ninth, the constant drizzle turned into a downpour. The soggy field quickly became a quagmire. Chance claimed the playing conditions were unsafe and asked the umpire to end the game, but O'Day allowed play to continue. Leach grounded toward Evers. "The Crab" slopped after and captured the ball, tossing to Chance for the first out. Chance muddled to his right to spear the second grounder, throwing to the galloping and high-stepping Fraser covering first. Two outs. The Pirates' last chance, Honus Wagner, stepped to the plate. By this time, spectators, players, and umpire O'Day were soaked to the skin. Fraser took a deep breath, made sure of his grip, and threw three strikes past the power-hitting shortstop. Three outs. Game over. Cubs win. Everyone raced for dry quarters.[24]

Still winning, the Cubs' team batting average had fallen to a paltry .211, second worse in the National League. Only the anemic-hitting (.200) St. Louis Cardinals trailed the Cubs. Left fielder Slagle had been to the plate 57 times in 15 games with only 7 hits (a .123 batting average). First baseman Chance (.173) and shortstop Tinker (.192) made three starting players hitting under .200. Bunched between .236 and .255 were right fielder Schulte, third baseman Steinfeldt, catcher Kling, and center fielder Sheckard. Second baseman Evers (.279) led the Cubs in hitting. He also led the team in stolen bases (7), tied with Miller Huggins of Cincinnati atop the National League.[25]

The ninth-inning downpour on Saturday was only the beginning of another storm in Pittsburgh. In Chicago, the first shirt-sleeve weather of the season had arrived. So, unable to play in Pittsburgh, both teams and umpire O'Day boarded a train Saturday night and headed to Chicago to play a doubleheader on Sunday afternoon. The Pirates remained the home team for both games. Customarily, the visiting team batted first, but National League rules allowed the home team the option of deciding which team hit first. The Pirates, as home team, chose to hit last.[26] Nice weather and two games for the price of one attracted the largest crowd of the season. Bugs packed the stands and overflowed the roped-off viewing areas in foul territory and behind the outfielders.[27]

Brown and Steinfeldt lead the Cubs to a 6 to 2 victory in the first game. "Brownie" held the Pirates scoreless for the first seven innings while Steinfeldt had a perfect day at the plate with three hits (two doubles) and a walk. Trailing 6 to 0, the Pirates managed to score single runs in the eight and ninth innings to avoid a shutout.[28]

In the second game, Pirates pitcher Vic Willis, aided by two stellar plays by left fielder Clarke, allowed the Cubs only two hits as the Pirates split the doubleheader with a 1 to 0 win. Twice the Cubs seemed destined to score, and twice Clarke saved the day. In the second inning, Hofman, playing first base for Chance, drew a walk. Dryden described how "Steinfeldt followed with a smash which sailed far out over left field with Clarke in full cry. Just as he reached the edge of the crowd the Pirate leaped and grabbed the ball, coming down on a promiscuous lot of corns, but spoiling the hit."[29] In the fourth inning after a walk to Sheckard, a sacrifice bunt by Schulte, and a pop out by Hofman, Steinfeldt again stepped to the plate. Dryden wrote, "again Steiny lifted a mighty one left fieldward. Again it sailed out to the overflow and again Clarke jumped and pinched it in broad day light. This time he went almost out of sight into the mass of humanity, all that was visible being his arms held aloft with the white ball gleaming against his black mitt."[30]

Jack Pfiester out-pitched Willis, and for six innings neither team scored. Steinfeldt made a sparkling play in the fifth to prevent a run. Pirate second baseman Ed Abbaticchio led off with a double and was sacrificed to third. Center fielder Wilson hit a slow roller toward third. Steinfeldt charged, grabbed the ball bare-handed, and fired to catcher Moran; the throw beat Abbaticchio by half a step. In the seventh inning, the Pirates' Leach stroked a triple just out of reach of the lunging Slagle. Pfiester then bore down and struck Clarke out, but intentionally walked the powerhouse Honus Wagner. Abbaticchio attempted a suicide squeeze bunt, but he missed. Leach was a dead duck as Moran easily tagged him for the second out, but Wagner hustled down to second base on the play. Abbaticchio redeemed himself on the next pitch sending a ground ball up the middle into center field. Wagner scored without a throw for the game's only run. The Chadwick Fund continued to grow; the penny contributions totaled $5.59 for the doubleheader.[31]

The Philadelphia Phillies arrived in Chicago for a four-game series on Monday, May 11, but just before noon a heavy shower deluged West Side Park, canceling the game. Charlie Kuhn's efforts could not restore the muddy diamond in time for the afternoon contest. A protective infield tarpaulin, like the one introduced by Barney Dreyfuss in Pittsburgh, would have allowed the game to be played, since the storm quickly passed. This was not lost on Charles Murphy. The fiscally conservative president reconsidered the value of purchasing an infield "raincoat."[32] Manager Chance found a few high spots in the outfield and had his weak-hitting team, second worse in the National League, take batting practice. Chance also announced his four-pitcher rotation. The starting quartet, led by ace Mordecai Brown, also included Orval Overall, Chick Fraser, and Jack Pfiester. Ed Reulbach, still struggling with his control, and Carl Lundgren were slated as reserve pitchers.[33]

Tuesday was Ladies Day. Females escorted by a gentleman paying full price received free admission. Ladies without escorts might attend, but they were required to purchase their ticket. The Cubs (i.e. Murphy) copied the idea of Ladies Day from their cross-town American League rival, the Chicago White Sox. Charles Comisky, the White Sox president, introduced Ladies Day the previous year as a way to increase attendance.[34]

Phillies manager Billy Murray sent his ace rookie George McQuillen to the mound. Promoted from the Eastern League near the end of 1907, McQuillen won all four of his starts that season with Philadelphia. He lost to the Giants on the opening day of 1908, but won his next five starts. Against the Cubs, he celebrated his May 1 birthday (23 years old) winning 6 to 2 to extend his consecutive victory streak to six. Phillies right fielder John Titus never had much to say, hence his nickname, "Silent John." But he made a bold statement in 1908, shaving his large handlebar mustache. The last player to sport the handlebar, so common to players of earlier days, he had been the only player with facial hair for a number of years.[35]

Overall had an even more impressive winning streak, having won his last ten starts of 1907 and his first four of 1908. But the Phillies hit Overall hard, scoring four runs in three innings, chasing Overall from the game. Coincidentally, or maybe not, the Phillies had handed Overall his last defeat, 4 to 2, on August 10, 1907.[36]

Unhappy with the lack of team hitting, Chance stunned Chicago bugs on Wednesday May 13 by announcing the first player changes in two years. I.E. Sanborn, the other half of the Chicago sportswriters team of Dryden and Sanborn, composed the headlines for the *Chicago Tribune*:

> SHAKEUP FOR THE CUB TEAM
> SLAGLE IS GIVEN A REST
> Hofman Is Slated To Play Center Field
> In Place Of The "Rabbit"[37]

Turning thirty-five in July, Jimmy Slagle had patrolled center field for the Cubs since 1902. Slagle possessed good speed ("Rabbit") and was a fine defensive outfielder. He hit .315 in his first season with Chicago. And his career batting average was a respectable .271, but he struggled at the plate this season, compiling a dismal .100 average, the lowest on the light-hitting team. Twenty-five-year-old Artie Hofman joined the Cubs in 1904. As a utility player, he had played every infield and outfield position, but he had never been a regular. His acrobatic catches in the outfield earned him the nickname, "Circus Solly." The previous season, Hofman played 134 games, 68 as an outfielder, hitting for a .268 average.[38]

Popular with Chicago bugs, Slagle's demotion prompted President Murphy to adamantly declare the move was temporary and assure everyone Slagle would return as soon as he regained his batting eye. Murphy emphasized

3. *Caught in the Rain* 55

that Slagle would not be traded or sold. Chance promoted Evers to the lead-off slot in the batting order and placed Hofman in Evers' former sixth position, but rain postponed Hofman's debut as a starter on Wednesday.[39]

The weather took three out of four games against the Phillies as the last scheduled game of the series was washed out on Thursday. Secretary Williams used the occasion to announce that Murphy and the Cubs had finally been convinced that the purchase of an infield tarpaulin was necessary to avoid postponements.[40]

The Brooklyn Dodgers and blue skies rolled into Chicago on Friday. Murphy pulled Brooklyn president Charles Ebbets aside before the game and persuaded him to give Arthur Evans, the unclaimed catcher, a trial. Evans donned a Brooklyn uniform for the day. The clear weather finally allowed Hofman to make his debut in center field. He had one hit, a single, in four at bats. As the lead-off hitter, Evers also had a single in four at bats. Slagle took his position as third-base coach for the bottom of the first inning and received loud applause from appreciative Chicago bugs. Applause also greeted Hofman as he made his way to the plate for his first at bat. But the new Cubs lineup failed as the last-place Dodgers scored a 5–3 victory, making three consecutive defeats for the Cubs. Chick Fraser suffered his first defeat of the year when second baseman Evers muffed a high pop fly against the bright, clear sky, allowing the Dodgers to score three unearned runs in the fourth inning. In the ninth inning, Hofman grounded back to the pitcher and deliberately ran out of the baseline, hoping the throw would hit him in the back and allow him to reach safely. Some of the baseball savvy Chicago crowd emitted loud hisses to show their disgust for the unsportsmanlike tactic. Unsuccessful in his attempt, Hofman was the last out of the game.[41]

The next day, Saturday, the Cubs ended their modest losing streak in dramatic fashion with the new center fielder making the difference. Sanborn's story featured the following headline:

> CUBS VICTORS IN
> BRILLIANT RALLY
> Strenuous Battle with Brooklyn
> Pulled Out of Fire in
> the Ninth, 4 to 3.
> HOFMAN IS HERO OF DAY
> Catches a Tall Fly and Makes a
> Startling Throw to Plate
> in Final Round[42]

Brooklyn scored single runs in the first, third, and sixth innings. The Cubs were given two runs in the fifth, one by the Dodgers and one by the umpire. After an out by Chance, Steinfeldt singled to left. Hofman forced Steinfeldt at second. Kling singled to right, placing runners on first and third with two outs. Tinker hit a slow roller toward shortstop Phil Lewis, who booted an easy play, allowing Hofman to score the first Cub run with Kling hustling all the way to third. Chance sent Del Howard to pinch hit for pitcher Jack Pfiester. Before Howard had a chance to swing the bat, Tinker and Kling attempted a double steal. Charles "Cy" Rigler, in his fourth season as an umpire, was the sole arbiter for this game. As Rigler focused his attention on Tinker going to second, he completely forgot the runner on third, turning his back to the plate. Kling clearly had not reached the plate before Tinker was tagged at second, and Dodger catcher Bill Bergen asked Rigler to make a call on Kling. Rigler, momentarily confused, allowed the run to score.[43]

Still, after eight innings, Brooklyn led 3 to 2. In the top of the ninth, the Dodgers looked to add to their lead against Ed Reulbach, who came on in relief of Pfiester in the sixth inning. Dodger first baseman Tim Jordan drew a walk to start the inning. Lewis popped a ball safely over the head of Evers into right field, and Reulbach issued another pass to second baseman Harry Pattee to fill the bases with nobody out.[44] Sanborn described the next play: "Pessimism ran riot through the stands, and many gave up and started for home. If they got far they missed the chance of a lifetime to perish of heart disease. Reulbach was well on the way toward giving Maloney a base-on balls and forcing in a run, when Billy took a crack at a shoot which came across the plate. He raised a tall fly to center. Hofman had time to camp under it and dig his feet into the turf preparatory to a supreme effort. Catching and throwing the ball with the same motion, he lined it to home like a rifle bullet, and it was so far ahead of Jordan that the runner hadn't a chance to score."[45] The double play relieved the pressure, and a minute later catcher Kling raced back close to the stands to make a one-handed catch of Bergen's foul fly ball to retire the Dodgers without a run scoring.[46]

Energized, the Cubs came to bat with new life. Sheckard lined a single to right. Schulte walloped a double over the head of center fielder Billy Maloney, and Sheckard stopped at third.[47] The *Tribune* observed that "the bugs, fanned to white heat by the doings in the first half, were buzzing like a boiler factory in action."[48] Chance ripped a line drive right at second baseman Pattee. It was a chance for a sure double play and a possible triple play, but Pattee dropped the ball. Recovering quickly, Pattee threw to third ahead of Sheckard, who tried to scramble back. A long rundown ensued, allowing Schulte to reach third and Chance to secure second base before Sheckard was tagged out. Steinfeldt rapped a grounder to shortstop Lewis. Schulte broke for the plate and slid across a fraction of a second ahead of the throw.

The score was tied, and the bugs were in riot. Stepping to the plate with Chance on third and Steinfeldt on first and only one out, Hofman hit another grounder to shortstop Lewis. Again Lewis threw to the plate, and again the runner, Chance, slid across the plate just ahead of the tag — this time with the winning run. The crowd erupted in joyous and prolonged pandemonium.[49]

Mordecai Brown pitched a near-perfect game on Sunday facing only twenty-eight men. Bill Bergen's third-inning single produced the only Dodger baserunner of the day. Meanwhile, Hofman, Evers, Tinker, and Brown each had two hits as the Cubs scored five times to defeat the Dodgers. "Brownie" almost joined some exclusive company. Only once since the modern pitching distance of 60'6" was adopted in 1893 had a pitcher retired twenty-seven men in a row. The great Cy Young, pitching for the Boston Americans, mowed down twenty-seven Philadelphia Athletics on May 5, 1904. At West Side Park, the Chadwick Penny Fund continued to grow. The two Cub victories over the weekend excited the bugs' generosity; the two days combined produced over eight dollars (Saturday $2.67 and Sunday $5.55).[50]

The wet weather returned on Monday, May 18, canceling the final game against Brooklyn. It was the tenth rain-out in Chicago and the fourteenth overall for the Cubs in the first five weeks of the season. The Cubs had a day off on Tuesday as groundskeeper Kuhn prepared for the World Championship Banner Ceremony set for Thursday. President Murphy, an Ohio man, announced that he would support and actively campaign for presidential candidate, William Howard Taft, a fellow Ohioan.[51]

Hofman had played well against Brooklyn, but playing full time caused his knee, injured the previous season, to become swollen and painful. Chance reinstated Slagle in center field, but kept Evers as the lead-off hitter for the next game against Boston. Slagle would bat in Hofman's number-six position.[52]

The moniker for the Boston team, the Doves, was taken from the name of their owner, George Dovey. Boston Doves, Chicago Murphs? No, only the year before, Chance had insisted that his team be officially known as the Cubs. Since 1905, when Chance became the player-manager, the team had been referred to in the press as both the Nationals, referring to the National League, and the Cubs, signifying the youth of the players. Originally, the charter Chicago team of the National League (1876) was known as the White Stockings after the color of their socks. In 1888, the team changed the color of their socks and their name to the Black Stockings. By 1890, the team was known as Anson's Colts, named after manager Adrian "Cap" Anson and his youthful players. The popular Anson was fired in 1897, and the next season the team was tagged the Orphans because of his absence. Highly successful Boston manager Frank Selee took over the Chicago team in 1902 and immediately began to rebuild the franchise. The press acknowledged Selee's reputation for success, calling the team Selee's Colts, just as the team had been Anson's Colts.[53] Almost all of the 1908 Cubs were brought to Chicago by Frank Selee between 1902 and 1905. He became seriously ill with tuberculosis in 1905 and by July had appointed Frank Chance as player-manager and retired from baseball. He died in 1909.[54] Frank Selee deserves full credit for assembling the players that dominated baseball from 1906 to 1910. During those five years, the Cubs won four National League pennants (finished second to Pittsburgh in 1909) and two World Series (1907, 1908).

Plagued by wildness since spring training, Reulbach started the first game against the Doves and, in a surprising reversal of form, threw strikes. Unfortunately, the Boston hitters were swinging and made contact often and effectively. After surrendering a single, double, and triple good for two runs in the third inning, Chance replaced Reulbach with Chick Fraser. Over the next six innings, Fraser allowed only three hits and one run. Meanwhile, first baseman Chance led the Cubs with three hits, including a double, and three runs scored, as the Cubs edged the Doves 5 to 3. The game ended with a ninth-inning double play: Tinker to Evers to Chance.[55]

A run by Chance in the sixth inning led to an unusual incident — hometown fans booing an umpire for calling a home player safe. Chance stood on second base. Slagle hit a slow roller toward second baseman Claude Ritchey, who charged the ball and whipped a throw to first to retire Slagle in a close play. Chance raced to third and, without breaking stride, made a brazen dash for home. First baseman McGann fired the ball to catcher Bowerman. Chance slid to avoid the tag and apparently never touched home plate. Everyone expected rookie umpire Rudderham to call Chance out, but he signaled safe and gave Chance the run.[56] Boston manager "Joe Kelley and his Doves ... flocked around the umpire, flew at his face and did other gyrations until he ordered Bowerman (Dove catcher) out of the game. A considerable section of the crowd sided against Chance and the umpire...."[57] Their sense of justice injured, many Chicago partisans from the sixth inning on loudly rooted for Boston to win.[58]

Why did Rudderham make that call? The rookie umpire had teamed with Rigler for the earlier Pittsburgh Pirates series (May 6–10), but he was the sole umpire for the Boston Doves series. Against Pittsburgh, Rudderham had ejected Chance after the "Peerless Leader" strenuously objected when the umpire called a Pirate runner safe at first. Perhaps Chance had intimidated Rudderham and the rookie ump made the classic mistake of making a bad call to make up for an earlier mistake. Maybe it was just a coincidence that Chance was involved in both situations and Rudderham simply called them as he saw them. But, it was unusual for Chicago bugs to root for the Cubs to lose. One Cub, the reinstated center fielder Jimmy Slagle, was applauded each time at bat, but crowd encouragement was not enough; his batting slump continued — three at bats, no hits.[59]

The weather man produced a fine spring day with blue skies and a dazzling sun for the raising of the 1907 World Championship banner on Thursday, May 21. West Side Park sparkled for the event with greenery, colorful bunting, and flowers everywhere. Stirring music from the band added to the

May 21— Boston Doves catcher Frank Bowerman (6'2", 190 pounds) foils Johnny Evers's attempt to steal home. The official exaggeration put Evers at five feet, nine inches, and he may have weighed as much as 125 pounds.

May 21— An unhappy Jimmy Slagle after going hitless against the Boston Doves. As his batting slump continued, the center fielder was replaced in the lineup by Arthur "Solly" Hofman.

festive atmosphere. In attendance were Charles Murphy, Boston president George Dovey, and National League president Harry Pulliam, who nursed a bad cold.[60] On cue, the Cubs formed a loose marching order behind the band and in front of their own bench. "Then, to a lively two step, they tramped across to the enemy's camp and picked up the visiting players as they passed. Straight out across the arena to the clubhouse the procession moved."[61] After a few moments of silence, the large tightly-folded banner came into view, slowly climbing the tall pole behind the new bleachers in front of the clubhouse. Out of sight behind the bleachers, Kuhn slowly hoisted the giant flag. Sanborn described the scene: "Just before it reached the top the bonds were loosened and with a grace as majestic as if the inanimate thing realized its own glory and the supreme honor of which it is emblematic, it shook out its folds one by one. As the great expanse of bunting swelled to the gentle breeze the band played the 'Star Spangled Banner' and scores of American flags were released from the folds of the pennant floating away into the air, like down from the thistle's bosom. Then the great cheer which had been swelling in the throats of the crowd broke loose and lasted until the return procession started."[62] Several Cubs carried on their shoulders a stretcher-like object, bearing a large chest covered in flowers, back toward home plate. A monster bunch of roses, so big it looked like a giant bouquet walking on two legs, came out to meet them. Murphy, escorted by Dovey, was summoned from the stands. The treasure chest contained 107 pieces of silverware, a token of appreciation from the players to their president. The chest was inscribed, "Presented to Charles W. Murphy, our president, with best wishes of his Cubs. May 21, 1908." The engraved plate also listed the twenty Cub players and Charlie Williams as the donors.[63]

A beautiful day, a grand ceremony, and a most disappointing baseball game. The Cubs played poorly, and the Doves shellacked Overall, Pfiester, and Reulbach, in their 11–3 victory. The usually reliable Tinker committed three errors, and the game was further marred by constant complaints from both teams and the crowd about umpire Rudderham's calls. At bat in the fourth inning, Evers registered a silent protest on a called second strike. Without a word or even a glance at Rudderham, he stepped to the front of the plate, bent over, and wiped the plate clean. Rudderham took offense at this gesture and expelled the second baseman from the game. Zimmerman replaced Evers at bat, fouled off one pitch, and missed the next for a strikeout.[64]

Shortstop Tinker made amends the next day, handling nine chances cleanly and leading the Cubs with three hits in four at bats. Brown, almost perfect in his last outing, gave up seven hits, but no walks and only one run, as the Cubs avenged their embarrassing defeat the day before with a 7–1 victory.[65]

Clarence Beaumont, the Doves center fielder, put on a hitting clinic on Saturday in the last game of the series: four hits, including three doubles and two runs scored. Boston collected ten hits in all and scored four runs, but the Cubs plated two runs in each of the fourth, sixth, and eighth innings to win 6 to 4. Slagle finally had a good day at bat with two singles, a pair of sacrifices, and a run scored.[66]

The Cubs rested comfortably atop the National League standings with eighteen wins and eight losses, a winning percentage of .692. The club ranked only sixth in team hitting, but they led the league in fielding (.972). Evers (9) and Chance (7) were among the league leaders in stolen bases. And Brown and Fraser ranked first and second among pitchers. Brown had an unblemished record of 4 wins and no losses. Fraser led the team with 5 victories against only 1 loss. Orval Overall ranked fourth in the league with a 4–2 record.[67]

NATIONAL LEAGUE STANDINGS

	W	L	PCT.
Chicago	18	8	.692
Cincinnati	15	13	.536
Pittsburgh	13	12	.520
Philadelphia	14	13	.519
Boston	15	16	.434
New York	14	15	.483
St. Louis	13	19	.406
Brooklyn	12	18	.400

After losing three out of four to the lowly Cardinals in St. Louis, the Giants limped into Chicago on May 24. The first-place Cubs, who had already won six of seven games against the Cardinals, expected to do well against the struggling sixth-place Giants. But the Cubs-Giant rivalry was one of the most intense in baseball, regardless of their team standing. Led by their fiery, pugnacious manager John McGraw and possessing one of the premiere pitchers in baseball, Christy Mathewson, the Giants were always formidable opponents, especially against the Cubs. The largest crowd yet turned out for the afternoon contest. Aware of the intense and often bitter rivalry, the National League office assigned two umpires for the four game series, Hank O'Day and Bob Emslie.[68] Close friends, O'Day and Emslie were tough, highly capable, veteran umpires, O'Day since 1888 and Emslie since 1891.[69]

The two teams did not disappoint, playing a hard-fought contest on Sunday. The Cubs attempted to gain an advantage in the very first inning. Fraser started for the Cubs, but, as the game began, Chance had Jack Pfiester warming up behind the outfield near the clubhouse. As the Cubs came to bat in the bottom of the first inning, Pfiester took a rest, sitting on a convenient chair. Umpire O'Day stopped the game and ordered Pfiester to continue throwing or leave the area. Pfiester resumed throwing. After a few moments, Pfiester returned to his seat. O'Day stopped the game again and this time banished Pfiester to the clubhouse. It seems Pfiester had been in an excellent position to steal the signals of Giants catcher Roger Bresnahan and relay them to the Cub hitters.[70]

Pitcher Luther Taylor started the game for the Giants. Taylor, a deafmute, carried the unkind nickname "Dummy." A nine-year veteran, Taylor pitched well for eight innings, allowing only four singles and an unearned run in the sixth inning. Meanwhile, his teammates collected thirteen hits against Fraser and scored six runs; the Giants would have scored more, but for the efforts of Cubs right fielder Schulte. In the eighth inning, Giants second baseman Larry Doyle reached first when Evers fumbled his grounder, and he was sacrificed to second. Taylor looped a single to right. Schulte hurled the ball on a line to Kling to nail the sliding Doyle at the plate for the second out. Left fielder Bill "Spike" Shannon singled, moving Taylor to second. First baseman Fred Tenney lined a single to right. Taylor tried to score from second, but Schulte's strong throw arrived so fast Taylor did not even attempt to slide.[71]

After eight innings, the Giants held a comfortable 5–1 lead. Bresnahan added a solo home run in the top of the ninth to expand the Giant lead to five, and a few bugs began to head for the exits. Steinfeldt walked, and Slagle rapped a single to right to begin the ninth inning for the Cubs. The crowd started to buzz; departing bugs stopped in their tracks. Kling walked to fill the bases. A few prematurely jubilant bugs threw their seat cushions into the air. Tinker fouled out, but Del Howard, batting for Fraser, received the third walk of the inning, scoring Steinfeldt. With the score 6 to 2, McGraw replaced Taylor with "Iron Man" Joe McGinnity. Evers lifted a pop fly to short left, but Shannon lost the ball in the sun, allowing the ball to fall safely for a single. Slagle crossed the plate, and the score stood 6 to 3 with the bases still loaded and only one out. Sheckard walked, forcing in Kling.[72] Sanborn described the scene and the conclusion of the game: "Every person in sight was splitting a throat and behaving like a circus clown. Schulte lifted a fly to Donlin in short right, and then there were two out. Still, a hit would tie the knot and Manager Chance stepped to the plate with the determination to tie it. There was a crack of the bat and a mad yelp from the crowd which died out almost instantly for the ball sailed high over left center and dropped noiselessly into Seymour's mitt."[73] Final score, Giants 6, Cubs 4.

A spectator, hit with a cushion during the frantic ninth inning, complained to President Murphy. Responding immediately, Murphy had signs posted the next day reading, in large type, "I am sorry." Smaller print underneath explained that was what a fan should say if he threw something which hit and hurt another person. The notice ended with a polite request that patrons curb their desire to throw any objects.[74]

On Monday, Joe Tinker beat the approaching darkness, the gathering rain storm, and the Giants with one timely swing of the bat. Tinker's second hit of the game, a single to center, scored Slagle from second in the bottom of the tenth inning in the gloomy twilight to win a slugfest, 8 to 7. Ten minutes after Slagle scored the game-winning run, a curtain of darkness and a heavy downpour fell.[75] But before that moment the two teams collected twenty-two hits for a total of twenty-seven bases against five pitchers, including a home run by Frank Schulte. In all, twenty-two players saw action. Steinfeldt led the Cubs' fourteen-hit attack with three hits, including a double. Slagle, Schulte, and Tinker each collected two hits apiece. The Cubs pounded seven hits and scored five runs in the first two innings against Christy Mathewson, arguably the best pitcher in baseball. Bill Malarkey replaced Matty to begin the third inning. Meanwhile, the Giants had scored once in the first inning and three more times in the third against Pfiester. Mordecai Brown, Chicago's candidate for the best pitcher in baseball, replaced Pfiester with only one out in the third. Malarkey held the Cubs in check for the next four innings while Brown temporarily silenced the Giants' bats. But the Giant hitters connected against Brown, scoring three runs in the top of the seventh inning to take a 7–5 lead. The Cubs answered, scoring two runs in the bottom half of the seventh to tie. Brown weathered the Giant storm and remained in the game. George "Hooks" Wiltse replaced Malarkey for the eighth. Neither team scored for the next two innings. Tied 7 to 7 after the regulation nine innings, the Cubs began their first extra-inning game of the season. Wiltse surrendered only two hits, but a tenth-inning walk and sacrifice bunt, followed by Tinker's single, gave the narrow victory to Brown and the Cubs.[76]

The Giants not only lost the game, but in the second inning Schulte fouled a pitch off Bresnahan's right wrist. The trainer sprinted from the Giants bench to assist Bresnahan, and quickly escorted him to the clubhouse for a closer medical evaluation. Tom "Deerfoot" Needham replaced Bresnahan behind the plate.[77] On Tuesday, the Giants announced that Bresnahan would be out of the lineup indefinitely. An examination of his wrist revealed a splintered bone and the forming of an abscess which would require lancing. Even without Bresnahan, one of their best hitters, the Giants smashed twelve hits that day and scored seven runs to defeat Ed Reulbach and the Cubs, 7 to 4. Reulbach also hit four Giant batters. Veteran center fielder Jim "Cy" Seymour felt Reulbach deliberately tried to hit him with a pitch that just missed his head in the fifth inning. Seymour let him know about it, and the two traded threats until umpire O'Day took charge and ordered the end of the yelling match. But the intense, often-bitter Cubs-Giants rivalry continued after the game as the "rival warriors walked off the lot hurling jeers and defiance at each other."[78]

3. Caught in the Rain 65

Combined, the Cubs and Giants scored ten, fifteen, and eleven runs respectively in the first three games. After their hitting jamboree of the three previous days, neither team had much swat left for the fourth and final game on Wednesday, May 27. Pfiester allowed the Giants only one run on five hits in eight innings, but it was one run too many as Wiltse pitched superbly. Wiltse also benefited from the stellar defensive play of rookie shortstop Charles "Buck" Herzog. Three times Herzog robbed Cubs batters of hits, each time throwing out the runner to retire the side as other baserunners were about to score. Al Bridwell, the regular shortstop, had returned to New York earlier to nurse a viral infection, giving the youngster Herzog his opportunity. Herzog's fielding and Wiltse's pitching allowed the Cubs only three hits and no runs. In the seventh inning Wiltse won his own game with an RBI double smashed down the third-base line past a diving Steinfeldt, giving the Giants the 1–0 victory.[79]

The last game against the Giants was played without the recently-raised 1907 World Championship banner waving from atop the flagpole behind left center field. Kuhn explained that the top halyard had broken, sending the giant flag floating into the street the previous day. The groundskeeper had retrieved the flag and announced the halyard would be repaired and the banner in place for the doubleheader on Sunday against the Pirates. Chicago fans also learned that former recruit Arthur Evans, given a trial by Brooklyn, had a signed contract to play for Columbia, South Carolina.[80]

Baseball is inexplicable. In a previous series at West Side Park, the Cubs won four straight games against the St. Louis Cardinals. Prior to arriving in Chicago, the Giants lost three out of four to the same team. And yet they turned the tables on the Cubs, winning three of four contests in Chicago. On Wednesday night, the Cubs boarded a train bound for St. Louis to play the Cardinals.[81]

Sheckard had strained the ligaments in his left side making a throw to the plate against the Giants and was unable to play in St. Louis. Center fielder Hofman remained in Chicago nursing his knee injury. Zimmerman replaced Sheckard in left field while Howard took Hofman's place in center.[82]

The hottest weather of the year greeted the Cubs in St. Louis. After surrendering two runs to the Cardinals in the first inning, Chick Fraser warmed up and held the Cards scoreless over the next eight. Meanwhile, the Cubs' bats were hot. Led by Kling (3 hits), Chance (2 hits), and Howard (2 hits), the Cubs defeated St. Louis, 8 to 2.[83] Umpire Jim Johnstone, who only a month before had undergone appendicitis surgery, worked the game alone. The next day, Bill Klem arrived to assist the still-recovering Johnstone.[84]

Johnstone appreciated the help — the game ran to eleven innings before

St. Louis scored an unearned run to gain a 4–3 victory. St. Louis plated a run in the first inning. The Cubs scored three times in their half of the third inning, but the Cardinals scored two more in the sixth against starting pitcher Carl Lundgren to tie the game. Chance decided to replace Lundgren with Brown to start the seventh. After two Cubs were retired in the eighth inning, Steinfeldt and Howard each singled to center, placing runners on first and third. The two singles were hits number eleven and twelve surrendered by the Cardinals' starting pitcher, Ed Karger. Superstitions St. Louis manager John McCloskey knew hit number thirteen meant another loss to the Cubs. He replaced Karger with his best pitcher, twenty-six-year-old right-hander Bugs Raymond, who had lost a one-hitter against the Cubs in St. Louis earlier in the season. St. Louis fans screamed with delight when Raymond retired Kling to end the eighth inning and the Cub threat. Brown and Raymond then matched each other pitch for pitch. Brown held the Cardinals scoreless for the eighth, ninth, and tenth innings. The Cubs bowed to Raymond in the ninth, tenth, and eleventh. Brown gave up a single to left fielder Joe Delahanty to start the Cardinal eleventh, but he quickly struck out both first baseman Ed Konetchy and catcher Bill Ludwig. With rookie shortstop Patsy O'Rourke at bat, Delahanty stole second base, beating Kling's throw by a whisker. Still, two were out and light-hitting O'Rourke (.195 average) figured to be an easy out against Brown. But O'Rourke held his own against Brown, rapping a sharp grounder to third. Steinfeldt made a good play, grabbing the ball above his head, but instead of throwing to first for the final out, the third baseman wheeled and made a bluff throw to second before hurrying his throw to first. Chance tried to field the low throw as it hit the dirt in front of his glove, but he could only block the ball with his shin. O'Rourke was safe on the throwing error, and Delahanty scampered to third. Meeting on the infield grass, Brown and Chance talked the situation over and decided to intentionally walk second baseman Billy Gilbert, loading the bases and bringing Raymond to the plate. In his last at bat, Raymond had struck out against Brown. But this time Bugs lined a single to left field, scoring Delahanty with the winning run. It was the first loss of the year for Mordecai Brown.[85]

The injured Artie Hofman made a surprise visit to St. Louis on Saturday and witnessed the Cubs' 4–3 loss. When asked why he came to St. Louis, Hofman, a St. Louis native, replied he had not seen his mother in four months and came to spend the holiday (Decoration Day) with her. The skeptical press immediately speculated a Cubs-Cardinals trade with Hofman coming to his home town. President Murphy denied any plans to trade Hofman. But the Cubs did acquire a player from St. Louis, catcher and sometime outfielder Bill "Doc" Marshall. A thirty-two-year-old journeyman,

Marshall was twenty-nine before he came to the major leagues. Starting in 1904 he played for five National League teams (Philadelphia, New York, Boston, St. Louis, Chicago) in four years. Chance wanted Marshall to bolster the catching corps behind Kling and Moran. Rookie Vin Campbell had made the team, beating out Arthur Evans as a catcher-outfielder, but Chance wanted someone else. In return for Marshall, the Cardinals received only a promise of a player later in the season.[86]

On Saturday, May 30, the Cubs easily swept a Decoration Day doubleheader from the Cardinals, scoring 10 and then 11 runs. The Cardinals managed to score only twice in each game. The two games were split into separate morning and afternoon affairs with a lunch break for players between games. Spectators paid for each game separately with few patrons attending both games.[87]

The first game started at 10:00 A.M. Overall blanked the Cardinals for two and two-thirds innings. The second hitter for St. Louis in the third inning, right fielder John "Shad" Barry, shot a vicious line drive right back at Overall. The big man managed to block the shot with his glove, retrieve the ball, and throw Barry out at first base before collapsing to the ground. Unable to continue, Overall was taken back to the hotel in a cab. Twisting violently to block the ball, he had strained a muscle in his lower back above his kidneys.[88]

Overall was the second Cub injured by Barry. The day before, baserunner Barry collided with Evers at second base. Evers sustained a bruised left hip, preventing him from playing on Saturday. Chance brought Zimmerman in from left field to play second base. Sheckard, still nursing his side injury, went back to left field while Howard continued to patrol center field for Hofman, still recovering from his knee injury. Zimmerman played second base flawlessly and collected three hits for the day. Reulbach replaced Overall, but Big Ed again had control problems, walking two hitters and giving up a single to fill the bases. Chance acted immediately, removing Reulbach in favor of his ace, Brown. Cardinal first baseman Ed Konetchy promptly lined a single to left, scoring two runs, but Brown struck out catcher Bill Ludwig to end the inning. Brown dominated the Cardinals from then on, allowing only three more hits and no runs for the final six innings. In the second game, Lundgren went the distance, surrendering six hits and two runs. Schulte was the hitting star, collecting six hits in eight at bats for the day. But the feature of the series was the fielding of Joe Tinker. At the end of the doubleheader and the four-game series against St. Louis, Tinker had handled forty-three chances without an error. He recorded thirteen putouts and thirty assists.[89]

Chapter 4

The Brawl

On Saturday evening, May 30, the bruised and battered Cubs boarded a home-bound train for a four-game series against the Pittsburgh Pirates. The sultry weather of St. Louis gave way to the damp, chilly Chicago air. Frank Chance caught a severe cold during the trip and could not play on Sunday. Artie Hofman, with his sore knee, played first base. Jimmy Sheckard nursed his strained side while playing left field. Del Howard remained in center, and Heinie "Big City" Zimmerman again played second base for the hip-bruised Johnny Evers. Pat Moran started as catcher, giving Johnny Kling a rest, but in the eighth inning of the first game he was spiked in his ankle on a play at the plate. Kling relieved Moran and played the second game.[1]

Unlike the split doubleheader in St. Louis, the games with the Pirates started at 1:30; fans received two games for the price of one. Jack Pfiester registered his first win of the season in the first game, beating the Pirates, 6 to 3. The Cubs bunched six of their nine hits against Pirates pitcher Vic Willis in the third inning to score five of their runs.[2] In the second game, Chick Fraser allowed four runs in four innings. In the fourth inning, Pirate left fielder, manager, and Fraser's brother-in-law, Fred Clarke, sent a bullet back to the mound, striking Fraser on his pitching hand. Fraser finished the inning, but he did not return to the mound. Chance called on Ed Reulbach to take over. Reulbach continued his string of poor performances, walking seven and giving up ten hits. The Pirates racked up nine more runs to score a 13–3 victory and a split of the two games.[3]

His first day in a Cub uniform, former Cardinal Doc Marshall spent the afternoon in the first-base coaching box celebrating his sudden jump from last to first place in the league standings.[4] From his box, Marshall also saw Chicago bugs providing some additional entertainment. In two separate incidents, spectators in the stands behind first base started fist fights. The first occurred between two men placing bets on the action on the field. One

During a fistfight with Heinie Zimmerman in the West Side Park clubhouse, left fielder Jimmy Sheckard was beaned with a bottle of ammonia. Hospitalized for several weeks, his eyesight did not fully recover for the rest of the season.

Twenty-one-year-old utility player Henry "Heinie" Zimmerman played four different positions over the 1908 season and had a .292 batting average. During a clubhouse fistfight, he hurled an ammonia bottle at Jimmy Sheckard's head. Zimmerman's teammates gave him a beating that hospitalized him for several weeks.

"welched," and the other took it out in punches. At the end of the second game, a bug threw a cushion at a Merry Widow hat, but missed. The unintended target took offense and fists started flying. Police arrived and dispersed the gathering crowd and two combatants with no arrests.[5]

Not only fans exchanged punches. The Cubs were tired and irritable; a few had been playing despite injury and illness, and they had just badly lost a game at the end of a long afternoon. In the clubhouse, Sheckard and Zimmerman exchanged heated words, which quickly escalated into a fist fight. During the scuffle, Sheckard threw something at Zimmerman. Retaliating in kind, Zimmerman grabbed a bottle of ammonia and hurled it at

4. The Brawl

Sheckard. The glass bottle shattered against Sheckard's forehead, sending a stream of ammonia down his face and into his eyes. Enraged, Chance went after Zimmerman, but, weakened by his cold, he got the worse of it. Several players rushed to their manager's aid, severely beating their teammate. Zimmerman was taken to a hospital, probably by trainer Bert Semmens.[6]

On Monday, June 1, Johnny Evers, still limping from the bruised hip he sustained in St. Louis, played second base. Zimmerman remained in the hospital. *Chicago Tribune* reporter I. E. Sanborn explained Zimmerman's absence and the premature return of Evers: "Zimmerman wrenched himself in one of the holiday games at St. Louis, and made the injury worse by playing the two games here on Sunday. He was unable to get around fast yesterday, so Evers went on the old job, and got through it despite a sore hip."[7] No explanation was given for Sheckard's absence and the appearance of Jimmy Slagle in left field. Hofman again substituted for Chance at first base. The players remained publicly silent about the clubhouse brawl.[8]

The Pirates' third baseman Tommy Leach slammed four hits in five at bats with a triple and home run, beating Chick Fraser and the patched-up Cubs, 8 to 6. His pitching hand recovered from the blow sustained off the bat of Fred Clarke the day before, Fraser pitched the full game. In the middle of the game, spectator attention suddenly focused on three young ladies, wearing Merry Widow hats and hobble skirts, slowly parading the length of the grandstand from their boxes behind first base to boxes behind third, ostrich plumes undulating on their hats. The smiling ladies enjoyed their stroll, as did the gentlemen in the crowd.[9]

On Tuesday, the injury-riddled Cubs lost their third-straight game to the Pirates, 12 to 6. Honus Wagner, the perennial National League batting champion and Pirate shortstop, led the Pittsburgh assault with three hits in four at bats, including a double and a home run into the right-field bleachers. Sore-hipped Johnny Evers also had a productive day at the plate, going four for five with a triple. Trailing 7 to 1 in the fifth inning, Chance considered the cause lost and decided to give Blaine "Kid" Durbin an opportunity to pitch in relief of Carl Lundgren. But then, in the bottom of the fifth, the Cubs scored four runs, closing the gap to 7–5. Durbin took the mound for the top of the sixth inning and completed his warm-up tosses when Chance beckoned him to the bench. Chance could not risk trying the youngster now; instead, he decided to go with Brown, his best pitcher. But even "Brownie" could not check the Pirates this day. Brown allowed three runs in two innings before giving way to Ed Reulbach for the final two innings and another two Pirate runs.[10]

Charlie Kuhn, the West Side Park groundskeeper, had repaired the flagpole halyard and, as promised, had the 1907 championship banner flying again for the Sunday doubleheader. But by Tuesday, Chicago fans, players, and press all attributed the club's recent misfortunes (injuries, losses and bad weather) to the purple-and-gold banner provided by the National Commission. Everyone saw not gold, but yellow, the color of cowardice, waving above West Side Park. At the end of the lopsided loss to the Pirates on Tuesday, President Murphy exclaimed, "That settles it! No more yellow pennant for me. I'll burn it or bury it. I haven't decided which, but there'll be nothing yellow about the Cubs or their plant hereafter. We'll use our own world's pennant in the future, even if we are found guilty of lese majeaty (sic), contempt of court, and every other crime in the National Commission's calendar.... It's a hoodoo color in baseball and we will hoist the red, white, and blue pennant which we had made for ourselves.... We've had nothing but accidents and injuries and tough luck weather ever since the pennant was raised and it began on the day we raised it."[11]

The Cubs' train departed Chicago at 5:30 P.M. on Tuesday, June 2, for a sixteen-game, four-city eastern tour of Boston, Brooklyn, Philadelphia and New York. Three Cubs did not board the east-bound train; Moran required stitches for his spiked ankle, Zimmerman remained in the hospital after his beating on Sunday, and Sheckard needed a doctor's care for his blurred vision. Sanborn still kept mum about the Sunday fight, writing that Sheckard "did not accompany the Cubs ... as his ankle was badly swollen from the wrenching he gave it sliding to third base the day before. No bones are broken, and Sheckard is expected to join the club in a week."[12] He did not mention Zimmerman at all.

The Cubs arrived in Rochester, New York, for an exhibition game on Wednesday, June 3. Of the starting lineup, only Tinker, Steinfeldt, and Schulte played in the 7 to 4 win against the Rochester nine. In the batting order, Kid Durbin led off and played center field; Slagle batted second and played left field; Schulte hit third in right field; Hofman at first base hit fourth; Steinfeldt at third hit fifth; Howard played second base and hit in the sixth slot; Marshall played his first game as a Cub, catching and batting seventh; and shortstop Tinker hit in his accustomed eighth spot. Exhibiting his best control of the season, Reulbach gave up eleven hits, but only four walks against five strikeouts in the complete-game victory. Doc Marshall hit a three-run home run.[13]

The National Commission finally announced its decision in the Arthur Evans case, declaring Evans a free agent and ruling that Wichita must pay Chicago $500. The ruling also required the Cubs to compensate Evans for ten days pay at the rate of $200 a month for a total of sixty-six dollars. In other Cub news, the *Chicago Tribune* proclaimed, "Reports in Local Circles Indicate Changes in Team-Zimmerman May Go to Cardinals." Sanborn explained that, due to "reports of a quarrel between Manager Chance and the utility man," the trade talk mentioned Zimmerman going to St. Louis in exchange for pitcher Ed Karger. When queried, Murphy only denied any plans to trade Slagle to St. Louis.[14]

On Thursday, June 4, the battered Cubs arrived in Boston. Before the game, Chance called his players to his hotel room and delivered a stern ten-minute lecture. Neither the players nor Chance divulged the contents of the lecture, but the grim, flushed, perspiring face of the manager conveyed the tone of his message.[15]

The game began under a sunny sky, but after the Cubs batted in the top of the first inning, storm clouds rumbled in and poured a heavy rain on the field. After a twenty-eight minute delay, the sun reappeared, and the game continued until darkness halted play after seventeen innings with the score still tied at one. After three hours and seventeen minutes of baseball, umpire O'Day dismissed the crowd as twilight faded to darkness. Both pitchers, Pfiester for the Cubs and Vive Lindaman for the Doves, pitched all seventeen innings. Both teams scored their lone run in the seventh. Howard poked a fly over the short left-field fence for a home run to give the Cubs the lead. The Doves tied it in their half. Center fielder Clarence "Ginger" Beaumont singled to start the inning. Manager and left fielder Joe Kelley walked. First baseman Dan McGann placed a bunt down the third-base line, sacrificing the runners to second and third with one out. Beaumont took a long lead off third, but southpaw Pfiester ignored him, concentrating on the hitter. Then Bowerman hit a sharp grounder to Steinfeldt at third. Normally a runner on third in this situation would be unable to score, but because Beaumont had such a huge lead against the left-handed pitcher, he sprinted for home upon contact. Steinfeldt never had a chance for a play at the plate. After thirteen innings, Pfiester had allowed only the one run and three singles. Lindaman had surrendered only two hits to the Cubs, including Howard's four-bagger. Doves second baseman Claude Ritchey came close to ending the game in the sixteenth inning. The Doves loaded the bases with only one out, but Bowerman popped out to Kling behind the plate. Ritchey, who was unsuccessful in his first five at bats against Pfiester, lofted a high fly over the left-field fence, but the wind blew it just outside the foul pole, preventing a grand slam. On the next pitch, Ritchey ripped a line drive to center, but Hofman raced in and made a shoe-top catch to retire Ritchey and the Doves. Chance returned to first base, and Evers stayed at second. Home-run Howard played left field, and weak-kneed Hofman patrolled center while Slagle remained on the bench.[16] At the end of the game, Doves management announced that the marathon tie game would not be completed the next day. Instead, the game would be continued on the Cubs' next visit to Boston.

Former heavyweight, bare-knuckle champion pugilist, John L. Sullivan attended the game on Friday. Escorted females were admitted at no charge on this "Ladies Day" in Boston. John L. and the ladies witnessed the Cubs end their winless streak with a 4 to 2 victory. Evers scored three of the four Cub runs, and Brown pitched a complete game, giving up five hits and single runs in the second and third innings. In the first inning, another player suffered a serious injury. Steinfeldt fouled a pitch, splintering the middle finger on the throwing hand of the Doves' catcher, Frank Bowerman. The prognosis indicated Bowerman would require several weeks to mend. George "Peaches" Graham relieved Bowerman.[17]

The Cubs sustained still another injury. Howard awoke the next morning with a swollen hand and wrist. A visit to a doctor confirmed trainer Semmens' diagnosis of no broken bones, but Howard would not be able to play for a few days. Chance wired Murphy to send Zimmerman to Boston.[18] He needed every available hand. The next day, word arrived that Zimmerman remained in the hospital and could not report to Boston. Murphy also informed Chance that Sheckard's eyes were improving, but his ankle remained weak and he also could not join the team.[19]

On Saturday, June 6, Howard's sprained hand forced Chance to play Slagle in left field. Even short-handed, the Cubs erupted for nineteen hits against four Boston pitchers, scoring a 14 to 0 victory. Slagle had one hit, a single, a base on balls, and scored one run; he also made two stellar catches in the ninth inning, picking balls off the left-field fence. Schulte went four for five with a double. Chance, Evers, and Steinfeldt each had three hits. Kling swatted a grand slam, and Hofman hit a solo home run. Fraser pitched seven scoreless innings and had an unassisted double play, catching a line drive and running to first, touching the base before the Dove runner could return. Reulbach pitched the final two innings, allowing a single and walking three, but preserving the shutout. Vin Campbell saw his first action of the season, pinch hitting unsuccessfully for Fraser in the eighth inning.[20]

Injuries and team turmoil aside, the Cubs had improved their team batting average to a respectable .236, the third best in the National League behind Philadelphia (.251) and Cincinnati (.242). Individually, Howard led the league in hitting with a .340 average. Playing as a substitute for several injured teammates, Howard had played in 16 games with 17 hits in 50 at bats. Among the regulars, third baseman Steinfeldt played every game and led the team with a .287 average, 40 hits in 139 at bats. Tinker had not missed a game either, but he struggled at the plate, hitting only .197. Schulte, the only other regular who had played in each of the Cubs' forty games, carried a .232 average. Evers (34 games) and Kling (35 games) were hitting .279 and .276 respectively. Chance had raised his average to .241. Sheckard played 36 games and hit .258 before his fight with Zimmerman. Playing in 11 games, Zimmerman carried a .290 average. Slagle had played in 23 games and had only fourteen hits (.140) in 100 times at bat, while his replacement, Hofman, sported a .222 average. Evers led the team with eleven stolen bases. As a team, the Cubs also placed third in defense with a .983 fielding percentage behind Boston (.987) and league-leading Pittsburgh (.989).[21] In the standings, Chicago remained in first place with a record of 25 wins and 15 losses, 2 games ahead of Cincinnati and 3 ahead of Pittsburgh.[22] The next day, Sunday, the Cubs and Doves idled about town; Boston did not allow baseball on the Sabbath.

Schulte awoke Monday morning, June 8, with severe stomach pain and immediately contacted a doctor. The doctor diagnosed Schulte with appendicitis, and prescribed complete rest. The ballplayer heeded the advice and remained in bed all day.[23] Schulte's absence caused a real dilemma for Chance; he was out of substitutes. Howard's sprained hand kept him on the sidelines. Forced to improvise, Chance placed the still-not-healed Pat Moran and his spiked ankle behind the plate and assigned catcher Johnny Kling to center field. Still hobbled by his knee, Hofman moved to right field. In Boston, the afternoon sun glared directly into right field, so Chance placed the more-experienced outfielder there and kept Kling in the shadows of center field.[24] The patched-up Cubs scored four runs in the first inning and added another run in the eighth inning. Brown surrendered single runs in the sixth and eight innings to win, 5 to 2.[25]

After the game, Schulte arose from his bed in time to board the New York-bound train with his teammates for the next series against the Brooklyn Dodgers. Kling and Hofman switched outfield positions for the first game in Brooklyn as Schulte required another day of rest. Kling moved to right field because in the Dodgers' Washington Park, right field had the least-direct sun glare. Pfiester held Brooklyn scoreless for the first six innings as his teammates scored single runs in the first, fourth, and fifth innings to lead 3 to 0. But after two outs in the Brooklyn seventh, catcher Lew Ritter, the eighth-place hitter, dropped a Texas leaguer behind third. Before Steinfeldt could retrieve the ball, Ritter reached second. Pitcher Harry McIntire surprised everyone with a single to left, scoring Ritter. Center fielder Al Burch followed with another single, moving McIntire up a base. Second baseman

Harry Pattee singled to right, and McIntire scored Brooklyn's second run as Burch raced to third. Kling's relay throw to Evers struck the second baseman on the end of a finger on his throwing hand, causing an excruciating pain. As the ball lay on the outfield grass, Burch realized time had not been called and scampered across the plate with the tying run. The Cubs scored the winning run in their next at bat in the top of the eighth inning. The first man up, Hofman, singled to center. Kling laid down a perfect sacrifice, sending Hofman to second. After Chance popped out for the second out, Steinfeldt came through in the clutch, sending a single into right field and scoring Hofman. Brooklyn failed to score in the eighth, and in the ninth inning Pfiester struck out three Dodgers to preserve a 4 to 3 win. Slagle finally broke out of his hitting slump, stroking three singles in four at bats. Bill Mack, the recently-signed collegiate pitcher from Syracuse University, joined the Cubs in Brooklyn. The lanky left-hander gave the Cubs their second southpaw, along with Pfiester.[26]

The Cubs' four-game winning streak came to a screeching halt on Wednesday, June 10, as George "Nap" Rucker pitched a four-hit shutout for Brooklyn, beating Chicago, 2 to 0. Moran had two of the Cubs' four hits, a double and single. Slagle and Steinfeldt had the other two hits, both singles, but the Cubs failed to score against Brooklyn's ace southpaw. Fraser matched Rucker, allowing only four hits, all singles, but the Cubs' defense allowed Brooklyn to score twice. Fraser retired the first hitter in the second inning. Then, after a walk to first baseman Tim Jordan and his steal of second, third baseman Tommy Sheehan hit a slow bounder wide of third. Instead of cutting the ball off, Steinfeldt allowed the ball to go to Tinker at deep short. Sheehan beat the throw to first, and Jordan went to third. With only one out, the Cubs played the infield in to cut off the run at the plate. Shortstop Phil Lewis popped a fly towards left behind the drawn-in infield. Tinker raced back and made the catch in short left field. Jordan took a gamble, tagged at third, and sprinted for home. Running full speed away from home, Tinker had to stop, pivot, and throw to the plate. Jordan arrived just ahead of the ball to score Brooklyn's first run. Two were out in the sixth inning when left fielder John Hummel singled and stole second. Hofman had been forced into service at second due to Evers's finger injury the day before. Right fielder Bill Maloney hit a roller to Hofman, who fumbled the ball, allowing Maloney to reach first. Hummel made for third on the play. Hofman finally grabbed the ball, but heaved it ten feet over Steinfeldt's head at third. Hummel scored easily on Hofman's double error. Fortunately for the Cubs, Schulte did not have appendicitis after all, only acute stomach cramps. Schulte volunteered to play, and, due to sun conditions, he was placed in left field. Kling was stationed in right field, and Slagle returned to his old center-field position. Moran put on the catcher's gear.[27]

On Thursday, June 11, the Cubs finally had their regulars, except for Sheckard, back in the lineup. Evers proclaimed his finger healed and returned to action; Slagle played Sheckard's left-field position. Moran's stitched-up ankle still bothered him. Although no bones were broken in Howard's hand or wrist, two nerves had crossed, causing pain and swelling. So the league's leading hitter returned to Chicago to recuperate along with Sheckard, whose eyes had not fully recovered, and Zimmerman, who still convalesced from his beating. Even rarely-used rookie substitute Vin Campbell was unavailable on Thursday, spending the day in a Boston hospital with stomach pains.[28]

Cold and intermittent light rain threatened to postpone the game from the start, but umpire Bob Emslie ruled playing conditions adequate. Lundgren and Brooklyn's Irvin "Kaiser" Wilhelm pitched superbly, and after nine innings each team had only managed to score one run. The Cubs took the lead in the second inning. Kling flied out, but Tinker followed with a double to right center field. Pitcher Lundgren tapped a slow roller down the third-base line and beat the throw to first. On the throw, Tinker went to third. Evers lined a single to center, scoring Tinker. Hofman followed with another single to center, but Lundgren, waved home by third-base coach Marshall, was thrown out by a wide margin at the plate. Schulte flied out to close the inning. Brooklyn tied the score in the sixth inning. Second baseman Harry Pattee walked to lead off the inning and was sacrificed to second. Right fielder Bill Maloney hit a high bounder to the hole at deep shortstop. Tinker got to the ball, but he was unable to throw anyone out; Pattee reached third. On the first pitch to first baseman Tim Jordan, Maloney stole second. After Chance ordered Jordan walked to load the bases, third baseman Tommy Sheehan came to the plate. Lundgren's first pitch to Sheehan hit the dirt in front of the plate and bounced over Kling's head; Pattee scored easily. Only Kling's hustle kept Maloney on third. Sheehan then rapped a sharp grounder down the third-base line. It would have been a sure double play before Lundgren's wild pitch. As it was, Steinfeldt made a brilliant back-handed grab and threw Maloney out at the plate. Shortstop Lewis popped out to end the inning.[29]

From there, Lundgren and Wilhelm traded scoreless innings until the top of the eleventh. Kling opened with a single and was sacrificed to second by Tinker. Lundgren gave himself and the Cubs the lead by lining a hit to left over the third-base bag, easily scoring Kling. Lundgren preserved the 2 to 1 win by retiring three consecutive Brooklyn hitters on fly balls in the bottom of the eleventh.[30]

It was only mid–June, and "Big Ed" Reulbach usually waited until the hot weather of July to master his control. But on Friday, June 12, with Overall unable to pitch due to lower back problems, manager Chance took a gamble and gave the ball to Reulbach. The formerly erratic pitcher responded magnificently, pitching a complete-game 7–1 victory. Brooklyn had six hits, but Reulbach did not issue a single walk. As inning after inning passed without a sign of the old wildness, Brooklyn spectators began to rub their eyes and inquire who was doing the pitching for Chicago. But Reulbach had made an extra effort. For several days, he had arrived at the ballpark an hour before anyone else and practiced throwing at a nail head in the center field fence.[31]

Chance and Hofman were the hitting stars in support of Reulbach. Chance had two hits, including a double in three official at bats. Hofman collected three hits in four at bats. Slagle contributed a single, driving in two runs in the first inning. Brooklyn's only run crossed the plate in the sixth inning after pitcher Jim Pastorious cracked a triple to right center field, followed by a single off the bat of center fielder Al Burch.[32]

After the game, Chance informed Vin Campbell he had been assigned to Springfield in the Three Eyes League (Iowa, Illinois, Indiana). The acquisition of Doc Marshall, a veteran catcher from the Cardinals, gave Chance four backstops (Kling, Moran, Marshall and Campbell). Campbell had appeared in only one game, as a pinch hitter, prior to Marshall's arrival; the chances of the rookie seeing any playing time with the Cubs was remote.[33]

After winning three of four games in Brooklyn, the Cubs arrived in Philadelphia to play a four-game series with the Phillies. The first game, on Saturday, June 13, was a marquee match-up of two premiere pitchers, Brown versus George McQuillan, the twenty-three-year-old Phillie phenom. Joining the Phillies at the end of the 1907 season, McQuillan won all 5 of his starts, including 2 victories against the Cubs. One of the wins over the Cubs was an exhibition game in Providence, Rhode Island. Just a month earlier, in Chicago on May 12, McQuillan out-dueled Overall, winning 6 to 2 and recording his third-straight win against the Cubs.[34] McQuillan, off to an impressive start, had recorded 11 wins against only 3 losses so far in 1908.

For six innings, Brown and McQuillan battled in a scoreless duel. The Phillies had only two harmless singles against Brown, while McQuillan pitched a no-hitter for five innings before surrendering a single to Tinker in the sixth. But the Cub did not score. Called out on strikes to end the Cub sixth, Hofman challenged umpire Bill Klem. In his fourth year, Klem, already known for his ability to call balls and strikes and control a game, did not hesitate to eject Hofman. Kid Durbin replaced Hofman in center field.[35]

Schulte hit a hot smash down the third-base line to open the seventh against McQuillan. Third baseman Eddie Grant managed to knock the ball down, but his throw to first was too late. Chance attempted a sacrifice bunt, but forced Schulte at second. Steinfeldt followed with a long single to right, sending Chance to third. Slagle delivered a timely single to center, scoring Chance with the first run. It was the only run McQuillan allowed. He shut out the Cubs for the final two innings. But old reliable Mordecai Brown outpitched the Phillies' young whirlwind on this day. Brown allowed only 3 hits, all singles, to blank Philadelphia 1 to 0. His record improved to 8 wins against a single defeat.[36]

From Philadelphia, the ocean resort town of Atlantic City is a short seventy-five-mile trip across the Delaware River and the state of New Jersey. On Saturday evening, the victorious Brown, several teammates, and treasurer Williams took a train to spend a leisurely Sunday on the boardwalk. Like Puritan Boston, Quaker Philadelphia forbade baseball on the Sabbath. Shortly after their departure, a telegram came from Brown's wife. His mother was seriously ill, and he needed to come home at once. Chance tried unsuccessfully to get in touch with his star pitcher by both telephone and telegram. Early Sunday morning, Chance and several other Cubs went to Atlantic City to deliver the bad news in person. Brown returned to Philadelphia by the first train and departed Sunday evening for his home in Rosedale, Indiana, to be with his ailing mother.[37]

Brown's absence waylaid Chance's pitching plans for the all-important upcoming series against the despised Giants. Chance had set the pitching rotation so Brown would pitch the opening game in Philadelphia, rest four days, pitch the first game in New York on Thursday, June 18, rest three days, and pitch the final game against the Giants on Monday, June 22. Overall's back injury further complicated Chance's pitching options. Out since May 30 (Memorial Day) when he wrenched his back stopping a line drive off the bat of Jack Barry in St. Louis, Overall pitched batting practice on Saturday in Philly. While he could throw fine, the instant he attempted to bend over, something caught at the base of his spine, causing severe pain. Without Brown and Overall, the Cubs' starting pitching corps dwindled to three: Fraser, Pfiester, and Lundgren. Reulbach's recent steady performance was a bright spot that gave Chance reason to believe he might fill the fourth pitching slot. Still, Overall's injury and Brown's departure would put the Cubs at a disadvantage against their hated New York rivals.[38]

A heavy rainstorm struck the East coast on Monday, June 15, washing out games in New York, Brooklyn, and Philadelphia. The storm lasted all day and kept the players caged in their hotel. Chance shared a telegram that provided some amusement for the bored players. Bill Bernhard, manager of the Nashville team in the Southern League, obviously aware of the clubhouse brawl in Chicago, asked Chance to loan Zimmerman to Nashville for the rest of the season. The brawl notwithstanding, Zimmerman was a valuable player, and the team missed his talent on the diamond. After some laughter, a suggestion was made to respond with a telegram asking if Nashville would consider taking Brown or Chance instead of Zimmerman. The Cubs spent the rest of the afternoon following the White Sox game on the ticker tape and rooting for their American League rivals to win their twelfth-straight victory. The Cubs, confident they would be National League champions, wanted the White Sox to win the American League pennant. Embarrassed by their 1906 World Series loss to the underdog White Sox (known as the "hitless wonders"), the Cubs, desperately wanted a rematch.[39]

On Tuesday, June 16, Philadelphia's Tully Sparks pitched a complete-game 2 to 1 victory over the Cubs. Pfiester also pitched well, allowing only three hits, and deserved a better fate. The Phillies scored both runs in the fourth inning. With two outs and runners on first and second, first baseman Bill "Kitty" Bransfield lifted a fly ball to right center field. Hofman trotted into position to make the catch for the final out of the inning, but the ball glanced off his glove. Otto Knabe scored the first run, and Bransfield and Sherry Magee stood on first and third. With center fielder Fred Osborne at bat, the two runners attempted a double steal. Kling fired the ball towards second, and Magee broke for the plate the instant the ball left Kling's hand. Tinker caught the ball and hurled it back to Kling. The ball and runner arrived simultaneously, but Magee made a magnificent sweeping hook slide, eluding the tag and brushing the edge of the plate to score the second run of the inning.[40] The Cubs managed only five hits and scored their only run in the eighth inning. After Evers was out, Hofman singled and reached third when Schulte doubled. Chance hit a grounder toward the hole to the right of second baseman Knabe. Knabe gloved the ball and threw Chance out, but Hofman scored on the play and Schulte went to third. The inning ended when Steinfeldt grounded out. Sparks took no chances in the ninth. He struck out three Cubs in a row: Slagle, Kling, and Tinker.[41]

In the fifth inning, Pfiester and the Cubs were victimized by the practice of assigning only one umpire to a game and using a single baseball for an entire contest. Fans did not keep foul balls; the umpire demanded balls hit into the stands be returned to the field of play. Another ball might temporarily be used to allow play to continue until the out-of-play ball was retrieved. Because a nine-inning game was usually completed in less than an hour and a half, and a two-hour game was rare, owners established the one-

4. The Brawl

umpire, one-baseball policy to save money. With the Cubs at bat, Pfiester fouled a pitch into the stands and then singled on the next pitch. While the foul ball was being retrieved, Evers came to bat. A fan threw the foul ball to the first-base coach, Orval Overall, who, not wanting to interrupt play, held on to it. Evers hit a grounder to first base. Bransfield fielded it and threw to second ahead of Pfiester. Evers beat the return throw to first, preventing a double play. The play completed, umpire Klem turned his back to first and walked back to the center of the diamond, behind the pitcher, to call balls and strikes and to be in position for any play at second. At this point, Overall rolled the retrieved ball on the infield grass toward the umpire. Second baseman Knabe thought this the game ball and dashed in to retrieve it. Evers bluffed a sprint towards second, but first baseman Bransfield still had the real ball in his glove. He tagged Evers, and Klem allowed the out. Manager Chance came off the bench disputing the call, claiming, since it was contrary to the rules to have two balls on the field while play was in progress, Klem should have ruled the play ended until he had the retrieved ball in his possession. But Klem made a distinction, ruling that if a Phillie player had rolled the out-of-play ball to the infield with the intent to deceive the runner, the out would not have been allowed. But since a Cub player rolled the ball, there was no deception and the out counted. Chance vehemently argued that the only issue was the rule against two balls on the field at the same time; it did not matter who rolled the retrieved ball back to the umpire. Chance lost the argument, but he was not ejected from the game — a rare reaction from Bill Klem.[42]

The most glaring weakness of the one-umpire system always occurred with runners on base. The umpire moved from his position behind the catcher to one behind the pitcher in order to call balls and strikes and to be able to make calls at the bases. If a ball was hit down either foul line, the umpire was in the worst possible position to rule fair or foul. After the bizarre two-ball incident in the fifth, the one-umpire dilemma in the next inning probably cost the Cubs the game. Hofman was hit by the first pitch of the inning. Umpire Klem moved from behind the plate to a position on the grass behind the pitcher. The next hitter, Schulte, caught the ball square and pulled it over the first-base line like a rifle shot. The ball was fair by a yard as it passed first base and remained fair by a foot on its second bounce, twenty feet behind first. But Klem had no time to get into position to make the call. All he could do was wheel around and make a guess. He ruled the ball foul and sent Hofman back to first from third and returned Schulte, standing on second, to the plate. The next day, in his column, reporter Sanborn lamented the shortcomings of the one-umpire system, castigated the owners for their frugal ways at the expense of the best interest of baseball, and strongly encouraged the owners to assign two umpires to every game.[43]

In the final game of the series, the Cubs and Phillies played their third consecutive one-run game. Fraser and the Cubs prevailed, 3 to 2. The Cubs scored a run on a double steal in the first inning and added two more in the sixth. Hit by a pitch, Chance scored on Steinfeldt's triple, and Slagle plated Steinfeldt with a single to center. Philly scored single runs against Fraser in the fourth and seventh innings to close to within one run. Phillies manager Billy Murray inserted his young ace, McQuillan, to pitch the final two innings, hoping his club would score again. McQuillan held the Cubs, but the Phillies did not score again.[44]

Two umpires, Klem and O'Day, worked the Cubs-Giants series — not because of the Philadelphia incident, but because two umpires were always assigned due to the intense and often bitter rivalry between these two teams. Reulbach, after his superb performance in Brooklyn, took the mound on Thursday, June 18, for the first of four games against the Giants. The Cubs scored four runs in the top of the third against George "Hooks" Wiltse while Reulbach held the Giants scoreless for the first two innings. But in the bottom of the third Reulbach, with a four-run lead, suddenly lost all semblance of control. Ten pitches in a row missed the plate by wide margins. The first two Giant hitters, catcher Roger Bresnahan and shortstop Al Bridwell, walked. The next two pitches to Buck Herzog, pinch hitting for the pitcher Wiltse, were wide of the mark. Clearly irritated by Reulbach's inability to throw strikes, Chance yanked him. Lundgren, only half warmed-up, came on and finished walking Herzog to fill the bases with no outs. First baseman Tenney stroked a single to center field, scoring Bresnahan and Bridwell. Second baseman Larry Doyle laid down a bunt to sacrifice Herzog to third; he promptly scored the third Giant run when center fielder Cy Seymour lifted a sacrifice fly to Slagle in left field. The next hitter, right fielder Mike Donlin, ripped a long drive to right center field. Schulte raced deep into the alley and made a spectacular leaping back-handed catch to save a sure home run and preserve the Cubs' one-run lead. Sanborn described Schulte's play as "a miracle ... the sweetest catch seen in years."[45]

Both teams scored single runs in the fourth and fifth innings. The Giants came to bat in the bottom of the seventh trailing by only one run, 6 to 5. Doyle singled and Seymour popped a fly into shallow right center field, too deep for second baseman Evers. Schulte tore in from his right-field position, made a head-long dive, and caught the ball. In center field, Hofman was closer to the short fly ball, but he had wrenched his bad knee running the bases in the top of the inning and could only jog. The next hitter, Mike

4. The Brawl

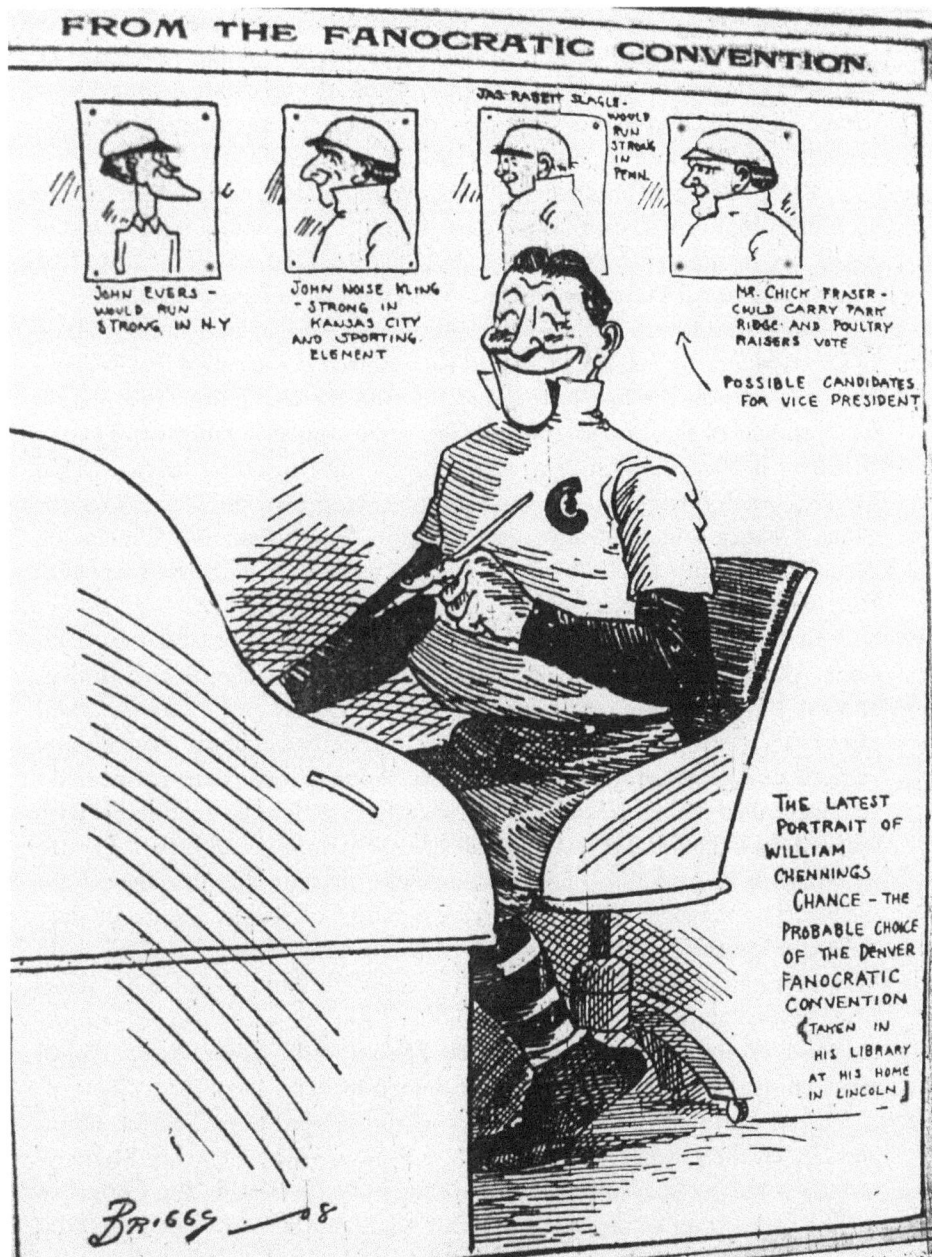

July 4 — Frank Chance is caricatured as William Jennings Bryan. The Democratic convention, soon to meet in Denver, would nominate Bryan to run against William Howard Taft, President Theodore Roosevelt's hand-picked successor.

Donlin, sacrificed Doyle to second base. Giant third baseman Art Devlin ripped a single into right field. Schulte charged quickly, grabbed the ball on the first bounce, and delivered a perfect throw to the plate, nailing Doyle for the final out. Even rabid Giant fans, momentarily forgetting their enmity, erupted into applause for Schulte's third brilliant play of the day.[46]

The Cubs scored another run in the eighth inning, and Lundgren retired six Giants in a row to capture the hard-fought 7 to 5 win. *Chicago Tribune* headlines trumpeted Schulte: "SCHULTE AS HERO SAVES THE CUBS. Three Sensational Plays Turn Tide in the First Game Against Giants."[47]

During the sixth inning while the Giants were at bat, umpire Hank O'Day temporarily suspended play and announced to the crowd that William Howard Taft, on the first ballot, had received the Republican nomination for President of the United States. Mild, polite applause followed. Then, a thunderous cheer greeted nineteen-year-old substitute first baseman Fred Merkle, pinch hitting for the pitcher, as he stepped to the plate. After the game, Chance sent the following telegram: "The Honorable William H. Taft. Washington, D.C. You have made a home run with the bases full. Heartiest congratulations from all the Cubs and myself."[48]

In his nine previous starts, Pfiester had 2 wins, 4 losses, and 3 no-decisions. All four defeats were by a single run: 2 to 1 to the Pirates and Phillies, and 1 to 0 to the Pirates and Giants. The Cubs won two of his no-decisions after Pfiester had left the game. In his best performance of the year, Pfiester pitched seventeen innings against the Boston Doves before the game, tied 1 to 1, was called due to darkness. On Friday, June 19, Chance made a bet with his hard-luck pitcher. He wagered that Pfiester's streak of bad luck had ended in Philadelphia and that Pfiester would win his start that day against the Giants. The manager offered Pfiester a new suit of clothes, valued at sixty dollars, if he beat the Giants. Trying further to break Pfiester's hard-luck spell, Chance took to the coaching lines for the game.[49] All to no avail. The Giants made several good plays to halt Cub rallies while the Cub defense committed three errors, including one each by Pfiester and Chance. At the end of nine innings, Pfiester suffered his fifth loss, 6 to 3.[50]

Over 20,000 fans, the largest crowd of the season, packed the stands and circled the playing field several rows deep to witness Christy Mathewson pitch a three-hit shutout on Saturday, June 20, beating the Cubs 4 to 0. The Cubs never came close to scoring; only one runner made it as far as second base. Matty struck out six and did not walk a single hitter.

In the fourth inning, Evers squawked about a strike call, and Klem threw him out of the game. When the Cubs took the field, Hofman moved from center field to play second base, and Marshall played center. Marshall,

4. The Brawl

a former classmate of Mathewson's, struck out twice against his fellow Bucknell College alum. The Giants hit Fraser hard in the fourth inning, but two stellar plays by shortstop Tinker kept the game scoreless. The first hitter, Fred Tenney, hit a sharp grounder toward the hole. Tinker made a brilliant back-hand catch and threw Tenney out. After two Giants reached base, Art Devlin hit a line drive toward left field, but Tinker leaped high in the air and caught the ball to end the inning with a sensational play. Fraser was saved again in the fifth inning, this time by third baseman Steinfeldt. The Giants had loaded the bases with two outs. Larry Doyle sent a shot down the third-base line. Steinfeldt made a diving back-handed catch and then scrambled to his feet to touch third base for the force out.[51] But the Cubs' brilliant defense could not prevent some questionable tactics in the seventh inning.

For six innings, the game was scoreless. In the seventh inning, the Giants loaded the bases with two outs. McGraw ordered Doyle, the next hitter, to get hit by the pitch to force in a run. McGraw felt one run would be enough to win the game with Mathewson pitching. Doyle stood close to the plate and tried to get hit with the first pitch from Fraser. He failed, but his attempt was so blatant that catcher Kling called the umpire's attention to it. Calling the pitches, umpire Bill Klem ordered play to continue. The next pitch Fraser delivered was over the plate and would have been a strike, but Doyle turned his back and deliberately stuck his hip into the ball. Playing at home in front of a large intimidating crowd, McGraw figured it would be difficult for the umpire to disallow the play. He was right. Klem gave first base to Doyle, scoring the run. Chance and the Cubs protested, but Klem would not change his call. Seymour followed with a single, scoring two more runs, and a passed ball by Kling allowed the fourth and final run of the inning and the game.[52]

On Saturday evening, a group of Cubs boarded a boat for a ride up the Hudson River to Troy, New York, Johnny Evers's hometown, for a Sunday exhibition game. New York City, like Boston, Brooklyn, and Philadelphia, did not allow Sunday baseball. Chance, Hofman, Kling, Fraser, Pfiester, and Lundgren did not make the trip. Every baseball bug in Troy turned out to honor their hometown hero. Evers had one hit and stole two bases. Only two pitchers went to Troy, rookie Bill Mack, a recent Syracuse University graduate, and Ed Reulbach. Mack pitched a complete game, allowing eight hits and four runs, as the hometown Trojans beat the major leaguers, 4 to 1. Catcher Doc Marshall scored the only run for the Cubs in the eighth inning. Schulte played first base, Moran and Reulbach split duties in right field, Durbin played center field, and Slagle patrolled left. Regulars Steinfeldt, Tinker, and Evers manned their normal positions.[53]

While the rest of the Cubs returned to Gotham, Evers stayed the night with his folks in Troy. Arriving at noon on Monday, Evers was hit with news of a three-day suspension. Umpire Klem had ordered Evers's suspension after ejecting the ballplayer from the Saturday game for commenting on his judgment. Evers wanted to return to his home immediately, but Chance refused his request.[54]

That afternoon, Evers sat on the bench and watched the Cubs lose their third-straight game to the Giants, 7 to 1. Even after losing three out of four to the Giants, the crippled team had compiled a creditable record on their sixteen-game East coast tour: 9 wins, 5 losses, a seventeen-inning tie in Boston, and a rainout in Philadelphia. Although they remained in first place, everyone looked forward to returning to Chicago.[55] After squeezing in a post-game dinner, the Cubs' train departed New York at 8:00 P.M. Monday; twenty-six hours later, they arrived in Chicago for a six-game home stand, one against St. Louis and five with Cincinnati.

An impressive West Side Park greeted the returning Cubs. During the road trip, the grandstand extension project and all the internal renovations, including the visitors clubhouse, were completed. President Murphy made good on his pledge to design and fly a new red, white, and blue championship pennant from the outfield flagpole.[56] The Cubs' injuries seemed to be on the mend. Del Howard, injured hand healed, returned to action playing left field against the Cardinals. Back in uniform, clubhouse brawl opponents Heinie Zimmerman and Jimmy Sheckard would take a day or two of practice before being ready to play. Hofman stayed at second base as Evers had one more day of his suspension to serve. Brown, his mother still seriously ill, decided to rejoin the team in Chicago, since he could return quickly to his home in Indiana, if necessary.[57]

St. Louis came to town having escaped the cellar, climbing ahead of Brooklyn into seventh place. On Wednesday, June 24, Art Fromme drew the starting pitching assignment for the Cardinals against Ed Reulbach. Fromme gave a strong performance, allowing six hits and only one run in nine innings. Reulbach matched Fromme, six hits and a single run. The Cardinals scored first in the sixth inning. Rookie shortstop Raymond "Chappy" Charles lined a ball to left center field. The ball took a weird bounce past center fielder Slagle. Howard gave chase, but before he could retrieve the ball, Charles rounded the bases. The Cubs tied the score in the bottom of the sixth. Chance and Steinfeldt singled, placing runners on first and third to start the inning. Kling popped out to shortstop Charles. Chance scored when Hofman rapped a grounder to Charles, who momentarily bobbled the ball before forcing Steinfeldt at second. Reulbach almost literally lost his head in the seventh inning. With one out and Reulbach on first, Slagle hit a grounder

4. The Brawl   87

to short. Charles shoveled the ball to second baseman Billy Gilbert. Trying for the double play, Gilbert's throw to first hit Reulbach in the head, knocking him to the ground, but Reulbach quickly regained his feet and stayed in the game.[58]

The Cubs won in the bottom of the tenth inning after two were out. Howard led off with a single, but he was forced at second when Schulte attempted a sacrifice bunt. Chance flied out. When Schulte tried to steal second, catcher Hoelskoetter hurled the ball high above the head of shortstop Charles, covering second, into center field. The ball also eluded center fielder Red Murray, and Schulte raced all the way home to score the winning tally. Manager Chance announced that Reulbach's performance, six hits, seven strike outs, and only two walks in ten innings, had earned him a position in the starting rotation.[59]

That morning, a few minutes before 9:00 A.M., Grover Cleveland, former President of the United States, died of heart failure at his home in Princeton, New Jersey. The seventy-one-year-old Cleveland had served as the twenty-second (1885–1889) and twenty-fourth (1893–1897) president.[60]

Fresh from a successful East coast trip, the Cincinnati Reds arrived in Chicago in fourth place with 31 victories and 27 losses. Any hopes the Reds had of advancing in the standings were quickly squashed. On Thursday, June 25, Brown pitched a six-hit shutout in the first game of the five-game series. The Cubs scored three runs in the first two innings, and the outcome was never in doubt with Three-Finger Brown on the mound. The only dramatic moment occurred in the fourth inning. Cincinnati rookie pitcher Jean Dubuc fielded a bunt by Slagle and suddenly collapsed on the field. In obvious pain, the pitcher had to be assisted from the field by several teammates and taken to the Cincinnati clubhouse. Umpire Klem immediately issued a call, "Is there a doctor in the stands? The Cincinnati club wants a doctor." As Reds manager John Ganzel offered an aside, "The Cincinnati club wants pitchers more than doctors," a young man jumped onto the field and headed through right field to the clubhouse amid the cheers of the crowd. Before he had gone far, another doctor appeared on the field and started for the clubhouse by way of left field. Older, he looked the part, wearing a full beard and carrying his kit. The first doctor possessed neither kit nor whiskers. The scene took on the appearance of a horse race as the two doctors rushed to aid the stricken Dubuc from different directions. Reporter I.E. Sanborn described the race: "Interest in this race distracted all attention from the game and the rooters began to cheer first one and then the other. The odds were on the whiskers until almost the finish, when the bare faced M.D. spurted quite professionally and imperceptibly and they pulled up at the entrance to the enemy's clubhouse in a dead heat. Just to show there was no enmity in the scramble, the two sawbones shook hands and disappeared arm in arm from the field." Upon examination, the two doctors announced Dubuc suffered no permanent disability, only a strained leg tendon which rest would heal.[61]

The next day, the Cubs, behind Chick Fraser, made it two in a row over the Reds, 8 to 5. Sheckard returned to the lineup for the first time since the clubhouse brawl with Zimmerman almost four weeks before, and in the fourth inning Zimmerman returned to action. Tied 3 to 3, the Cubs came to bat in the fourth. Steinfeldt led off with a single. Kling flied out, but Evers singled, placing runners on first and second. Pitcher Bob Spade tried to pick Steinfeldt off second base, but he threw the ball into center field. Steinfeldt advanced to third, and Evers made for second base, sliding in ahead of the throw. During the slide, Evers twisted the ligaments of his leg and ankle so severely he had to be assisted from the field and leave the game. Zimmerman came in to run for Evers and scored, along with Steinfeldt, when Tinker singled to right field. Fraser sacrificed Tinker to second. Slagle singled, scoring Tinker with the third run of the inning and a lead that Fraser never surrendered. Hofman finished the game at second base for Evers. Shortly after the game, Brown received the sad news of his mother's death and caught the first available train for Rosedale. His teammates sent a large floral arrangement for the funeral.[62]

Evers, on crutches, could only watch as Reds pitcher Andy Coakley pitched a four-hitter, beating the Cubs 4 to 1 on Saturday, June 27. Chance doubled home the Cubs' run in the first inning after Sheckard had singled, but Coakley allowed the Cubs only two hits for the rest of the game. Cincinnati bunched three runs in the fifth and another in the eighth to defeat Lundgren.[63]

Sunday baseball was legal in Chicago, and Cubs fans witnessed a sweet doubleheader victory to take four of the five games against Cincinnati. In the first game, Cincinnati out-hit the Cubs 7 to 5, but the Reds could score only a lone run in the second inning to take the lead. Steinfeldt objected to one of Klem's calls in the eighth inning and was ejected from the game. Manager Chance shifted Hofman from second base to third, Howard from center field to second base, and inserted Durbin in center field. Johnny Evers, his ankle in a cast, watched the action from the stands.[64] In another strong performance, Reulbach pitched his second consecutive one-run game, while his teammates, led by Sheckard's seventh-inning home run and Kling's run-scoring eighth-inning double, bunched their hits in their last two at bats to score a 3 to 1 victory.[65]

Pfiester took charge in the second game, pitching a three-hit shutout. Chance did not play. Howard started at first base, but in the third inning, after Hofman reached third base on a muffed fly ball, Chance sent Zimmerman in to bat for Howard. Zimmerman laced a ball through right center field, scoring Hofman with the first Cub run. Zimmerman tried to make it a homer, but he was thrown out at the plate. On this day, one run was enough for Pfiester, but in the eighth inning Steinfeldt doubled and scored on Kling's single to add an insurance run. Tinker ran his consecutive-game streak without an error to twenty-two. He last made an error in the ninth inning against the Pittsburgh Pirates on June 1. During those twenty-two games, Tinker made 48 putouts and 77 assists for a total of 125 chances, handled flawlessly.[66]

Overnight, the Cubs and Reds traveled to Cincinnati to play three more games. Pitcher Orval Overall, unable to play since he injured his lower back on Memorial Day, made his return. After a twenty-minute rain delay, the sun poked through the clouds again, the grounds crew applied sawdust to the infield, and the game got underway. The Cubs took the lead in their first at bat. Slagle led off with a triple and scored on an infield out, but Jack Doscher, making his pitching debut with the Reds, bore down and retired the Cubs.[67] Doscher began his career in 1903 with the Cubs, but he was traded to Brooklyn after pitching only one game for Chicago. He spent four years in Brooklyn before joining Cincinnati.[68]

In the bottom of the first inning after two outs, Overall walked both third baseman Hans Lobert and left fielder Dode Paskert. Ganzel singled to right, but Schulte made a strong throw to the plate, and Kling tagged Lobert trying to score. Umpire John Rudderham ruled Lobert safe. Kling threw the ball to Steinfeldt at third to hold Paskert there while he and Overall surrounded Rudderham to discuss the call. Steinfeldt, still carrying the ball, came to the plate and joined the discussion with zest, pointing out the slide marks indicating Lobert had missed the plate. While Steinfeldt, his back to the plate, argued with Rudderham, Paskert quietly sneaked down the third-base line and crossed the plate with the second Cincinnati run and the lead. The Cubs scored to tie the game in the fifth inning, but the Reds answered with a run of their own in the bottom of the fifth to regain a one-run lead. They scored single runs in the next two innings to make it 5 to 2. The Cubs tallied one more run in the eighth inning to edge closer, but Doscher retired the side in order in the ninth to win his first start in Cincinnati, 5 to 3. In the seventh inning, Tinker misplayed a grounder off the bat of Paskert, ending his string of error-free games.[69]

The month of June ended badly for the Cubs. In Tuesday's game, pitcher

Bob Spade allowed only four hits to deal the Cubs their second-straight defeat in Cincinnati, 4 to 2; for the first time, the Cubs relinquished first place. The Pittsburgh Pirates, second to the Cubs in 1907 and considered their strongest rivals for the National League championship, slipped into first place. On July 1, the league standings told the story.[70]

TEAM STANDINGS

	W	L	Pct.
Pittsburgh	40	24	.623
Chicago	37	23	.617
New York	37	27	.578
Cincinnati	34	30	.531
Philadelphia	27	28	.491
Boston	27	37	.422
St. Louis	24	40	.375
Brooklyn	22	39	.361

Chapter 5

Backs, Legs, and Thumbs

On the morning of July 1, Mordecai Brown, returning from his mother's funeral in Indiana, rejoined his teammates for the final game against Cincinnati. Frank Schulte suffered a severe groin pull and had returned to Chicago for rest and treatment; Del Howard played Schulte's right-field position. Ed Reulbach turned in another strong performance, pitching a two-hit complete game, a 5–1 victory over the Reds. The Cubs scored two runs in the first inning to give Reulbach the lead. Johnny Kling and Joe Tinker lead the Cubs' hitting attack with two hits apiece, including a double for each. Reulbach contributed a triple to his own cause.[1]

After the game, President Murphy informed Harry Steinfeldt that he was no longer a fugitive from justice in the state of Alabama. The summons that Steinfeldt had avoided being served in Birmingham during spring training, for his role in a dispute with a local umpire, was null and void. Largely through the efforts of Harry Vaughn, the manager of the Birmingham team, the $5,000 lawsuit filed by the umpire against Steinfeldt and Del Howard (Howard had been served his summons in Birmingham) had been dismissed.[2]

Trailing the Pirates by two percentage points, the second-place Cubs left Cincinnati for a five-game series in Pittsburgh. The players considered the Pirates their toughest opponents and respected the individual abilities of the Pittsburgh players, but they were determined to reclaim first place. Baseball pride fueled the Chicago-Pittsburgh rivalry, unlike the intense personal animosity between the Cubs and the despised Giants of New York.[3]

The battle for first place began with a doubleheader on Thursday, July 2. Brown pitched a shutout in the first game, winning 3 to 0. Brown allowed only six hits, two by Honus Wagner, but he did not issue a single base on balls. The Cubs scored all the runs Brown needed in the fourth inning. Howard and Chance singled with one out. Steinfeldt drew a walk to load the bases. Kling rapped a grounder to short for a sure inning-ending double play, but the ball glanced off Wagner's knee, allowing two runs to score and putting Steinfeldt on third. The hometown scorers awarded a hit to Kling instead of an error to Wagner. Steinfeldt scored the final run of the inning and the game when Hofman grounded out. Kling did not finish the game; in the sixth inning, a foul tip off the bat of Tommy Leech caught Kling squarely on his right thumb, sending him to the hospital. Doc Marshall finished the game behind the plate.[4]

Pittsburgh easily won the second game of the day, scoring four runs in the first inning. Eventually, the Pirates collected thirteen hits and another five runs against Pfiester in their 9 to 4 victory. Trailing 8 to 1 in the sixth inning, Chance, his problematic toe hurting, took himself out of the game. Hofman moved from second base to first, and Heinie Zimmerman finished the game at second.[5] The Cubs remained in second place.

The next day, July 3, broken-thumbed Johnny Kling sat in the stands with President Murphy to watch Vic Willis, the ace of the Pirate pitching staff, shutout the Cubs. Willis allowed five hits, but only a stellar defensive play prevented the Cubs from scoring. In the third inning, with the Pirates ahead 2 to 0, the Cubs loaded the bases with two outs. Chance cracked a drive toward the gap in left center field that looked to clear the bases, but center fielder Roy Thomas raced to his right and at the last instant made a back-hand stab at the ball. It stuck; the only Cub threat of the day was over.[6] Meanwhile, Orval Overall, in his first appearance since injuring his lower back on Memorial Day, was ineffective, giving up three runs in three innings. Carl Lundgren relieved Overall for the fourth inning and promptly surrendered two more runs to the Pirates. Pittsburgh scored a final two runs in the eighth inning to win easily, 7 to 0.[7]

The loss dropped the Cubs one and a half games behind the Pirates. But with a sweep of the Independence Day doubleheader, the champions could return to their accustomed spot atop the league. Chance started Brown in the Saturday morning game. Just two days before, Brown had shut out the Pirates in the first game of the series. One day's rest was enough, and the three-fingered wonder did not disappoint. One hour and thirty-five minutes after the game started, the Pirates had only two hits, a single by right fielder Owen Wilson and a double by shortstop Honus Wagner. For the second time in three days, the Pirates failed to score a run against the Cubs' star twirler. The Cubs scored two runs in the first inning to win the first game of the day, 2 to 0.[8]

Between games, the Cubs enjoyed a luncheon of club sandwiches and pickles at the ballpark, courtesy of Pirate president Barney Dreyfuss. In the one o'clock afternoon game, led by Hofman's two doubles, a single, and four runs batted in, the Cubs tallied nine runs, five in the first inning, to sweep the two games and recapture first place. Ed Reulbach again pitched well. Ahead 7 to 0, Reulbach allowed single runs in the sixth, seventh, and eighth innings to record his sixth straight victory, 9 to 3. The *Chicago Tribune* blared: CHAMPS SCUTTLE PIRATES' CRAFT. Triumphant Cubs Take Both Ends of Double Bill ... LEAD THE LEAGUE AGAIN.[9]

Managers Chance and Clarke agreed to play another doubleheader on Sunday, July 5, to make up two games postponed by rain earlier in the season. Since Pittsburgh did not allow Sunday baseball, both teams boarded different trains Saturday evening and headed for Chicago. Arriving in Cleveland at 10:30, Reulbach, Semmens, and Williams disembarked, without their tickets, to grab a late-night snack of fried chicken. When they returned, the train and their tickets were gone. Their only option was to buy new tickets and catch a later train. Semmens had only $1.55 in cash, well short of the $10 ticket price. Dismayed, Semmens returned the chicken and requested a refund, but he was rebuffed. Fortunately, the American League Cleveland Naps were at the depot on their way to St. Louis, and several hungry Cleveland players happily bought the chicken. Unfortunately, Semmens was still short, and Reulbach's pockets were entirely empty. Secretary Williams let the two men sweat for a while before coming forth with $30 to cover three tickets to Chicago.[10]

Slagle pulled a muscle chasing a fly ball in the fourth inning of the second game on Saturday and joined the list of injured Cubs. On Sunday, during pre-game infield practice, Chance stretched to receive a low throw, and the crowd heard a loud popping noise. The Cub leader lay on the ground with intense pain in his lower back. Helped to the dugout, Chance refused to leave the ballpark, but he did change his mind about playing a doubleheader. Five Cub regulars — Chance, Kling, Schulte, Evers, and Slagle — were invalids. The replacements — Hofman at first base, Zimmerman at second, Moran behind the plate, Marshall in right field, and Howard in center — were talented players, but they were substitutes. Chance decided to play only a single game on Sunday. Pirate manager Fred Clarke objected and filed a protest with the league office, demanding the Cubs forfeit the second game.[11]

In constant and occasionally severe pain, Chance still remained in charge. A doctor sat next to the "Peerless Leader" in the dugout throughout the game, attending as best he could to the fallen manager's lower back. At the end of eight innings, the Pirates maintained a three-run lead, 5 to 2, but then erupted for five runs in the ninth against Jack Pfiester. The Cubs managed to tally three runs in the bottom of the ninth, including a home run by Joe Tinker, but the 10–5 victory gave Pittsburgh the league lead. The Cubs trailed by one-and-one-half games as they boarded the train for Chicago.[12]

Marshall had turned his ankle during the Cubs' loss to the Pirates, and Chance, diagnosed with a popped vertebrae, stayed in bed for the next game. A Chicago specialist, Dr. McKinloch, expected the Cub boss to miss only a few days, and fortunately the team began an extensive home stand, playing their next seventeen games at West Side Park.[13]

Brooklyn arrived in Chicago on Monday, July 6, for a four-game series. Evers, wearing a pink rubber ankle boot, took part in pre-game batting practice, but his pink boot rendered him immobile for game competition. Howard moved from center to right field, and twenty-one-year-old Durbin played Slagle's center-field position. The seven hits and four walks in seven innings allowed by Chick Fraser let Brooklyn take a 5–1 lead. The Cubs rallied in the bottom of the seventh. Durbin singled, as did Tinker. Fraser gave way to pinch hitter Marshall, who promptly tripled, scoring his two teammates. Sliding into third, Marshall re-injured his tender ankle. The game was delayed while trainer Semmens worked his magic; Marshall remained in the game. After Hofman flied out to Phil Lewis at shortstop, Marshall scored when Sheckard's pop fly fell just beyond the reach of Lewis and the charging left fielder Al Burch. With three runs home, the Cubs trailed by one with a runner on first and only one out. But Howard lined out to second baseman John Hummel and Zimmerman grounded out to the pitcher. Brown held Brooklyn scoreless for their last two at bats, but the Cubs failed to score in either the eighth or ninth inning, giving Brooklyn the edge, 5 to 4.[14]

The next day, one sub-line in the *Chicago Tribune* read, "SUPERBAS WIN BY 5 TO 4," but the headline announced the Cubs had been, "LICKED BY THE DODGERS." So which team were the Cubs playing? When Brooklyn first joined the National League in 1890, they were tagged the Bridegrooms by Francis C. Richter, a Philadelphia baseball writer; the previous season, four Brooklyn players had married. In 1899, a popular vaudeville troupe, "Hanlon's Superbas," was all the rage in Brooklyn. When Ned Hanlon, no relation to the actors, managed Brooklyn to the National League pennant the same year, local scribes assigned the "Superbas" moniker to their baseball heroes. Hanlon left Brooklyn in 1905, but the name stuck for a few years. A complex tangle of trolley lines at the end of the Brooklyn Bridge caused passengers much confusion, and citizens of Brooklyn became known as "Trolley Dodgers." Gradually, the name was applied to the baseball team as well, and eventually "Trolley Dodgers" was shortened to "Dodgers."[15]

On Tuesday, rain prevented the second game against the Dodgers.

National League president Harry Pulliam ruled against the Pittsburgh protest that the Cubs should forfeit the doubleheader game not played on Sunday. Since the Cubs never scheduled the doubleheader with the league office, Pulliam reasoned, "Under the conditions, I do not see my way clear to order this game forfeited to the Pittsburgh club."[16]

Chance felt the Cubs needed some insurance in the catcher department. The Kling and Marshall injuries left only Pat Moran to stand behind the plate. Instead of calling up one of the Cubs' minor-league catchers (Monte Beville, a former major leaguer, was the choice of the *Chicago Tribune*), Chance selected Delancy Gunning of the Streator Reds, a Chicago-area semi-pro team. Gunning joined the Cubs in time for their 6 to 3 victory over the Dodgers.[17]

On Wednesday, July 8, Chance returned to the dugout, but not the game. Led by their super-subs, the Cubs scored three runs in the first, another in the second, and two final tallies crossed the plate in the sixth. Meanwhile, Reulbach allowed the Dodgers only single runs in the fifth and seventh innings to lead 6 to 2. But in the eight inning, Reulbach walked the bases full with only one out, and Chance called Brown to the rescue. Brown struck out the first man he faced, pinch hitter Harry Pattee, for the second out. Left fielder Burch then flied out to end the inning and Philadelphia's threat. In the ninth, center fielder Bill Maloney spiked a ball to the alley in left center field and, in a daring baserunning sprint, circled the bases, just beating the relay throw to the plate. It was the first run scored against Brown in over four games and the last run of the day for the Dodgers. The 6 to 3 Cub win, coupled with the doubleheader defeat of the Pirates in Philadelphia, returned the Cubs to their first-place perch.[18]

Umpire Cy Rigler stood behind the plate, calling balls and strikes for the Brooklyn series. Umpires wore a regulation windpad inside their shirt for protection from the batters' foul tips. All, except Rigler. He choose to forego the issued windpad and instead inserted a register, the kind used in hotels for guest sign-ins, inside his shirt. Rigler wore the register backside out and received his supply from hotel clerks around the league.[19]

After eight innings on Thursday, July 9, Brooklyn held a 3 to 1 lead, and the Dodgers, in last place, looked forward to winning two out of three from the first-place Cubs. Ace southpaw George "Napoleon" Rucker had surrendered a lone run to the Cubs in the first inning and then pitched superbly, blanking Chicago for the next seven innings. But in the bottom of the ninth, the Dodger defense collapsed. Third baseman Tommy Sheehan fielded a routine ground ball off the bat of Steinfeldt and promptly threw the ball over the head of first baseman Jordan for a two-base error. Moran skied to center field for the first out, and Rucker struck out Brown, pinch hitting for Durbin. With two outs, a runner on second, and a two-run lead, Rucker still seemed poised to record the victory. But Tinker singled to left. Evers, pinch hitting for Pfiester and still wearing the pink rubber cast on his left ankle, took a pitch on his hand. Evers hobbled to first and, in obvious pain, tucked his sore hand under his armpit. The bases were full with two outs, and the Cubs still needed two runs to tie. Shortstop Lewis fielded Hofman's ground ball and threw to second to force Evers and end the game. But second baseman Hummel broke too late to cover and allowed the crippled Evers to beat him to the bag. Steinfeldt scored on Hummel's mental error, and the bases remained full. Rucker temporarily lost his control and walked Sheckard to force in run number two, knotting the score at three. Del Howard strode to the plate, hoping to cop the heroes laurels, but Rucker composed himself and struck him out.[20]

Failing to win the game in the ninth inning, the Cubs presented an unusual defense in the tenth. Howard moved from right to center field, and Evers, pink cast and all, limped to right field. After pinch hitting for center fielder Durbin, Brown pitched the tenth inning, retiring the Dodgers in order. Zimmerman singled to begin the Cubs' tenth, and Steinfeldt followed with a sacrifice bunt to place Zimmerman on second. The Chicago bugs sensed victory and rose to their feet, yelling encouragement. Zimmerman took third when Rucker threw a wild pitch, and, when Pat Moran hit a deep fly ball to right field, he scored on the sacrifice fly to win the game. Outfielder Lumley made the catch, but made no throw. Zimmerman trotted home to give the Cubs a come-from-behind 4–3 victory.[21]

Chance felt better. The pain in his lower back eased, and the Cubs' leader expected to return to action soon. His injury, however, did not prevent him from cruising about Chicago in his newly purchased automobile. But after a few nervous test runs, Chance decided he would employ an expert driver to steer him about town.[22]

Just as his right ankle was healing, Evers developed a bruised left heel, preventing the second baseman from returning to the everyday lineup. The Cubs' three catchers were still hobbled; only Moran could play, and his ankle injury made manager Chance nervous. At least he had the new, untried Delancy Gunning as a back-up. Reporter Dryden lamented the fact that Arthur Evans had been sold and was no longer available to rejoin his spring training team.[23]

On Friday, July 10, the Phillies arrived in Chicago for a lengthy five-day, six-game series. Brown began the series against a twenty-four-year-old rookie, southpaw Billy Foxen. The Cubs scored two runs in the first inning against Foxen, but the youngster gathered himself and shutout the Cubs for the next nine innings. Meanwhile, the Phillies scored single runs in the fourth and sixth against Brown to knot the score at two apiece. Neither team scored in the tenth. Brown retired the Phillies again in the eleventh inning. Tinker lead off the Cub eleventh with a triple. Then Brown grounded to the hole between first and second. First baseman Bransfield knocked the ball down and held Tinker at third; Brown safely reached first. Hofman followed with a game-winning single, scoring Tinker. It was a tough loss for the rookie in his first start against the Cubs.[24]

The Phillies took revenge on Saturday, scoring five runs on eight hits in the first three innings, knocking Reulbach from the box. Philadelphia ace right-hander George McQuillen allowed only single runs in the first and third innings to record the 6 to 2 victory. One bright spot for the Cubs was the return of Orval Overall to the mound. Overall relieved Reulbach and pitched five shutout innings with no back pain.[25]

During the contest, umpire Jim Johnstone, a six-year veteran, tried to make himself comfortable in the July heat. After the Phillies' half of the first inning, Johnstone halted play while he removed the baseballs from his pockets, built two small pyramids of balls behind home plate, and shucked his coat. Reporter Dryden described umpire Johnstone's subsequent attempts to remain cool: "Mr. Johnstone then resumed in blue cotton shirt, suspenders, and a little whisk broom sticking out of his starboard hip pocket. Even this outfit proved too heavy in the first half of the second round. Johnstone called another halt after the fourth successive swat off Reulbach while the ump pulled off his celluloid collar and piled it on top of the discarded coat."[26]

On Sunday, July 12, the Cubs and Phillies split a doubleheader. After completing just three innings on Saturday, manager Chance sent Reulbach to the mound again for the first game on Sunday. This time, Reulbach did not disappoint, pitching a complete game, a four-hit shutout for the 3–0 win. The *Chicago Tribune* waxed lyrical: "It was much like eating cantaloupe a la mode under the shade tree at home. When Edward is right there is nothing to match his éclat."[27] Zimmerman played second base and "pole[d] wild pitches after the manner of Mr. Lajoie,"[28] managing three singles and a run scored.[29] "Mr. Lajoie" referred to Larry Lajoie, current second baseman and manager of the Cleveland's American League team and three-time American League batting champion, including a .422 average in 1901.

In the second game, luckless Jack Pfiester suffered a tough 2 to 0 loss. In the second inning, Pfiester struck out the side, but he gave up four hits and two runs as well. The Phillies did not score again, but the Cubs did not score at all. Frank Corridon allowed the Cubs only five hits, all singles, as nine zeros went up for the Cubs on the scoreboard. The Cubs threatened to score in the eighth inning, loading the bases with two walks and a single and none out, but Howard flied to short left for the first out. Zimmerman tagged a hard shot to right field, but John Titus made a leaping catch for out number two. Steinfeldt rapped a grounder to third baseman Eddie Grant, who stepped on third base for the final out. Chance returned to action, pinch hitting in the ninth inning, but the Peerless Leader struck out. Durbin played center field in both games and had one of the five Cub singles in the second game as his dad, visiting Chicago from his home in Kansas, watched his son perform.[30]

Overall celebrated his recuperated back by becoming the second Cub player to purchase an automobile. "O. Overall has followed the example of Mr. Chance and purchased a beautiful automobile. The fashion is spreading. Next thing we know Dreamer Durbin will be wizzing around on a velocipede."[31] Unlike Chance, Overall enjoyed the new sport of driving and saw no need to hire a chauffeur.

When interviewed by Charles Dryden, Kling explained that his injured thumb needed another week to heal. During his convalescence, Kling had ample time to ponder his future. He played billiards well. So well, in fact, that he was considering leaving baseball, opening a billiards parlor, and playing the sport professionally.[32] It was easier on the digits.

On Monday, July 13, the fourth Olympic games began in London. The Cubs and Phillies made up one of their earlier rained-out games in Chicago. Trainer Semmens declared Slagle and Schulte fit for duty, but both needed some practice time before returning to action. The Cubs collected fourteen hits and scored five runs, but lost 6 to 5. Lundgren gave up fifteen hits, including a triple to third baseman Grant and a home run to first baseman Bransfield. The Cubs, trailing 6 to 3, rallied in the ninth inning and had an opportunity to win the game. Two Cubs crossed the plate, making the score 6 to 5, and runners perched on second and third with two outs. Steinfeldt came to bat needing only a single to score a dramatic come-from-behind Cub victory. But Phillies pitcher Tully Sparks needed only one more out. Steinfeldt swung at a good pitch, but he hit under the ball, lifting a lazy pop fly behind the plate. Catcher Red Dooin drifted back toward the stands to catch the ball and preserve the Philadelphia victory.[33]

Chance and Evers returned to the lineup for the last game of the Phillies series on Tuesday. After his encouraging five-inning outing in relief of Reulbach on Saturday, Overall took the mound for the Cubs. Hofman moved from first base to center field. Durbin and Zimmerman returned to the bench; both had played well in the absence of Chance and Evers. Howard remained in right field while Frank Schulte prepared to return. Although healthy, Slagle joined Durbin and Zimmerman as a substitute.[34]

The Chicago bugs welcomed the return of Chance and Evers with enthusiastic applause and looked forward to watching a healthy Overall perform. Southpaw Billy Foxen, loser in eleven innings to Brown in the first game of the series, started for the Phillies. The Phillies scored two runs in the second inning and then exploded for six runs in the fifth against Overall. Leading 8 to 0, Foxen allowed the Cubs only single runs in the sixth and seventh innings. Bill Mack, the Syracuse rookie, made his first appearance as a Cub, relieving Overall in the fifth and striking out Foxen to end the inning. Mack pitched the final four innings, surrendering another three runs, as Philadelphia won its third-straight game, 11 to 2, and took four out of the six games.[35]

On Wednesday, July 15, the Cubs looked to recover their momentum against the next arrivals in town, the haughty New York Giants. Instead, the Giants scored two runs in the first inning to begin the massacre that saw the Cubs lose their fourth-straight game, a humiliating 11–0 loss that knocked them from first to third place. Brown had a rare poor performance, surrendering five runs in only four and two-thirds innings of work. Pfiester gave up another four runs in four innings, and Overall allowed the final two runs pitching the ninth. George "Hooks" Wiltse tossed the shutout for the Giants, allowing the Cubs only seven hits, four to Johnny Evers. A cartoon in the *Chicago Tribune* portrayed the despondent Cubs trailing in line behind the jovial second-place Giants and the league-leading Pittsburgh Pirates.[36]

The score was closer on Thursday, 4 to 3, but the Cubs still lost their fifth-straight game. Steinfeldt, down with a fever, missed his first game of the season. The ever-versatile Hofman played third base, and Slagle returned to center field. Trying to break the losing streak, Chance exercised the home team's batting prerogative and had the Cubs hit first. It almost worked. The Giants scored two runs in the first inning and another two runs in the fifth against Reulbach. Giant pitcher Doc Crandall picked up where Wiltse left off, blanking the Cubs for the first six innings. In fact, over the last three games, the Cubs had failed to score in seventeen consecutive innings. Finally, in the seventh inning, the Cubs pushed across a run on Slagle's sacrifice fly after Pat Moran tripled.[37]

Trailing 4 to 1, the Cubs came to bat in the ninth inning. Evers opened the inning with a slow roller to Al Bridwell at shortstop. Bridwell hurried his throw and chucked the ball over first baseman Fred Tenney's head. Evers trotted to second. Moran followed with another grounder to Bridwell. Run-

July 16 — After being in first place for most of the season, the Cubs suffer a humiliating defeat, 11–0, against the Giants on July 15, falling from first to third place.

ning the bases aggressively, Evers broke for third and was an easy out in the ensuing rundown between second and third base. But Moran did make second base during Evers's baserunning blunder. Tinker walked, and Durbin, hitting for Reulbach, reached first when Crandall hit him with a pitch on his chin. The bases were loaded with only one out.[38]

The Giants lead had looked secure as the ninth inning began. Christy Mathewson, scheduled to pitch the next day, figured to get a head start on his teammates and take his post-game bath as the Cubs came to bat in the ninth. But suddenly, the Cubs loaded the bases, and, just as quickly, Giant manager McGraw issued the call for his most dependable pitcher to end the Cub uprising. Told that Matty was already in the clubhouse, McGraw sent two couriers to fetch him; they returned to tell McGraw that Mathewson was bathing. Irate, McGraw began stalling. The Cubs complained to plate umpire Jim Johnstone and, when McGraw continued to delay, asked Johnstone to declare a forfeit. Forced to act, McGraw sent for Joe McGinnity, who was also in the clubhouse but not yet in the tub. Instructed to take his time, McGinnity slowly made his way to the mound. Finally, Johnstone forced McGinnity to throw. Slagle hit a slow roller wide of first base; Tenney fielded the ball and tossed to second baseman Doyle covering first. Base umpire O'Day ruled that Slagle and the ball reached first base simultaneously, making Slagle safe. Moran scored on the play; the score was 4 to 2, and the bases were still full. Doyle expressed his unprintable dissent to O'Day and was promptly ejected from the game. Substitute Dave Brain came on to play second base as the Giants continued their delaying tactics.[39]

A few innings earlier, the skies had grown dark and a light mist began falling. Suddenly, in the fading light, an apparition seemed to appear, trotting across center field from the clubhouse towards the pitcher's mound. All eyes turned to watch the ghostly figure come into focus. Wearing a trench coat over his uniform, the Giants' savior, Christy Mathewson, made his dramatic entrance. The recently boisterous crowd grew quiet as the great Mathewson took the mound. Every Cub player and bug sensed doom. Somehow, after two strikes, Sheckard put bat to ball, hitting a weak grounder to first baseman Tenney for out number two; Tinker scored, but it hardly mattered. The next hitter, Howard, fouled the first pitch. "Then Matty looked his victim in the eye and started to wind the fade-away ball with steam on it...."[40] Howard heroically swung at the next two pitches, but he never came close to hitting the ball — three strikes, three outs, game over. In awe, the hushed spectators silently departed from West Side Park.[41]

The next day, under a brilliant sun and blue sky, President Murphy's upper terrace flower garden added color and cheer to the scene. In a better mood, the bugs looked forward to a classic pitching duel between Mathewson and their own star hurler, Brown. The two heroes did not disappoint, both pitching magnificently. The game, completed in one hour and twenty-six minutes, saw only one runner cross the plate. After making a brilliant defensive play in the fourth inning to prevent the Giants from scoring, Tinker circled the bases in the fifth inning for the only run of the game. Tinker's home run was one of seven hits allowed by Mathewson. Brown performed just a little bit better. The Giants managed only five hits. The 1–0 Cub victory ended their five-game losing streak.[42]

Charles Dryden reported that reserve catcher Delancey Gunning, after only nine days in uniform, was no longer with the Cubs. Chance and Overall were not the only automobile owners in Chicago. Fans started arriving at the ballpark in their new machines, parking on Lincoln and Polk streets. A problem immediately arose with "boy thieves who rummage through the tool boxes or repair kits and take whatever accessories they think they can sell. The thefts mostly are from machines left on Polk street, as the police maintain a fairly efficient watch on Lincoln street. One instance reported yesterday was of an owner who hired a small boy to watch his car while he saw the game. Soon a gang of larger boys came along and slugged the watch, stealing an electric lighter and other tools. The thefts have become so frequent President Murphy is having signs printed calling the attention of owners to the fact that the automobile entrance is on Taylor street, where a club attendant has charge of a free auto enclosure."[43]

Lacking the price of a ticket, fourteen-year-old Willie Hudson had climbed to the roof of a three-story building at 451 Wood Street to watch Mathewson and Brown battle. Excited, Willie leaped in the air when Tinker hit his long drive into center field in the fifth inning. The young boy, already standing on the edge of the roof, fell fifty feet, head first, fracturing his skull. Police carried Willie to the county hospital, where he was pronounced dead.[44] Hudson's death caused the police to close rooftops to spectators.

Tinker and the Cubs made it two in a row against the Giants on Saturday, July 18, to gain a split in the four-game

In 1908, shortstop Joe Tinker led the Cubs with six home runs and 68 runs batted in. He often made the game-winning hit, most famously hitting a home run against legendary New York Giants pitcher Christy Mathewson for a 1–0 win on July 17, 1908.

5. Backs, Legs and Thumbs

July 18 — Hero Joe Tinker protects a vulnerable first place from the crude advances of the New York Giants. The day before, Tinker hit a home run off of Christy Mathewson to beat the Giants 1 to 0, keeping the Pirates in first and the Cubs in third.

series. Kling returned to action, but his sore thumb prevented him from catching. Chance placed him in right field to get his bat in the lineup, and Kling delivered, going 2 for 3 with a double and a walk, but Tinker won the game with a clutch double in the ninth inning to give the Cubs a dramatic come-from-behind victory. Reulbach pitched poorly, giving up seven hits and three runs before the end of the third inning. Wiltse held the Cubs scoreless for five innings, but in the sixth, the heroic Tinker tripled, and Slagle, with two outs, singled to left field, scoring the Cubs' first run. Southpaw Pfiester relieved Reulbach in the third and ended the Giants' scoring for the next four innings. The Giants did push across a lone run in the eighth inning to take a 4 to 1 lead, but in the bottom of the inning, the Cubs rallied. After one out, Zimmerman batted for Pfiester and reached first on a dropped third strike. Slagle drew a walk, and Sheckard's ground ball forced Slagle at second base, placing Cub runners on first and third with two outs.

Kling laced a double to left center field, scoring Zimmerman and sending Sheckard to third. Chance hit a hard grounder to third baseman Devlin, who missed tagging Kling as he raced for third. Chance reached first, and Sheckard scored the Cubs' third run. Chance then stole second, placing Cubs on second and third, but Hofman lifted a pop fly to first baseman Tenney to end the inning. The Cubs still trailed, 4 to 3.[45]

Overall came on to pitch the ninth and retired the Giants in order; catcher Bresnahan grounded out to Evers, and outfielders Donlin and Seymour struck out. The stage was set. Evers walked to start the bottom of the ninth. Moran shot a double down the third-base line, and Evers stopped at third. On the first pitch, Tinker connected, sending the ball bounding into the gap in left center field. Evers and Moran scored, ending the game and sending the jubilant crowd into a frenzy. A shower of black seat cushions cascaded onto the field.[46]

The Cubs remained in second place, one game behind the Pirates, but in team statistics they led the league in both hitting (.250) and fielding (.967). Among the regulars, Evers's .302 batting average led the team. Tinker's timely hitting, his home run against Mathewson and his game-winning double the next day, produced two Chicago victories, but the shortstop carried only a .206 season average. Among pitchers, Mathewson led the league in victories with 17 against only 5 losses, but Brown, (13 wins and 2 losses) had a better winning percentage. Reulbach led the other Cubs' pitchers with 9 wins and 3 losses. Fraser had a winning record (9–8), while Lundgren (6–6) and Overall (5–5) managed only an even winning/losing percentage. Pfiester's pitching efforts deserved a better fate than his 3–9 record, and Pfiester and the Cubs hoped that his last performance against the Giants had broken his season-long hard-luck spell.[47]

Delighted with Tinker's heroics in the two wins against the Giants, Chicago bugs were nevertheless relieved when John McGraw and his boys left town. The Boston Doves arrived in town on Sunday to begin a four-game series. The Doves rested in sixth place, ahead of only Brooklyn and St. Louis, and Cub fans relaxed, expecting their boys to easily handle the second-division visitors. Scheduled to pitch the first game against Boston, Overall tinkered with his automobile on Sunday morning, planning to drive his new machine to West Side Park. But a wrench slipped and knocked the head off a spark plug. Overall caught the trolley. Tinker arrived at the ballpark sporting a new cane. Reporter Dryden remarked, "look out for the monocle next week."[48]

During the pre-game warm-up, a thrown ball struck first baseman Chance on his index finger. The manager moved Hofman from third to first base and inserted Zimmerman at third for the still-ailing Steinfeldt. Moran remained behind the plate, and Kling stayed in right field as Schulte remained incapacitated. Overall's injured back appeared healed and mechanically he was in good form, but he lacked control, walking five Doves. Boston scored single runs in the second, third, and sixth innings. The Cubs collected seven hits, three by Kling, but they could only score twice, losing 3 to 2. Umpire Klem added to the Cubs' frustration as he lost track of the ball-and-strike count with Boston right fielder Jack Hanifan at bat in the ninth inning in a one-run game. No harm occurred, but Hanifan did have an extra swing of the bat. As he made his way through the stands after the Cubs failed to score in the bottom of the ninth, vocal hometown fans let Klem know what they thought of his math skills.[49]

A month earlier, on June 18, Boston had traded three-year-veteran pitcher Irv Young to Pittsburgh in exchange for rookie pitcher Tom McCarthy. As a Pirate, McCarthy had appeared in two games without a decision. But he became a rookie phenom with Boston, winning his first five starts. On Monday, July 20, the twenty-four-year-old McCarthy took the mound for his first start against the Cubs and suffered his first loss of the season. After three walks, five hits, and three runs in only four innings, Jake Boultes replaced McCarthy. Playing first base, Hofman led the Cubs' attack with three hits, including a double and triple. Chance, his finger still sore and mangled, managed from the bench. Steinfeldt returned to the lineup, but he went hitless in four at bats. Reulbach pitched well, allowing only two walks and five hits, three by Doves second baseman Claude Ritchey.[50] Final score, 5 to 2.

On Tuesday, Ladies Day attracted large numbers of big-hatted women to West Side Park. Everyone anticipated another Cubs' victory with Brown pitching. Instead, Boston's Vive Lindaman turned in the performance Cub fans were expecting from their own pitching star. Brown pitched poorly, giving up five hits and three runs in four innings. Lundgren surrendered another two runs in three innings of relief, and Mack pitched the final two innings, holding the Doves scoreless. Mack also made a bid for a home run in the bottom of the ninth inning. After two outs, Mack drove a ball over the head of center fielder Ginger Beaumont. Mack raced around three bases and headed for home, but Beaumont quickly retrieved the ball, threw to shortstop Dahlen, who then made a perfect throw to catcher Graham. Mack could not avoid the tag and registered the final out of the game. Lindaman shut out the Cubs on five hits as the Doves won for the second time in three games and defeated the Cubs' best pitcher.[51]

The defeat placed the Cubs back into third place, two and one-half games behind Pittsburgh, but only a half game behind New York. The condition of the Cubs' pitching staff was of most immediate concern. Dryden reported, "Fraser and Brown have ailing arms, Pfiester is hoodooed, and Lundgren lacks effectiveness."[52] Murphy missed the Ladies Day game; instead, he traveled to St. Louis to meet with Cardinals owner Stanley Robison. There, Murphy made an offer to purchase pitchers Eddie Karger and "Bugs" Raymond. Robison stated to the press that he might enter into a trade with the Cubs, but that he was not interested in sending any Cardinal players to Chicago for cash only. Murphy denied he was in St. Louis to make any player deals, claiming he was merely meeting with the Cardinal owner to discuss "some new baseball legislation with the local magnate."[53] Perhaps the two owners discussed possible spitball legislation.

Almost everyone wanted to ban the spitball, except the pitchers who threw it. Hitters hated trying to hit the thing. Infielders claimed the slippery sphere often caused throwing errors. Managers, including Frank Chance, favored outlawing the pitch. Baseball writers seeking to ban the pitch often used a humorous ploy. Reporter Dryden claimed Frank Bowerman, the Boston Doves catcher, "is in favor of legislating the spitball out of existence for sanitary reasons. He says the by-product of the flying sphere often lodges in the eyes of catchers and batsmen, and unless the pitcher can show a clean bill of health there is danger of infection."[54]

Visiting team players slept in Chicago hotels but used the visiting team dressing room at West Side Park prior to each game. Fresh towels, provided by the hotels, sparked a lively competition among hotel delivery boys. Those receiving the delivery assignment trundled the clean towels to the park and collected the soiled ones, and they were allowed to remain and watch the game.[55]

The Cubs eighteen-game homestand ended on Wednesday, July 22. The Cubs had been at home since July 5, posting a record of 7 wins and 10 losses, including 5 consecutive defeats. After Wednesday's game, both teams would head east, the Doves returning to Boston to host the Cincinnati Reds and the Cubs traveling to Brooklyn to begin their East coast trip. The usual 3:30 game time was changed to three o'clock on Wednesday and a end of game time limit was set at 4:45 P.M. to allow each team to catch their departing trains. The average nine-inning game required an hour and forty minutes to play.[56]

Starting pitchers for the final game of the series were the same as the first, Boston's Flahery versus Chicago's Overall. The Cubs scored a lone run in the second inning without getting a hit. Hofman walked to start the inning, moved to second on Steinfeldt's ground out, reached third when

5. Backs, Legs and Thumbs

July 22 — The pennant race, with the Pittsburgh Pirates and the New York Giants neck and neck for first, and the Cubs right behind.

shortstop Dahlen booted Evers's grounder, and scored when umpire Klem ruled Moran safe at first after his grounder to short forced Evers at second. Howls of disapproval rose from the Boston bench. Gus Dorner, a pitcher, was selected by Klem to leave the premises.[57]

Overall held the Doves scoreless for six innings. But in the seventh, Boston tied the score on a pair of singles and a wild pitch from Overall. Both Flaherty and Overall worked quickly from the mound, and players from both teams hustled about their business. At four o'clock, after only an hour of play, eight innings were completed, but the score remained tied at one. Boston failed to score in the eighth and ninth innings. The Cubs loaded the bases in the bottom of the ninth with two outs. Overall came to the plate and made a bid to win his own game. Orvie hit a fast ball from Flaherty square, sending the ball deep into left field, but the Doves' Johnny Bates raced back and made an impossible over-his-head running catch. Then, in the top of the tenth, Bates smashed a single, scoring third baseman Bill Sweeney and giving Boston a 2 to 1 lead. Sweeney reached first on Hofman's muff of Tinker's throw and promptly stole second. From there, he scored on the hit by Bates.[58]

Conceding nothing to Boston, Chance inserted himself to bat for Slagle to begin the bottom of the tenth. But his injured finger made it difficult to firmly hold a bat, and the Cubs' leader meekly lofted an infield pop-up for the first out. Chance's next move sent Zimmerman to hit for Sheckard. Zimmerman singled to give hope to the Cub fans, but Howard flied out for out number two. As Hofman came to bat, fans hoped he would redeem himself for his error that led to Boston's second run. Hofman did not disappoint. He walloped a triple over the head of center fielder Beaumont, scoring Zimmerman, and again the game was tied. Overall retired the Doves in the eleventh and then came to bat with two outs and a runner at third in the bottom of the inning. Tinker had singled, stolen second, and advanced to third when Doves' catcher Graham threw high over second base into center field. Overall had another chance to win the game, but he struck out.[59]

The clock read 4:43 P.M. Both teams prepared to leave the field, but Klem ordered the Cubs to take the field and begin the twelfth inning. Two minutes expired as Overall dawdled to the pitcher's mound. Klem then announced the time limit had been reached, officially declared the game a tie, and allowed the players to leave the scene.[60]

That same day, Brown received word of the second death in his family this season. His sister died suddenly, only a few weeks after his mother's passing. Brown left immediately for another funeral in his hometown.[61] The coroner's jury receiving the case of Willie Hudson, the young fan who fell to his death the week before, ordered the rooftops surrounding West Side Park permanently closed.[62] Hofman re-injured his knee chasing a pop-up from his first base position in the last game against Boston and went to Cleveland for treatment by the renowned baseball doctor, John "Bonesetter" Reese, of Youngstown, Ohio.[63] Back from his negotiations with Robison in St. Louis, Murphy joined his team for the East coast trip. Murphy had a lot on his mind. Robison had offered to trade a pitcher to Chicago in exchange for Zimmerman, but Murphy declined. The Cubs expected to play an exhibition game on Thursday against the minor-league Bisons in Buffalo before beginning their series against the Brooklyn Dodgers on Friday. At two o'clock in the morning, as they rolled down the tracks, the club received a telegram from Buffalo reminding the Cub management that the exhibition game had been canceled six weeks before. Murphy had forgotten, and he sheepishly acknowledged the fact.[64]

When the Cubs reached Buffalo at 8:00 A.M., Williams made valiant efforts to keep the team's special car attached to the train, but Buffalo railroad officials still had orders to decouple the car, and decouple it they did.

5. Backs, Legs and Thumbs

Williams scurried to make other travel arrangements, but for two hours the Cubs' players walked the streets of Buffalo. At 10:00 A.M., most boarded another train for New York. Steinfeldt, accompanied by his wife, remained in Buffalo and enjoyed a trip to Niagara Falls on the unexpected day off. Evers spent the day of leisure in his hometown of Troy. Murphy and Chance decided to remain in Buffalo for the day and watch the local nine, the Buffalo Bisons, play the first-place Eastern League team from Providence, Rhode Island. They witnessed a magnificent pitching performance from the Bisons George McConnell as he shut out the Providence team 2 to 0.[65] McConnell turned thirty-one in 1908 and began his six-year major-league career the next year with the New York Highlanders.

Right fielder Schulte remained in Chicago recovering from his groin injury, and catcher Kling, while traveling with the team, still nursed his sore thumb. Howard and Moran filled in for the two ailing regulars. Chance returned to first base, so the wobbly knees of super-sub Hofman, finally, could be rested. He had played four different positions as a utility player: center field for Slagle, second base for Evers, third base for Steinfeldt, and first base for Chance. Back from Cleveland, he now had time to recuperate after his treatment from "Bonesetter" Reese.[66]

The Cubs began their second East Coast swing of the season with a dramatic come-from-behind extra-inning victory against the Dodgers. Pfiester pitched seven strong innings, allowing only a single run in the second, but lady luck still seemed against him. Marshall hit for Pfiester in the Cubs' eighth inning. With the Cubs trailing 1 to 0, Reulbach replaced Pfiester.[67] For eight innings, the Dodger's Kaiser Wilhelm pitched superbly. Chicago did not come close to scoring during the first eight innings, and they were retired in order in the sixth, seventh, and eighth. Some Brooklyn bugs rejoiced over Wilhelm's dazzling performance against the reigning champions and slowly began to amble toward the exits as the ninth inning began. They stopped briefly when Chance singled to left and was sacrificed to second by Evers, but resumed their slow exit march after Steinfeldt flied out with Chance remaining on second. Howard came to the plate with two outs. He worked the count to three balls and two strikes and then fouled off five consecutive pitches. On the next pitch, the ball found the meat of the bat, and the left-handed hitting Howard lined the ball past first base. Right fielder Lumley charged the hard-hit ball and could have thrown Chance out at the plate, but the ball skipped by the anxious outfielder and rolled all the way to the fence, giving Howard three bases. Tinker showed no heroics in this at bat and popped out to end the inning.[68]

After the Cubs tied the score in the ninth inning, neither team scored in the tenth. Kaiser Wilhelm continued to pitch for the Dodgers. Evers lead off the eleventh inning with a single to center field. Steinfeldt laid down a sacrifice bunt, sending Evers to second base and bringing Howard to the plate. This time, Howard rolled a ground ball to first baseman Jordan for the second out. The next batter, the right-handed hitting Tinker swung a little late on a fast ball from Wilhelm, which sent the ball over Jordan's head down the right-field line for a double, scoring Evers with the go-ahead run. Moran popped out to end the inning. Reulbach retired three-straight Brooklyn hitters in the bottom of the inning to give the Cubs a 2 to 1 victory.[69]

Repairs to the grandstand roof at Washington Park could not wait. Throughout the game, a group of carpenters sawed and hammered on top of the grandstand directly behind home plate. Occasionally, the carpenters became "dodgers," ducking foul balls hit in their direction. In the fifth inning, a two-by-four fell, landing on the protective screen just above the heads of the reporters in the press area. The carpenters, Dodger fans, temporarily halted work in the ninth and eleventh innings as the Cubs first tied, then won, the game. As the disappointed Brooklyn bugs departed Washington Park, the disappointed carpenters resumed their work.[70]

It rained hard that night, flooding the ballpark. By daylight on Saturday morning, the deluge had ended and Charles Ebbets made plans to have the field repaired for play that afternoon. Start time was delayed an hour to give workers extra time. Umpire Cy Rigler inspected the field as the grounds crew completed their work and declared conditions satisfactory for play. Almost immediately afterwards, the skies opened and within three minutes drowned out all the workmen's efforts. Ebbets announced a doubleheader would be played on Monday, July 27. Baseball was not played in Brooklyn on Sundays, giving the players two consecutive days of rest.[71]

Hofman needed the time off. Returning from his appointment with "Bonesetter" Reese, Hofman reported that the doctor was amazed that he had been playing, since the super-utility man had two strained ligaments in his knee. Describing his treatment, Hofman recalled how "the doctor seized the leg, twisted it to all points of the compass at once, then gave it a sharp twitch, and it made a noise like a pair of rifle shots. Then he was told he was all right-and he was."[72] Reese wrapped Hofman's knee with woolen tape and told him to rest for a few days.[73]

Chance announced that as a member of the National League Rules Committee he would work for legislation to abolish the spitball for the 1909 season. His timing may have been influenced by Kaiser Wilhelm's Friday's performance, but Chance had declared his personal opposition to the wet pitch several weeks earlier.[74] Later Sunday afternoon, Murphy announced the purchase of twenty-four year old pitcher Carl Spongberg, who had been playing in Ogden, Utah. A right-hander, Spongberg stood six feet two inches and weighed 208 pounds. Best of all, Murphy had acquired a pitcher without trading any of his players.[75]

Brooklyn newspapers, for reasons known only to the reporters, had stated that Mordecai Brown had left the Cubs in a huff to go to his home in Indiana, without informing their readers of the real reason, the unexpected death of Brown's sister. The bereaved Cub pitcher rejoined his teammates Sunday night.[76]

The Washington Park grounds remained damp on Monday. The belowground concrete player coops (dugouts) attracted droves of mosquitoes, and the Cubs could stay on their bench only by building smudge fires with paper and grass to drive out the pests.[77]

Each team won a game on Monday. Reulbach and Jim Pastorius locked up in a pitcher's duel in the first game. Pastorius pitched a perfect game with five strikeouts for the first four innings. Reulbach, almost as good, allowed a single hit in four innings. Evers, batting fourth in the lineup, began the Cubs' fifth inning with a single. Steinfeldt sacrificed him to second. On Howard's single to right field, Evers raced around third and crossed the plate, but he neglected to touch third base. The Dodgers third baseman called for the ball, stepped on third base, and appealed the play to umpire Rigler, who ruled Evers out. Instead of the first run, Evers was the second out of the inning, and the game remained scoreless. But Tinker singled, placing Howard on third. Tinker and Howard then executed a double steal. Brooklyn catcher Bill Bergen threw to second, but Tinker beat the throw, and Howard scored the first run of the game. Brooklyn tied the score in the seventh. In the Cubs' eighth inning, Reulbach led off with a double. Slagle bunted toward third to advance Reulbach and landed safely at first when Jordan dropped the throw from Tommy Sheehan. On a check swing, Sheckard sent a slow roller to Pastorius, who threw him out at first, but with Slagle going to second. Chance scored Reulbach and Slagle with a single, giving the Cubs a 3 to 1 lead. Reulbach finished strong, retiring the Brooklyn hitters in order in the eighth and ninth innings to preserve the 3 to 1 victory.[78]

The second game, following the first-game pitching duel, produced a classic "Casey at the Bat" scenario, but with a happy ending for Brooklyn fans. Tim Jordan, the muscular six-foot, one-inch first baseman and the most popular player in Brooklyn, hit a two-run home run over the right-field fence in the second inning against Carl Lundgren to give the Dodgers the lead. The Cubs rallied, scoring three runs in the fifth and single runs in the sixth and seventh innings to amass a 5 to 2 lead. Jordan came to bat in the Dodger seventh and hit his second home run over the right-field fence, 5 to 3.[79]

With two Dodgers out in the bottom of the eighth inning, right fielder John Hummel singled to center. "Alperman was next, and the eyes of the rooters reminded one of the poem entitled 'Casey.' If only Alperman could get 'on' it would bring up Jordan, and what Jordan would do the fans all knew. But poor, despised Alperman had not done much all day, and the rooters turned sick with the thought of how easy he would be for the third out." But, "the white haired substitute fooled them all by popping a measley little fly just inside the foul line and just out of Chance's reach as he tore back for it. The ball struck only six inches inside the line, and safe ... Such a roar as went up when the fans realized their dreams had come true and the mighty Tim had come to bat with a chance to win the game with another poke over the fence. Lundgren was going to be game, and was in a fair way to give a lifelike rendition of 'Casey at the Bat,' for he had two balls and two strikes called on Jordan, when Tim pulled a terrific foul...."[80] Manager Chance intervened after Jordan just missed his third home run of the day against Lundgren and ordered the power hitter walked to load the bases. Brooklyn manager Patsy Donovan sent left-handed hitting Harry Lumley to pinch hit for third baseman Sheehan. Lumley replaced Jordan in the hearts of Brooklyn fans, at least for the moment, when he sent the ball between Howard and Slagle in right center field for a bases-clearing double. Brooklyn fans erupted in joyous pandemonium as the Dodgers grabbed the lead, 6 to 5, and the victory when three Cubs (Steinfeldt, Zimmerman, and Kling) struck out in the ninth inning. The Cubs may have lost the second game, but Kling returned to the lineup and threw out several runners; his sore thumb had healed. [81]

Chance had a tough day on the basepaths. In the first game, he overran first base on his game-winning hit and was thrown out before he could return safely. In the fourth inning of the second game, on first with a single, he misjudged a line drive to right by Evers. Right fielder Hummel caught the Evers drive and whipped a throw to Jordan at first for the double play. Later, in the eighth inning, after drawing a walk, Chance strayed too far from the bag. Brooklyn's left hander, Nap Rucker, threw to Jordan, and Chance was tagged out in a run down. [82]

As three Cubs were striking out in the final inning of the second game, Evers commented on umpire Rigler's method of judging strikes. Rigler immediately expelled him. As Evers departed for the clubhouse, he stopped at the plate to whisper something in the umpire's ear. Rigler submitted a four-page description of Evers's use of the English language to the National League office in New York City. The next morning, Evers received notice of another three-day suspension.[83]

Tinker made five hits during the doubleheader on Monday, hitting in the number-seven slot in the lineup. On Tuesday, July 28, manager Chance promoted Tinker to the clean-up position. Evers had been hitting fourth before his suspension. His replacement at second base, Hofman, took the number-seven spot in the lineup and showed no ill effects from his recently repaired knee injury.[84]

Both teams scored in their half of the second inning, one run for the Cubs, two for the Dodgers. Neither team scored for the next five innings as Brooklyn's Harry McIntire and Orval Overall matched each other pitch for pitch. Kling ended the scoreless string with a drive over the head of left fielder Al Burch after Del Howard had singled. Howard scored, and Kling raced for third as Burch retrieved the ball. Kling never hesitated, rounding third as the relay throw came to third baseman Sheehan. The ball and Kling arrived simultaneously at home, but the throw was high and Kling slid safely under Bergen's tag. Overall continued his string of shutout innings in the eighth and ninth. The Cubs added an insurance run in the ninth to garner the win, 4 to 2. His lower back problems behind him, Overall pitched effectively with ten strikeouts, no walks, only six hits, and eight shutout innings.[85]

The Cubs headed for Boston, having won three of four games from the Dodgers. Pitcher Bill Mack and outfielder-pitcher Kid Durbin were sent back to Chicago; the health of the Cubs' pitching staff had improved, and the recently signed rookie pitcher, Carl Spongberg, would meet the team in Boston. The schedule provided for five games against the Doves, including a make-up of the seventeen-inning tie game in June.[86]

Slagle, Tinker, and Brown dominated the first game in Boston. Slagle hit three singles in four trips to the plate. Tinker continued his hitting rampage with another four singles. In his last twelve games, Tinker hit safely 21 times in 45 at bats for a .467 batting average. Brown took the mound with his right (pitching) wrist bandaged. Brooklyn's mosquitoes had feasted on him while he sat in the dugout on Monday and Tuesday. The soaked bandage, applied by trainer Semmens, kept the swelling down and had no effect on Brown's delivery. Brown dominated the Boston hitters and pitched the Cubs to a 6 to 0 victory in one hour and thirty-four minutes. Boston managed only four hits and never threatened to score. The Cubs scored their runs in bunches, two in the first inning and four in the fifth.[87]

The Cubs and Doves played two games on Thursday, July 30. One was a replay of the June 4 seventeen-inning tie game. There were no ties this day as the Cubs swept the doubleheader, 13 to 4 and 6 to 3. The Cubs' hitters

July 31—The Cubs finally shake things up by winning a doubleheader against the Boston Doves. They move into second place, only half a game behind Pittsburgh.

held a slugfest against Doves pitcher Gus Dorner, scoring thirteen runs in six innings in the first game. Sheckard, Steinfeldt, and pitcher Reulbach each had three hits. Steinfeldt's hits included an out-of-the-park home run. Slagle, Chance, and Hofman (playing second base for the suspended Evers) had two hits apiece. Moran added a single to the hit parade. Only two of the Cub starters failed to hit safely against Dorner: right fielder Howard and

5. Backs, Legs and Thumbs

shortstop Tinker, who ended an eleven-game hitting streak. After six innings, Chance rested himself, Reulbach, Hofman, and Moran.[88]

A much closer contest, the second game required a come-from-behind effort by the Cubs to secure the victory. Boston's rookie pitcher, Tom McCarthy, had only one loss for the season, but that had come against the Cubs in Chicago a month before on June 20. McCarthy surrendered two runs to the Cubs in the fourth inning, but the Doves scored three against Pfiester in the fifth to take a one-run lead. A fielding error by McCarthy led to the Cubs scoring three runs in the seventh inning to regain the lead. Chance inserted Kling at first base for the second game, but he came in to pinch hit for Pfiester during the Cubs' rally in the seventh inning, drawing a walk. Overall held the Bostons scoreless for the last three innings, and the Cubs added an additional run in the ninth to win, 6 to 3. McCarthy suffered his second loss to the Cubs, as yet the only team able to beat the rookie sensation. The double victory drew the Cubs within a half game of the league-leading Pittsburgh Pirates. Both teams had 36 losses with the Pirates winning 56 times and the Cubs 55. Carl Spongberg, the Utah pitcher, joined his new team on Thursday evening.[89]

On Friday, the last day of July, the Cubs made it four in a row against Boston and extended their winning streak to five games, winning 3 to 1. After pitching the final three innings of the second game on Thursday, Overall came back to pitch another nine innings on Friday. The Doves managed only a solo run in the second inning against Orvie. Evers returned after his three-day suspension and had two hits. Kling hit a towering home run over the left field fence in the seventh inning, giving the Cubs the lead: "...two strikes were called on Kling before he caught one between the eyes and raised it several hundred feet above sea level. John stood calmly on the plate and watched it sail out over the railroad track until it disappeared from sight, then trotted around the diamond with the run that spelled victory."[90]

After the game, Chance made a deal with his acerbic-tongued second baseman. Chance promised to buy Evers a $60 suit of clothes if the combative infielder was not ejected from any more games during the season, but he quickly added, "That doesn't mean you are not to do any more talking, however."[91]

The third catcher behind Kling and Moran, veteran Doc Marshall, turning thirty-three in September, was not seeing much playing time, and President Murphy needed someone to scout some local talent in Pennsylvania. After Friday's game in Boston, Murphy sent Marshall ahead as his scouting envoy with instructions to rejoin the team in Philadelphia on Sunday. On Monday, the Cubs would begin a five-game series against the Phillies.[92]

CHAPTER 6

Bottomed Out

August began badly for the Cubs. Not only did their five-game winning streak come to an abrupt halt, but the Cubs were humiliated by the Boston Doves, losing the last game of the five-game series, 14 to 0. After seven consecutive victories at Boston's South End Grounds, the Cubs lost in stunning fashion. Carl Lundgren pitched to only four hitters, allowing two hits, two walks and a wild pitch. Chance replaced the ineffective Lundgren with Chick Fraser. Before Fraser registered the first out, Boston scored six runs, but Chance stayed with Fraser until the end of the inning, Boston scoring one final run. With the Cubs seven runs behind after the first inning, Chance decided to debut his Utah rookie pitcher. Carl Spongberg pitched the next seven innings, but he was ineffective: walking seven batters, hitting two with a pitch, allowing eight hits, including a home run, while Boston tallied another seven runs. After the score reached 14 to 0 in the sixth inning, players from both teams purposely made outs on the basepaths to end the game sooner. In the eighth inning, Johnny Kling hit into a force play and remained at home plate to ensure a double play. Spongberg did have a good day at the plate, hitting two singles in three at bats. Boston pitcher Cecil Ferguson pitched the shutout, allowing a total of five Cub hits.[1]

After the Saturday game, Johnny Evers, a twenty-seven year old bachelor, departed for Troy, New York, to spend Sunday's off day planning for his autumn wedding. The rest of the Cubs boarded the Federal Limited and made their way to Philadelphia. The City of Brotherly Love did not permit Sunday baseball, so normally Cub players spent their Sundays traveling the short distance across New Jersey from Philadelphia to cavort on the beach and boardwalk in Atlantic City.[2]

But the next ten games for the Cubs were against rival first-division teams, beginning with the fourth-place Phillies, and the players realized the fate of the season might well depend on the outcome. After the Phillies, the

Cubs were scheduled to play four games against the Giants and two more in Pittsburgh before heading home to Chicago. Cavorting in Atlantic City could wait. Every Cub player remained in Philadelphia on Sunday gathering strength.[3]

Reliable Mordecai Brown pitched the first game against Philadelphia on Monday, August 3. Brown limited the Phillies to six singles and, but for some questionable ball-and-strike calls by rookie umpire John Rudderham in the seventh inning, would have pitched another shutout. A walk, a stolen base, and a single netted the Phillies their only run of the day in the Cubs' 5 to 1 win. Center fielder Slagle used all his speed to make a stellar catch in the sixth inning. After one out, Eddie Grant, the Phillies third baseman, beat out a slow roller to Steinfeldt and stood on first base. The next batter, right fielder John Titus, hit a Brown fastball square and sent the ball soaring towards deep center field. Grant and everyone in the ballpark expected the ball to fall safely far beyond the reach of Slagle. "There apparently was no way for any one to get that ball and Grant began reeling off a ten second gait for the plate. But Slagle was not of the same mind regarding that wallop. He gave chase at top speed and to the astonishment of everyone except the Rabbit himself he got where he could grab it with one final desperate jump as the ball was speeding over his head. Grant was over third base by this time and had no chance to get back to first base alive, so submitted to fate gracefully. The Cubs made a peculiar double play out of it just for fun. Slagle's throw was relayed by Evers to Tinker, who called Brownie back from his trip to the bench, and handed him the ball on first base for the third out."[4]

The Cubs scored four runs against Philadelphia's ace, George McQuillan, in the fifth inning, and they tallied their final run in the ninth on a triple by Tinker and a single by Kling. The Cubs' ninth inning ended in the same fashion as the Phillies' sixth when Slagle made his great catch. Ironically, Slagle was the victim in the ninth. With one out and Brown on first base, Slagle sent a line drive towards right field. Second baseman Otto "Dutch" Knabe raced for the ball, jumped to make the catch, and relayed the ball to first to complete a double play on Brown.[5]

On Tuesday, August 4, the Cubs released rookie pitchers Bill Mack and Carl Spongberg. Mack had appeared in two games, pitched six and one-third innings, and had an earned run average of 2.84. Spongberg had been with the Cubs only five days and had a poor seven-inning showing against the Boston Doves in the embarrassing 14–0 Cub loss the previous Saturday. Manager Chance and Brown felt especially bad about Spongberg's release. He obviously was not ready to pitch in the major leagues, but he had been highly recommended, traveled such a great distance, and been with the Cubs such a short time. Both Chance and Brown, each unaware of the other's efforts, made phone calls to secure Spongberg a place on a minor-league team. The Springfield, Illinois, team agreed to take Spongberg.[6] Neither Bill Mack nor Carl Spongberg ever returned to the major leagues.

With help from umpire Rudderham, the Phillies won the day's game, 4 to 2. Rudderham, who teamed up with O'Day for the Philadelphia series, had a day that began badly and got worse. In the second inning, he raced across the diamond to make a call at first base and fell flat on his face. In the Cubs' sixth, Evers walked to begin the inning. Steinfeldt, the next batter, hit a sharp grounder over second base. Knabe knocked the ball down to one side of the bag, then scrambled for it. "Before he could pick it up Evers was standing over him, looking at him. Rudderham, however, called John out."[7] Evers, having made a recent pact with Chance not to get ejected, showed remarkable, if unusual, self-restraint, uttering not a word and trotting off the field to the Cubs' bench. Howard followed with a single that would have scored Evers. Instead, runners were on first and second with one out. Tinker then hit into a double play to end the inning.[8]

The bottom of the sixth inning witnessed an ugly episode. With a runner on first, John Titus hit a sharp ground ball to Chance at first base. Chance grabbed the hard-hit ball and fired to Tinker at second to force the runner. As Reulbach raced to cover the bag at first, he and Titus collided, knocking both from the basepath. Chance was able to take the return throw and tag Titus before he could recover and reach first base. Incensed, Philadelphia fans jeered Reulbach and the Cubs. When Chance sent Overall and Hofman to warm up out by the fence in right field in case Reulbach was not able to continue pitching after his collision, the fans first yelled verbal insults at Overall and Hofman and then began throwing glass pop bottles. A bottle hit Overall, but did no damage. Police arrived to quiet the crowd as Overall and Hofman moved over to the area by the center-field fence, where there were no fans.[9]

The second poor Rudderham call occurred in the bottom of the seventh inning. Trailing 2 to 1 against Reulbach, the Phillies, after a single and a walk, had runners on first and second. Center fielder Magee took his lead off second base. Reulbach made a snap throw to Tinker at second, catching Magee "so far off second that Magee did not even try to get back to the bag after over sliding it, thinking he was out. The arbitrator called him safe."[10] After the favorable call, Philadelphia went on to score three runs to win the game. Rudderham was the brother of the Phillies' trainer—a fact Rudderham was reminded of each time the Cubs felt victimized by the rookie umpire.¹¹ The headline in the *Chicago Tribune* read, "Unspeakable Ump Has Something to Do About Score of 4 to 2.¹²

Wednesday's game began under ominous black clouds. Slagle and Sheckard made outs. Chance singled to right and stole second with Evers at bat. Then the sky exploded with lightening and an ear-spitting crescendo of thunder. Rain began to fall as Evers flied out to short right field. Before the Phillies could come to bat, at precisely 4:05, the deluge began, sending fans and players to cover. Reporter I. E. Sanborn cleverly used Rudderham's name to describe the umpire's flight for cover: "...Rudderham shipped the front part of his name and paddled the rest of it to the grand stand after suspending play."¹³ It continued to rain hard, and after thirty minutes umpires O'Day and Rudderham called the game off.¹⁴

On Wednesday evening, Charles Murphy announced the Cubs had signed pitcher Floyd Kroh of the Johnstown, Pennsylvania, team in the Tri-State League. The left-handed Kroh, three weeks short of his twenty-second birthday, was a former pitcher with Boston's American League team. Kroh compiled a 1 and 0 record in 1906 and slipped to only 1 win against 4 losses in 1907. Boston had sent Kroh to Johnstown for the 1908 season.¹⁵

The next day, Thursday, August 6, the Cubs and Phillies played a doubleheader to make up the previous day's wash out. Veteran umpire O'Day took charge and, to the relief of both teams, abandoned the custom of rotating umpires for a doubleheader and called balls and strikes for both games. Rudderham avoided controversy serving as basepath umpire.¹⁶

The Cubs had their worst fielding performance of the season, making five errors in the first game and six in the second. The Cubs' pitching and bats could not overcome the poor fielding and suffered a double loss, 7 to 5 and 5 to 3. Shortstop Tinker made three errors in the first game, as did third baseman Steinfeldt in the second. At the end of the day, the Cubs were mired deep in third place, a full three games behind first-place Pittsburgh. And, to make matters worse, Reulbach suffered a line-drive blow to his knee in the third inning, knocking him to the ground. The right-hander limped noticeably, but he was able to complete the game.¹⁷

The Cubs hobbled out of Philadelphia's Baker Bowl after losing three straight and headed for the Polo Grounds in New York. It rained on Friday, canceling the first game. President Murphy announced the Cubs had purchased Tom Catterson, a minor-league outfielder playing with the Brockton team in the New England League, but the New York papers reported the same Catterson had been purchased by the Brooklyn Superbras. It looked like the National League directors would have to settle the conflicting claims to Catterson.¹⁸

Another legal matter required Murphy's attention. Curt Elston, the rookie outfielder released by the Cubs eight days before the season began, filed a petition with the National League claiming back pay for the required ten days notice of release. Murphy claimed that since player contracts did not begin until the regular season started, Elston was not due any salary. But National League president Harry Pulliam expressed the opinion that if the ten days' notice extended beyond the opening of the league season, Chicago must pay players from such date to the end of the ten days' notice of release. In Elston's case, that meant Murphy owed the young outfielder two days pay, since he was given notice of release eight days prior to the April 14 league opening date.[19]

On Saturday at the Polo Grounds, poor fielding continued to haunt the Cubs. Tinker, Hofman, and Kling all made miscues in the first inning, allowing the Giants to score three runs. Evers and Howard contributed errors in the next inning. By the end of four innings, the Giants had amassed a 4 to 0 lead to the delight of over 25,000 rabid Giant fans. Brown allowed only six hits, but without defensive support he could not prevent the Cubs' fourth-straight defeat, 4 to 1.[20] The jeer "acid thrower" greeted Zimmerman when he pinch hit for Brown in the eighth inning, referring to the now publicized account of the Cubs' great clubhouse brawl in June. Chicago reporter Sanborn acknowledged the jeering, but denied the validity of the taunt: "Zimmerman was addressed as 'acid thrower' by fans here, who still believe the wild yarns about Zim's attack on Sheckard...."[21]

The large crowd included four carloads of employees and friends of the elevated railroad. "They were run out on a spur track back of the left field bleachers and given a fine view of the game."[22] The overflowing on-field crowd encroached on the field of play all day and in the ninth inning had to be restrained by the extra Giant players to allow the game to be completed. Early in the game, usually stoic umpire O'Day stunned the Cubs second baseman Evers by smiling and addressing him as "Johnnie." Evers responded to the umpire's ice-breaking gesture, and they "were like two old college chums all day."[23] After the game, Murphy received a telegram from the Brockton club stating that Brooklyn had closed the deal for outfielder Tom Catterson before Murphy's offer had been received; therefore, Catterson belonged to Brooklyn.[24]

On Sunday, the Cubs won a game, but they had to travel to Waterbury, Connecticut to do so. Since it was only an exhibition game against a minor-league team, Chance, Tinker, Steinfeldt, and Kling did not play. Howard played first base; Zimmerman, shortstop; Hofman, third base; and Moran, catcher. Marshall played right field. Fraser pitched the Cubs to a 5 to 1 win.

Howard and Evers led the Cubs' hitting attack, each with three hits, including a triple by Howard.[25]

Art Nichols, a former Cub, was the captain and first baseman of the Waterbury team, and he bantered with members of his former team throughout the game. The thirty-seven year old Nichols joined the Cubs in 1898, the same year as Chance. Nichols and Chance were both catchers in 1898 and competed for the number-two catcher position behind the regular backstop, Tim Donahue. After a double in the ninth inning, with the Cubs leading 5 to 0, Fraser gave Nichols an opportunity to look good for his home crowd, grooving a fastball over the heart of the plate. The veteran responded, hitting a line drive to center field and scoring Waterbury's only run of the game.[26]

George "Candy" LaChance, former major league first baseman with the champion Boston Americans of 1903 and 1904 and a Connecticut native, sat on the Cubs' bench chatting with the current champions. James Burns, brother of deceased former Cubs player Tom Burns, made the trip to Waterbury from New Britain to visit with some of brother Tom's old friends. Burns, an infielder, played twelve years for the Cubs from 1880 to 1891 and then managed the Cubs for two seasons, 1898 and 1899. Tom Burns passed away just short of his forty-fifth birthday in 1902. Another former major leaguer, thirty-six-year-old pitcher Frank McPartlin, did not pitch against the Cubs, but he was on the Waterbury pitching staff. McPartlin spent a brief period as a New York Giant in 1899.[27]

The Cubs and Giants resumed play on Monday, August 10, with Overall going against Mathewson. After an hour and twenty-five minutes, New York secured the victory, 3 to 2, extending the Cubs' losing streak to five. Overall out-pitched Matty, allowing the Giants only a single hit, a double in the first inning to catcher Roger Bresnahan. But that double, combined with some shaky Cub defense, netted the Giants three runs in the first inning. After a line out to Slagle in center field, Overall walked second baseman Buck Herzog. Bresnahan pulled a line drive just inside the third-base line past a diving Steinfeldt. Umpire Cy Rigler stopped Herzog at third base after one of the security police, thinking the ball was foul, ran in, scooped it up in foul territory, and tossed it back toward the infield. "Instead of expected applause for his ability that cop got an awful roasting, in which McGraw was the toastmaster."[28] Right fielder Mike Donlin then hit a high bouncing ball back to Overall. Herzog immediately broke for the plate and slid across, a split-second ahead of Kling's tag. Donlin made a long turn toward second on the play at the plate, and Kling whipped a throw to Chance at first base, catching Donlin in a run down. Bresnahan advanced to third on the play at home and made a wide turn at third. As he was about to tag Donlin, Evers turned and fired the ball toward third, trying to nail Bresnahan. But the ball sailed high over Steinfeldt's head and into the stands. Bresnahan scored, and Donlin went to third. The next hitter, Cy Seymour, sent a fly ball to center field. Slagle made the catch for the second out and made a strong throw to the plate when Donlin tagged up on third. Kling caught Slagle's throw on the fly and tagged Donlin. Rigler called Donlin out, then reversed his call when Kling dropped the ball, giving the Giants their third run of the inning. Frank Chance made a fine catch of a low line drive over the first-base bag off the bat of Art Devlin to end the inning.[29]

Overall held the Giants scoreless and hitless for the rest of the game. "And when Overall closed that round (bottom of eighth inning) with a goose egg and finished his work with only one hit tabbed against him there was a roar of applause from every part of the closely packed stands." In addition, Tinker had a perfect day at the plate against Mathewson with three hits, including a triple, and a run scored. But, despite a ninth-inning rally, the Cubs could not overcome the Giants' three-run first inning. Sheckard led off the ninth with a double down the right-field foul line. Chance dumped a ball in front of the plate and was thrown out at first, but Sheckard moved to third. Evers then beat out a slow roller toward first, and Sheckard scored the Cubs' second run. With only one out and Evers on first, the Cubs needed one more run to tie, but Matty bore down and struck out both Steinfeldt and Howard, each for the third time, to end the game.[30]

Overall departed for Chicago immediately after the game. Before the game, Overall had received news that his wife's illness had taken a turn for the worse, and he prepared to catch the noon train. Just as he was leaving the hotel, a messenger boy stopped him with another message containing slightly encouraging news. Overall showed the message to his manager and said he would stay for the game. Chance immediately changed his pitching rotation, started Overall instead of Pfiester, and told the still-anxious husband to leave that evening.[31] Elsewhere in New York, National League president Harry Pulliam hosted a meeting in his office on Monday to explore steps to be taken to form a Baseball Writers' Association of America (originally the Base Ball Writers Association of America). The purpose of the new organization was to obtain better telegraph service in some cities and to promote uniformity of scoring. Charles Murphy announced the club had signed another pitcher, "Cy" Young. Not the original Cy Young, but a promising recruit from a Milwaukee Lake Shore league team and a University of Wisconsin graduate. This Cy Young recently pitched a twenty-one inning game against Toledo and allowed only seven hits.[32]

Murphy believed in luck, good and bad. The Cubs' luck seemed to be all bad on this eastern road trip. The Cubs' recent record, 8 wins and 7 losses, including the last five in a row, bedeviled Murphy. Only once were the Cubs able to win a game against another first-division team. Murphy felt strongly that his presence contributed to the recent ill fortunes of his team. His players did not disagree with him. On Tuesday, August 11, before the game began, the Cub boss boarded a train to return to Chicago. But the departure of the Jonah was not enough for Moran. He sent for Schulte's puppy, a Boston Terrier and a gift to Schulte from Moran, to join the team as a good-luck mascot. The small black dog, named "Cub," sat on the team bench throughout the game. The combination worked. The Cubs halted their losing streak, defeating the Giants, 4 to 0. And, they were lucky. Leading 2 to 0 after two innings, rain threatened to halt the game before the completion of the five innings, required to make the game official. But the rain gods waited until the Cubs were batting in the seventh inning before opening the heavens and halting play. The two runs the Cubs scored in the sixth added to their lead and proved the margin of victory. The season's hard luck for Pfiester turned as well as he pitched superbly against the Giants, allowing only two hits in the rain-shortened game.[33]

Frustrated by Pfiester, Giant players had begun verbally baiting the Cubs, who responded in kind, hurling insult for insult. The bitter feelings between the two teams were deep and real, stemming from 1906 when the Cubs dethroned the Giants as National League champions. John McGraw, the swaggering, bellicose, egotistical manager of the Giants, hated losing. And neither did he win graciously. After winning the 1905 championship, McGraw had his team wear uniforms with "Champions" emblazoned across their chests to intimidate other teams in 1906. The Cubs not only took the crown from the Giants in 1906, but again in 1907, beginning the intense rivalry. On this day, emotions ran high. Reporter I. E. Sanborn wrote: "Some of the verbal bouquets handed back and forth by the warring athletes fairly burned the atmosphere in spots."[34] As the Cubs took the field for the fourth inning, McGraw yelled at Chance, "You've got a bunch of Germans with their heads down," to which Chance retorted, "Aw, why don't you go out and pay some of the debts you owe," referring to McGraw's well-known habit of horse race-gambling. Other words between the two men were personal and quickly escalated to the brink of fighting. Umpire O'Day took charge of the situation and banished McGraw to the clubhouse.[35]

Their losing streak ended, the Cubs boarded their train Tuesday evening and headed for Pittsburgh to play two games against the Pirates. Chance announced that John "Tacks" Neuer would travel with the team to Pittsburgh and continue on with the Cubs to Chicago. The thirty-one-year-old left-hander pitched for New York's Highlanders in 1907, posting a 4 win, 2 loss record with a 2.17 earned run average, but the Highlanders released him prior to the 1908 season. Chance invited Neuer to tryout for the team once the Cubs returned to Chicago.[36]

Chicago's new mascot, Schulte's puppy Cub, sat on the front seat of the players' bus as the Cubs rode to Pittsburgh's Exposition Park for the first game against the Pirates. Cub then joined the players on the bench to ensure continued good fortune for the team. The Cubs played flawless baseball behind Brown's three-hitter and scored a 3–0 win. Not only did the Cubs play error-free baseball, but Steinfeldt, Howard, and Sheckard all made outstanding plays. Steinfeldt made a fine running catch of a pop foul and speared a low line drive. Howard robbed Tommy Leach of a hit by making a spectacular catch of a line drive off his shoe tops. But the feature play of the day belonged to Jimmy Sheckard. Honus Wagner lifted a tall foul fly toward the left-field stands. After a hard run, Sheckard made a final desperate lunge for the ball, caught the ball in his mitt, and finished with a somersault, coming to rest at the base of the stands for the final out of the game.[37]

Moran was more than ever convinced that the puppy was a good luck charm. Others were just as sure the departure of Charles Murphy had changed their fortunes. Brown pitched as he always did. Back in Chicago, Murphy felt chipper again and released a statement praising the team and predicting another pennant for the Cubs. "The team is now in good condition except for Schulte, almost for the first time this season, and that's what we want. We'll move to the front in the stay on our home grounds, and then its up to us to make good on the last eastern trip. Chance explains our poor showing in New York by over anxiety of the boys, following the many breakups in teamwork by injuries."[38]

Albert "Lefty" Leifield pitched one of his better games against the Cubs the next day, scattering four hits as he shut out Chicago, 1 to 0. Reulbach surrendered only five hits to the Pirates, but the one run in the first inning proved the difference. Center fielder Roy Thomas received a walk to begin the inning. Tommy Leach sacrificed Thomas to second, and player-manager Fred Clarke lined a single into center field, scoring Thomas with the only run of the day. Tinker tried to score a run all on his own in the fifth inning. With one out, Tinker singled and promptly stole second and third base while Moran stood in the batter's box. Moran took three strikes for the second out, sending Reulbach to the plate. Taking a big lead, Tinker made a daring dash for home in his unaided attempt to tie the score. Leifield's pitch to Reulbach happened to be low and inside. Catcher George Gibson caught the ball just as Tinker slid into the plate and Gibson's glove. Still, the call could have gone either way, but umpire Jim Johnstone ruled Tinker out by a whisker. Johnstone, who had only recently been released from the hospital after suffering from appendicitis, was the sole umpire the previous day, so he appreciated the help of Bob Emslie, who had been sent by the National League office to Pittsburgh to assist the still-recovering umpire.[39]

The Cubs boarded the 8:00 P.M. train for Chicago. The eastern swing had produced a record of 10 wins and 8 losses. Six of those losses could be directly attributed to the Cubs' poor fielding. Still, except for Frank Schulte, the Cubs were finally healthy, and they rested in third place, four and a half games behind the first-place Pirates. And Schulte expected to play in another week.[40]

Business manager Charlie Williams secured accommodations in two special sleeper cars for the journey home. "Business Manager Williams' success in securing sleeping accommodations and avoiding the ball players despair, upper berths, has earned him around the circuit the title of world's champion business manager."[41]

On Saturday, August 15, Chance switched the batting order to begin the homestand against the Philadelphia Phillies. Rewarded for his recent hard hitting, Tinker moved from the number-seven position in the batting order to third, taking the spot formerly occupied by Chance. Slagle and Sheckard remained in their customary first and second slots. Evers stayed in the clean-up position, while Steinfeldt hit fifth, followed by Howard, Chance, and Kling. The new lineup produced only four hits and a single run against the Phillies. Brown gave up six hits and single runs to the Phillies in the second, fourth, and seventh innings, losing 3 to 1.[42]

The next day, Sunday, Chance used the same lineup except Hofman played first base and hit seventh in place of Chance. Hofman's double in the third inning was the only hit allowed by the Phillies' McQuillen, as the Cubs were shut out for the second time in the last three games and lost their second-straight game to the Phillies, 1 to 0. Pfiester pitched a fine game, allowing only three hits. Unfortunately, two of them, a double followed by a single in the second inning, produced the Phillies' winning run. In sixteen games against Philadelphia this season, the Cubs managed only 5 victories against 11 defeats. This loss put the Cubs six full games behind the Pirates and three games behind the second-place Giants. McQuillen's one-hit victory brought the Phillies within one-half game of the Cubs and third place.[43]

The two losses over the weekend brought the Cubs to the precipice of fourth place. On Monday, August 17, manager Chance switched back to the old lineup, trying to prevent the fall. Tinker went back to hitting in the seventh position, Chance reclaimed his number-three slot, and Hofman led off and played center field. Light-hitting Jimmy Slagle sat on the bench. The Cubs scored a run in the second inning and three more in the third. Pitching duties fell to Ed Reulbach, who responded magnificently. Going into the seventh inning, Reulbach had a no-hitter and a 4–0 lead. The Phillies managed a hit and a run in the seventh, but they failed to score in the final two innings, while the Cubs scored in the eighth to lead, 5 to 1. Reulbach finished with a two-hitter, allowing a lead-off single to John Titus in the ninth, but Titus was erased on a sharp double play: Reulbach to Tinker to Chance. The old lineup change worked. Howard and Tinker led the hitting attack, Howard with two singles and Tinker with a triple. Hofman and Evers added a single apiece to the Cubs' hit total.[44]

Umpire O'Day earned a round of applause from the crowd for fielding a foul grounder behind the plate off Reulbach's bat in the seventh inning and quickly tossing the ball back to the pitcher, while Phillies catcher Red Dooin looked around for the ball. Two innings earlier, O'Day gained the respect of players and crowd when Philadelphia shortstop Mickey Doolan sent a ball screaming down the third-base line. O'Day immediately called the ball foul. The Phillies started to disagree, but O'Day calmly walked down the third-base line to the outfield grass and pointed to the exact spot the ball had struck, one sixteenth of an inch from the foul line. Reulbach still had his no-hitter.[45]

Tully Sparks, the winning pitcher for Philadelphia in the first game of the series on Saturday against Brown, pitched the final game on Tuesday, August 18. The veteran thirty-three-year-old right-hander, a mainstay of the Phillies' pitching staff since 1903, won 22 games in 1907, leading the team in victories. Headlines in the *Chicago Tribune* announced the results of Tuesday's game: "CUBS GET LACING FROM MR. SPARKS, PHILADELPHIA PITCHER TRIMS CHAMPS FOR SECOND TIME DURING SERIES, WIDE MARGIN OF 8 TO 3."[46]

Overall was scheduled to pitch, but instead he spent the day by his wife's bedside at the hospital for her operation. Lundgren started for the Cubs. When O'Day announced the starting batteries (pitcher and catcher) for the two teams, the fans made some remarks, "unfit for publication," concerning Lundgren's pitching abilities. For three innings, Lundgren silenced his critics, but in the fourth, Philadelphia erupted for three runs which "produced a resumption of the flow of decayed utterances from the spectators."[47] Lundgren lasted until the sixth, when Chance replaced him with Chick Fraser, after Lundgren walked the lead-off hitter and allowed a single to place runners on first and second. Before Fraser recorded three outs, the Phillies scored five times to surge into the lead, 8 to 2.[48]

After Steinfeldt singled in the second inning, Tinker hit a terrific drive into the left-field pavilion to give Lundgren a two-run lead. Chance hit well against Sparks with a double and triple, scoring the Cubs' third and final run in the sixth, but otherwise Sparks controlled the game. Warm applause greeted Schulte when he trotted into right field to begin the seventh inning. Out of action since he pulled a groin muscle in Cincinnati on July 1, Schulte gingerly played the final two and a half innings, testing his leg. No hits came his way in right field, but he batted twice (no hits), including producing the final out of the game against Sparks. After winning three of the four games, Philadelphia continued to press the Cubs for third place, only a half game behind.[49]

On Wednesday, August 19, Howard resumed his role in right field for the first of four games against the visiting Boston Doves. Schulte needed at least another week to heal. Brown allowed four hits and one run in the third inning, but it was the only run Boston scored as the Cubs piled on five runs, with a three-run outburst in the bottom of the eighth, to win, 5 to 1. Tinker again led the Cub hitting assault with two doubles. Sheckard joined Tinker, producing his own two doubles. Rudderham and Rigler umpired the Boston series, and, unlike Rudderham's last performance with the Cubs, no incidents marred the opening game with Boston.[50]

Overall reported his wife's successful operation and returned to uniform. Pitcher John Neuer, recently invited by Chance to tryout with the Cubs, was released to the Johnstown team of the Tri-State League. In Johnstown, pitcher Floyd Kroh received word to report to the Cubs.[51]

Thursday's game was the replay of the eleven-inning tie game on July 22. Harry Pulliam watched from the promenade deck and made no public comments on the contest or the on-duty detectives among the crowd. Murphy had posted signs in the stands warning patrons that betting was prohibited and violations would be punished. Detectives were strategically stationed in the stands where gamblers were known to operate.[52]

Cub hitters produced ten runs, and Pfiester had an easy day on the mound, winning 10 to 2. Led by Hofman's four hits in four tries with a walk, three hits apiece for Evers and Tinker, and a double and triple from Chance, the Cubs scored often, giving Pfiester an easy cushion to work with. After gaining a big lead, Chance gave his sore toe a rest. Hofman went from center field to first base, and Slagle returned to his old position in center field.[53]

Thursday was the deadline for purchasing minor-league players, and Murphy announced the purchase of two minor-league pitchers and the sale of a third to the Boston Doves. Forrest More, a twenty-four-year-old right-handed star with the Springfield, Illinois, team of the Three-Eyes League had won 17 of 21 games, including a streak of fourteen in a row. Late in the evening, just before the deadline, Murphy signed his second minor leaguer, another right-handed pitcher, twenty-year-old Zeriah Zequiel Hagerman from Topeka of the Western Association. Lastly, Murphy exercised his option on pitcher Joe Donahue, the Chicago rookie who was lent to the Montreal team of the Eastern League early in the season. A member of the Cubs after the season started, Donahue was never given a chance to pitch before he was demoted. Murphy sold Donahue to the Boston Doves for an undisclosed amount.[54] Donahue never pitched in the major leagues.

The next day, Friday, August 21, Reulbach pitched erratically, walking four and allowing six hits in just over two innings. But the Doves left the bases loaded in the first without a run scoring and left the bases full again in the second inning, scoring only a single run. When Reulbach started the third inning, allowing two hits and a walk and another run scored, Chance called for Overall to rescue Reulbach. The fans cheered as Overall made his way to the mound, and they were not disappointed. Orvie quickly retired the Doves in the third and kept Boston scoreless for the next five innings. The Cubs scored a run in the first inning after two were out. Chance walked and scored after singles by Evers and Steinfeldt. The Cubs added two more runs in the fourth and fifth innings. The Doves managed to push across a lone run in the ninth against Overall, but it was too little, too late, as the Cubs won their third straight from Boston, 5 to 3.[55]

The Cubs and Brown went for the four-game sweep on Saturday. Boston started a six-foot, three-inch, twenty-four-year-old rookie left-hander, Tom Tuckey. After only three weeks in the major leagues, the English-born Tuckey went against the Cubs' star pitcher. Tuckey possessed a wide sweeping curve ball, good speed, and an excellent change-of-pace pitch.

Brown rang up seven consecutive zeros on the scoreboard, but the Boston youngster matched him pitch for pitch until the Cubs' seventh inning when Chicago scored the first run of the game. After one out, Tinker singled and went to third when Kling followed with a single to right field. Brown fouled out to catcher Graham for the second out. Graham walked out to the mound to offer instructions to Tuckey in case the Cubs tried a two-out double steal. During the conference, Kling walked away from first base toward second. Tuckey, the ball in his hand, unsure what to do, turned completely around and fired the ball toward third. The ball sailed into the outfield, and Tinker trotted home. Tuckey regained his composure and retired Hofman on a ground ball.[56]

After seven shutout innings against the light-hitting Doves, a one-run lead for Brown seemed safe enough for confident Cub fans. But the Doves fluttered in the eighth inning to score a run and tie the score at one all. Left fielder Johnny Bates doubled and sprinted home on a single by first baseman Dan McGann. But that was all. Brown and Tuckey both stiffened, and at the end of the regulation nine innings the score remained tied. For the next five innings, both pitchers shut out their opponents.[57]

The Cubs had a chance to end the game in the bottom of the fourteenth inning. Steinfeldt struck out to begin the inning, but Howard bounced a sharp hit off of Tuckey's glove. Tinker singled to right, his fourth hit, sending Howard to third. Kling was intentionally walked, filling the bases with only one out. Chance wanted to send Zimmerman to the plate to pinch hit for Brown, but Mordecai pleaded to stay in the game and Chance gave in. Brown, a good hitter, gave a valiant effort, but struck out swinging at a wicked Tuckey curveball. Still, the bases remained loaded as Hofman came to the plate, but Tuckey retired Hofman on a pop up to shortstop Bill Dahlen.[58]

Johnny Bates, the Dove left fielder, made his fifth consecutive hit off Brown to begin the fifteenth inning. Center fielder Ginger Beaumont followed with a single to left center. Dan McGann sacrificed, placing runners on second and third with one out. Brown deliberately passed second baseman Ritchey to pitch to shortstop Dahlen. Hitless against Brown all day, now Dahlen ruined the strategy by sending a ball between short and third into left field. Bates and Beaumont both scored with Ritchey going to third. Third baseman Sweeney lifted a fly to center field. Ritchey tagged and raced for home, but Hofman made a strong, accurate throw to Kling, who applied the tag for the third out.[59]

The Cubs made a two-out rally in the bottom of the fifteenth inning. Evers beat out an infield hit, and one of Tuckey's curves nicked Steinfeldt, putting Cubs on second and third. The next hitter, Howard, had three hits already, so Chance, playing the percentages, decided to pinch hit Moran. But Tuckey struck out Moran to end the game, beating Brown and the Cubs, 3 to 1.[60]

Umpire Rudderham had another difficult day with several close calls at first. In the tenth inning, Brown and Chance both went for a bunt, forcing Evers to cover first. Chance tossed to Evers, but it appeared the runner beat the throw. Rudderham ruled the runner out to the displeasure of both the Boston players and the spectators. In the fifteenth inning, Chance tapped a slow roller on the infield grass, wide of first base. McGann fielded the ball, changed direction, and raced Chance to the bag. Again, it appeared the runner arrived first, but Rudderham signaled Chance out.[61]

Tinker, who had been hitting the daylights out of the ball, received word he had been hit with a lawsuit. Business manager Charlie Williams informed Tinker that wholesale liquor and cigar dealers had filed suit to tie up the shortstop's September salary to satisfy bills accrued by Tinker as former part-owner of a saloon at Van Buren and Leavitt streets. As team treasurer, Williams was also named in the suit.[62]

The Brooklyn team arrived in town for a doubleheader on Sunday, August 23, with an identity problem. The team name was in transition. They were called Superbas, their former name, and Trolley Dodgers, often shortened by newspaper reporters to Dodgers. Regardless of name, seventh-place Brooklyn lost both games on Sunday to the Cubs by identical 2–0 scores. Overall pitched a two-hit shutout in the first game, and Reulbach nearly matched him, pitching a four-hit shutout in the second contest. Overall struck out eleven Superbas (or Dodgers) while Reulbach fanned five. Evers provided the firepower, collecting five hits in the two games.[63]

Frank Chance sat on the Cubs' bench in citizen's clothes on Monday. At the end of the fifteen-inning game against Boston on Saturday, Chance, using colorful language, told umpire Rudderham what he thought of his umpiring skills. Rudderham promptly filed a report with National League president Harry Pulliam, who just as promptly suspended Chance for three games.[64]

Brooklyn scored two runs in the fifth inning on Monday to take the lead and break a string of forty-two consecutive scoreless innings, twenty in Pittsburgh and twenty-two in Chicago. The Cubs answered with a single run in the bottom of the fifth when Kling tripled and Zimmerman, batting for Pfiester, singled. Fraser blanked the Dodgers in the sixth and seventh innings. Propelled by Steinfeldt's lead-off triple in the bottom of the seventh, the Cubs tallied three more runs. Slagle pinch hit for Fraser during the rally, bringing Overall to the mound for the final two innings. Overall continued where he left off the day before, striking out three Dodgers in two innings to preserve the 4–2 victory.[65]

Schulte played right field for a full game for the first time since his groin pull on July 1. He failed to get a hit in four at bats, but he received a walk and had one put out in right field. More importantly, he maneuvered naturally on the basepaths and in the outfield. Howard moved from right to center field with Hofman playing first base for the suspended Chance.[66]

After Monday's games around the National League, the league standings changed. The Cubs remained in third place, but the Giants won a doubleheader in Pittsburgh and vaulted into first place, ahead of the Pirates for the first time. The Cubs trailed the Giants by three and a half games.[67]

6. Bottomed Out 131

Floyd Kroh arrived from Johnstown, Pennsylvania, on Tuesday, August 25, his twenty-second birthday, donned a Cub uniform, and demonstrated his left-handed pitching delivery before the start of the game. Observing the six-foot, two-inch youngster perform, Sanborn declared, "He looked good enough ... and has the height and wide, sweeping delivery which often is a left hander's best stock in trade."[68]

Reulbach started the game badly. He hit Brooklyn's lead-off batter, Whitey Alperman, with a pitch. Then right fielder Harry Lumley drove a single to center. The next hitter, left fielder John Hummel, attempted a sacrifice bunt, but popped the ball toward first. Hofman, at full speed, made a fine catch just before the ball hit the ground. Then, he turned and fired the ball to Tinker at second base in time for a double play on Alperman. Tim Jordan followed with a tremendous wallop a dozen feet over *The Tribune* sign in right center field scoring two runs.[69] Reulbach maintained his composure and finally found his groove in the second inning. Five of the nine men to face Reulbach in the next three innings struck out, and the Dodgers did not score the rest of the game.[70]

The Cubs scored a single run in the third inning when Reulbach tripled and scored on a sacrifice fly off the bat of Jimmy Sheckard. In the sixth inning, the Cubs tied the score when Sheckard tripled and Schulte stroked a single through the drawn-in infield. At this point, Brooklyn's pitcher, George "Farmer" Bell, lost his control and walked three Cubs in a row, scoring Schulte. Another single by Moran and several misplays by Brooklyn allowed three more runs to score before the Cubs finished the inning. The Cubs added a set of double runs in the next two innings to win easily, 10 to 2.[71]

The Cubs won their fifth in a row, 6 to 4, sweeping the five games from Brooklyn. On Wednesday, August 26, Overall started the final game, but he had difficulty with his control, constantly falling behind the hitters in the count. Brooklyn scored a run in the first inning and two more in the second, taking a 3–0 lead. Overall continued to struggle, with the Dodgers threatening but failing to score in the next four innings. In trouble again after three consecutive hits and a run scored in the Brooklyn seventh, Overall made his exit. Serving the last game of his suspension, Chance called on Brown to save the day. The Cubs scored single runs in the second, fourth, and sixth innings and bunched three runs together in the third. Brooklyn's run in the seventh inning made it a two-run game with the tying runs on base. But Brown rescued Overall, ending the Dodger rally in the seventh and blanking Brooklyn the final two innings to preserve the 6–4 win. Bob Emslie, umpiring behind the plate, took a hard foul tip in the second inning.[72] "The ball hit him in the thigh just at the outer edge of his protector and doubled the umpire up with intense pain for several minutes. For once the rabid rooters did not gloat gleefully, but actually cheered Bob when he was ready to go on with the play."[73]

The Giants strutted into Chicago in first place, having won four in a row in Pittsburgh. The Cubs remained in third place, but trailed the Pirates by only two percentage points and the Giants by three and a half games. The Giants were confident, even cocky, having already won ten of the fifteen games played against the Cubs so far this season. Both teams were healthy and eager for battle.[74]

By three o'clock on Thursday, lines of fans a block-and-a-half long formed in front of each ticket window, eagerly anticipating the most important game of the year. Every Cub fan knew last year's champions had to win at least two of the three games with the Giants to have a chance of retaining their crown. Crowds squeezed into every nook of West Side Park, then overflowed onto the field. Management sent for extra police to confine fans to foul territory, but to no avail. "Soon the dammed up stream burst its barriers and flowed around the entire field."[75] O'Day and Emslie, two of the National League's best umpires, were assigned to the Cubs vs. Giants series. O'Day usually preferred to umpire solo, but he and Emslie were friends, and the Cub-Giant rivalry needed two sets of eyes.[76]

Pfiester drew the first-game pitching assignment against Wiltse. Neither team scored for the first three innings. In the bottom of the fourth, the Cubs drew first blood. After Chance grounded out, Evers sent a line drive just inside the third-base line and into the crowd encircling the field for a ground rule double. Steinfeldt singled to right, scoring Evers with the first run of the game. Howard fouled out, but then Tinker singled to center, advancing Steinfeldt to second base. Kling drove a ball past the outfielders in the gap between left and center field and into the on-field spectators. Kling circled the bases with an apparent three-run homer, sending the partisan fans into jubilant hysteria. But the ground rules agreed to before the game began required any ball reaching the overflow crowd behind the outfielders to be ruled a double. Umpire O'Day sent Tinker back to third and Kling to second, allowing only Steinfeldt to score. Pitcher Pfiester grounded out to end the inning.[77]

The Giants got one of the runs back in the top of the fifth. Shad Barry singled to left. Al Bridwell grounded a ball to Steinfeldt, who threw to Evers at second to start a double play; but Evers dropped the throw, placing Giants on first and second. Pfiester prepared to deliver the next pitch. Tinker suddenly broke for second base behind the runner, Barry. Pfiester wheeled around and threw toward Tinker, but the ball struck Barry in the back and bounded away toward left field. Both runners advanced a base as Tinker retrieved the ball. The next hitter, pitcher Wiltse, helped his own cause, lifting a fly ball just deep enough to Hofman in center field to allow Barry to tag and score. Pfiester struck out first baseman Fred Tenney for the second out. Larry Doyle sent a line drive toward right field with an apparent hit that would have tied the score, but Howard made a diving catch, landing flat on his stomach, to preserve the Cubs' 2–1 lead.[78]

With the help of a wild throw, the Cubs scored three more times in the bottom of the fifth. Hofman singled off Bridwell's glove, and Sheckard walked. Chance laid down a sacrifice bunt, fielded by Wiltse. Second baseman Doyle covered first base, but Wiltse threw wide of first, forcing Doyle into the basepath. Chance and Doyle collided, and the ball sailed into foul territory. Hofman scored and Sheckard went to third before the ball was retrieved. Umpire O'Day called time to allow Doyle time to recover after his collision with Chance, who outweighed the Giant second baseman by twenty-five pounds. The next hitter, Evers, grounded to first baseman Fred Tenney, who held Sheckard at third and stepped on first ahead of Evers for the first out. Chance advanced to second. Then Steinfeldt scored both Sheckard and Chance with a single to left. Howard and Tinker made ground outs to end the productive fifth inning.[79]

Leading 5 to 1, Jack Pfiester shut out the Giants for the final four innings, earning the nickname that remained with him for the rest of his career, "Jack the Giant Killer." When Evers threw out Doyle for the final out in the ninth inning, the West Side Grounds exploded with joy. Bugs cheered long and loud, while some of the more excited fans expressed their delight and let fly their seat cushions. The crowd was the largest of the season, filling the 14,200 spectator capacity of West Side Grounds and spilling another estimated 10,000 rooters onto the field down both foul lines and on the outfield grass behind the outfielders. Chicago had not witnessed a crowd this large since the previous October for the World Series against the Detroit Tigers.[80]

Several thousand more fans gathered on the corner of Dearborn and Madison Streets to watch the game on the Tribune Electric Score Board, a new invention in 1908. Shaped like a baseball diamond with electric lights at each position, the giant board recorded each play almost simultaneously as it happened at the ballpark. Lights also indicated the ball-and-strike count, the number of outs, and runners on base. Lineups for both teams and the player positions were listed in foul territory on the board. A teletype operator watching the game at West Side Grounds sent a message on every pitch, and another operator at Dearborn Street recorded the information, in lights,

on the scoreboard. In the fourth inning, the street fans "watched" Evers double and score the first run. A glowing light bulb by his name indicated Evers at bat. As the Cubs second baseman sent the ball down the third-base line for a double, a light followed Evers around the basepaths to first and then second base. The next light went on by Steinfeldt's name as he batted, while lights recorded balls and strikes. When Steinfeldt singled to right field, a light recorded his position on first base. And Evers's bright light on second base advanced to third and then home as a number 1 lit up in the Cubs' run box. Street fans erupted into applause as if they really witnessed the run score.[81]

On Friday, August 28, an off day, the Cubs practiced for two hours in the morning, preparing for the next contest, while the Giants took a full day to relax. *The Tribune* used the off-day to erect a second electric scoreboard on top of the Illinois Central railroad station on Randolph Street and announced the fact on the front page of their newspaper. According to *The Tribune*, "Every movement of every man on the field is faithfully and instantaneously reproduced on a miniature diamond

August 28 — After the Cubs beat the Giants 5 to 1 behind "Jack the Giant Killer" Pfiester, jubilant fans threw seat cushions from the stands. Fans on the receiving end were less than jubilant.

August 29 — Sunrise illuminates a long line of fans, waiting in front of West Side Park to purchase tickets for the big game. Cub fans were not disappointed as pitcher Mordecai Brown beat the Giants' Christy Mathewson, 3 to 2.

so accurately that but little imagination is needed to picture the scene itself."[82] Fans who could not attend the game in person appreciated the new innovation, but every one would much rather be in the ball park. After all, the new scoreboards did not show Hank O'Day striding from behind the plate on Kling's hit into the crowd on Thursday, holding up two fingers to rule the hit a double and sending Tinker back to third and Kling to second base, after both had crossed home plate.[83]

Chicago went baseball mad for the second Cub-Giant game, matching the two best pitchers in baseball. Ticket lines were longer than for the first game, and more police were required to maintain order. Ticket speculators worked the lines, making a hefty profit on each ticket sold, while avoiding the attention of Chicago's finest. Baseball was the sole topic of conversation, eclipsing business issues and even presidential politics in this election year.[84] "Chicago Fandom Eager for Second Battle in Thrilling Race for Pennant." "BROWN VS. MATHEWSON." "Record Breaking Throng Expected to Witness Duel of the Mighty Twirlers." "For the second encounter Mordecai

Brown and Christy Mathewson will be the opposing slabmen, and that means a battle royal between two of the greatest exponents of the pitching art in the world."[85]

The second-largest crowd in Cubs' history, Chicago's legendary Cap Anson among them, jammed West Side Grounds to watch the pitching titans perform. Anson received loud applause as he entered the ballpark, giving "ample proof that he has not been forgotten, even by the generation of rooters which knows him only by renown."[86] Brown started slowly, giving up a run in the first inning. Tenney led off, hitting a high bouncing ball into the hole at deep shortstop. Tinker managed to field the ball on the outfield grass, but Tenney beat his throw to Chance at first base. Hofman recorded the first out, catching a shallow fly ball off the bat of Larry Doyle, but Bresnahan singled to right, sending Tenney to third. Mike Donlin smashed a long fly over Hofman's head into the crowd for a ground-rule double, scoring Tenney and placing runners on second and third with only one out. Cy Seymour popped a fly into shallow right center field where neither outfielder, Hofman in center or Howard in right, could make the play. But second baseman Evers raced into the outfield, made a fine over-the-shoulder catch, and immediately threw home to keep Bresnahan from scoring. Confident the ball would land safely, Donlin ran to third before he realized Evers had caught it, and he could not return to second before Kling threw the ball to Evers, who stepped on second base for the double play. Still, the Giants had a one-run lead with Matty pitching.[87]

Hofman, Sheckard, and Chance were easy outs, with both Sheckard and Chance striking out swinging against Mathewson in the Cubs' first inning. Brown recovered and retired the Giants without a hit in the second. Evers, Steinfeldt and Howard were Cub outs. New York threatened to score again in the third, but a fine play by Tinker saved the day. Tenney walked, and Doyle sacrificed him to second. Then Bresnahan received the second walk of the inning, placing Giants on first and second. Donlin hit a ground ball into the hole at shortstop; Tinker made a fine back-handed catch, but he had no chance to throw out the speedy Donlin at first. Instead, Tinker threw to Steinfeldt covering third. The ball arrived just ahead of Tenney for the force out. Seymour flied out to Hofman for the final out. In the bottom of the third, Matty made it nine outs in a row, retiring Tinker, Kling, and Brown on ground balls. Mathewson threw out Tinker and made a fine play knocking down a hard shot off the bat of Brown and retrieving the ball in time to throw to Tenney at first.[88]

The tables turned in the fourth inning. Brown found his form and easily set down Devlin, Barry, and Bridwell in order, while Cub hitters bunched five hits and scored three runs to take a 3–1 lead. Hofman pulled a line drive over the head of Shad Barry into the crowd in left field, beginning the fourth inning with the first Cub hit, a ground-rule double. Sheckard sacrificed Hofman to third. Chance followed with a single just out of Bridwell's reach, scoring Hofman with the tying run. Evers sliced a grounder between Tenney and the first-base bag which disappeared into the crowd in foul territory. Normally a double without fans on the field, the ground rules gave Evers only a single and stopped Chance at second base. Steinfeldt ripped a line drive into right field; Donlin charged the ball and threw to Bresnahan at home to make a play on Chance, but his throw, wide of the mark, allowed Chance to slide safely across the plate with run number two. Evers and Steinfeldt advanced a base on the play at the plate, placing Cubs on second and third. Howard duplicated Evers's hit, placing a line drive between Tenney and first base and, again, into the crowd in foul territory. Like Evers, Howard received a ground-rule single, and the runner on base, Steinfeldt, was allowed to advance only one base, to third. But Evers scored from third with run number three. Tinker tried a squeeze bunt to score Steinfeldt, but popped up the ball to Tenney. Kling grounded out to shortstop to end the inning.[89]

The Giants scored another run in the fifth inning, and, but for a brilliant catch and throw from Jimmy Sheckard, would have scored several more. Brown struck out Mathewson to begin the fifth, but Tenney singled to left and Doyle to right. Howard charged Doyle's hit and held Tenney at second, but Brown walked Bresnahan, filling the bases. The next hitter, Mike Donlin, walloped a fly towards the crowd in left field. If the ball fell safely into the crowd, Donlin would receive a ground-rule double and two runs would score. But Sheckard had other ideas. He retreated past the fringe of spectators into the crowd and pulled down Donlin's drive. Tenney and Doyle tagged their bases on the catch. Much too deep to make a throw to the plate, Sheckard fired the ball on a line to Steinfeldt at third to nail the sliding Doyle, complete a double play, and end the inning. Tenney did score the Giants second run. Score, 3 to 2.

Both Brown and Mathewson dominated the hitters for the final four and a half innings, with neither team mounting any scoring threats. The Cubs' close victory brought them within a game and a half of the first-place Giants and tied the Cubs with the Pirates, who split a doubleheader in Philadelphia, in second place. The Cubs and Pirates had identical records, 69 wins against 47 losses. Brown recorded his 18th win of the season with 6 losses. Mathewson lost his seventh game of the season, after compiling 26 wins before the end of August.[90]

One hundred blue-clad policeman, guests of President Murphy, con-

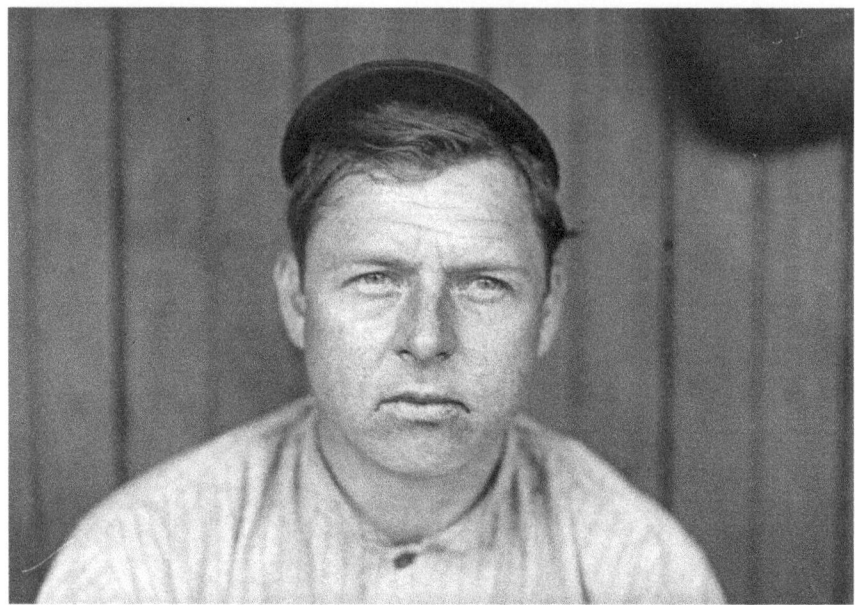

Ace Mordecai Brown led the team with a 1.47 earned run average and 29 wins with only 9 losses.

trolled the large crowd, preventing most rowdy behavior. Most spectators appreciated their presence, but not all. "A large feminine fan with a merry widow lid of pronounced blue tint, two stories high, and adorned with sweeping feathers, insisted on standing directly in front of some of the box seats on the third base side of the catcher. She was deaf to all remarks and requests to remove the beautiful creation, but when a policeman politely asked her to take it off or sit down she and her escort left in a terrible huff, looking for President Murphy or anybody else to pay damages for her fatally injured feelings."[91]

While the Cubs inched closer towards first place, they already led the league in hitting with a team batting average of (.251). Zimmerman appeared in 40 of the Cubs' 116 games, with 32 hits in 93 at bats for a .327 average, and led the team in hitting. Only Pittsburgh's Honus Wagner, the National League's leading hitter, had a higher batting average (.336). Among the Cubs' regulars, Evers (.315) led all other Cubs and stood fourth in the league. Individual Cub averages were as follows: Howard (.273); Kling (.269); Tinker (.266); Steinfeldt (.257); Moran (.250); Chance (.241); Sheckard (.239); Hofman (.235); Schulte (.232); and Slagle (.199). Reulbach was the best-hitting pitcher at .280, followed by Brown at .235. In the pitching depart-

6. Bottomed Out

In 1908, Solly Hofman (holding the bat), one of the great utility men of his day, played 68 games in the infield and another 50 in the outfield. His "catcher" in this photo, pitcher Jack Pfiester, would earn the nickname "Jack the Giant Killer" after late-season victories against arch-rival New York.

ment, Brown led with his 18 wins. Reulbach followed with 16 wins against 6 losses. Overall compiled 12 wins versus 8 losses, followed by Fraser (10–8), Lundgren (6–9), and Pfiester (6–10).[92]

On Sunday, August 30, the Cubs fulfilled the city of Chicago's sweetest dream with a 2–1 victory and a sweep of the three-game series against the Giants. Pfiester made it three in a row of his own against New York. On July 18, after relieving Reulbach in the third inning, Pfiester had beaten the Giants 5 to 4 in Chicago, and on August 11 he pitched a 4–0 shutout in New York, the only Cub win against the Giants in that series. This day, Pfiester pitched a five-hitter, allowing the Giants only a single run in the second inning. Donlin walked, advanced to third on Seymour's single to center field, and scored on a lightening double play executed by Evers, Tinker, and Chance. The Cubs scored one run in the first. Hofman walked, advanced to second on a hit-and-run fielder's choice by Sheckard, and scored on a Chance single. The Giant run in the second tied the score. In the fifth inning, Tinker beat out an infield hit, and, after Kling flied out, Pfiester set up the winning run with a sacrifice bunt, sending Tinker to second. Hofman provided the game-winning hit, a sharp single past the mound to center field, scoring Tinker.[93]

"Jack's Pitching Is Brilliant," beamed the *Chicago Tribune* of Pfiester's performance. And *Tribune* reporter I. E. Sanborn decreed, "for the rest of time and part of eternity the Mr. Pfiester of private life will be known to the public and the historians solely as Jack The Giant Killer."[94]

The slightly smaller crowd on Sunday had exhibited good behavior throughout the contest. They seemed to enjoy themselves without the raucous cheering and yelling in evidence for the first two Giant games. But after the game was over and the blue-clad barriers removed, a mob flooded the diamond, venting their enthusiasm and rejoicing in a battle of seat cushions. "[M]any a hat was smashed and many a bruise suffered good naturedly with small thought of the danger of serious injury or of the spirit of reckless ruffianism which it typified."[95]

CHAPTER 7

Touching Second, Twice

On Monday, the last day of August, the Cubs continued their winning streak, making it nine in a row and twelve out of their last thirteen games. Chicago's baseball fever of the previous ninety-six hours subsided with the arrival of the National League's tail-enders, the St. Louis Cardinals. Frank Chance took the day off from playing, rested his sore finger and foot, and inserted the ever-versatile Artie Hofman at first base. The Cubs-Giants series umpires, Hank O'Day and Bob Emslie, were replaced by Cy Rigler and the much maligned rookie umpire, John Rudderham. Orval Overall pitched a four-hit shutout against the light-hitting Cardinals, striking out eleven. The Cubs managed only five hits, two by Evers, against Cardinal pitcher Bugs Raymond, but scored single runs in the first and sixth innings to record their ninth consecutive win, 2 to 0.[1]

Rigler umpired solo for the next game and for the rest of the Cardinal series, including a doubleheader on Thursday. The *Chicago Tribune* made no mention of Rudderham's absence, but simply omitted his name from the box score for Tuesday, September 1.[2] Later in the month, the National League office confirmed that Rudderham had been released. Umpiring alone, Rigler missed a call in the fourth inning. Johnny Evers led off with a walk and went to second base on an apparent Steinfeldt single to center field. Evers saw the ball hit the ground before being fielded on the short hop by center fielder Al Shaw, but he missed the umpire's call. Rigler thought Shaw made the catch before the ball hit the ground and ruled Steinfeldt out. Shaw returned the ball to shortstop Walter Morris, who applied the tag to Evers, standing on second base. Rigler called Evers out, precipitating a vigorous protest from the Cubs. Doc Marshall, the most vocal, was ejected and sent to the clubhouse.[3]

Pat Moran led the Cubs' hitting attack with three singles as the Cubs scored single runs in the first, second, fifth, and sixth innings, taking a 4–0 lead. Ed Reulbach shut out the Cardinals on only four hits for seven innings, and the Cubs appeared headed for ten wins in a row. But the Cardinal bats came to life with eight hits in the next three innings. The Cardinals scored one run in the eighth and three more in the ninth to tie the score, sending the game into extra innings. In the top of the tenth, Red Murray tripled between Schulte and Howard (playing center field) to right center field. Reulbach struck out first baseman Konetchy for the second out, but then Joe Delahanty lined a single to center, scoring Murray with the go-ahead run. Johnny Lush pitched the ninth and tenth innings in relief of starter Fred Beebe and retired six Cubs in a row to secure the come-from-behind St. Louis victory, 5 to 4. While the Cubs suffered their first loss in ten games, New York and Pittsburgh were sweeping doubleheaders in Boston and Cincinnati. As a result, the Cubs dropped back into third place after being only a half game behind the first-place Giants two days before.[4]

After one day of rest, Chance returned to the lineup on Wednesday, September 2, but Joe Tinker missed his first game of the season with a wrenched back. Heinie Zimmerman played shortstop. Hofman's return from first base to center field gave the Cubs their regular outfield of Schulte in right, Hofman in center, and Sheckard in left, for the first time since the benching of Jimmy Slagle. Twelve-year veteran Chick Fraser turned in a fine performance to return the Cubs to their winning ways. He shut down the Cardinal batters with three hits while his teammates crossed home plate eight times for the 8–0 win. It was his eleventh victory of the season against 8 losses.[5]

The thirty-seven-year-old Fraser, the senior Cub, began his career in 1896 with Louisville before that team's move to Pittsburgh in 1900. A teammate of Honus Wagner in 1897 and 1898, Fraser was traded to Cleveland's National League team in the middle of the 1898 season. The next year, Fraser moved to Philadelphia. He played two seasons with the Phillies, one with the Athletics, and three more with the Phillies before being traded to the Boston Doves in 1905. Fraser had his best seasons in Philadelphia, winning 21 and 22 games in 1899 and 1901. He pitched in Boston one season, moved to Cincinnati in 1906, and joined the Cubs in 1907, compiling an 8 win, 5 loss season. Fraser's three-hit shutout victory against the Cardinals turned out to be his last win of the season and the last win of his major-league career. In 1909, Fraser pitched only three innings for the Cubs, with no record, before he retired. After Tuesday's game, President Murphy announced that pitcher Andy Coakley would join the Cubs in Pittsburgh on Friday. Murphy purchased the six-year, right-handed veteran from the Cincinnati Reds. The cash amount was not disclosed.[6]

7. Touching Second, Twice   143

The Cubs completed their series with the Cardinals on Thursday with a doubleheader victory. Overall pitched a four-hit shutout in the first game, winning 5 to 0, but the contest remained in doubt until the eighth inning when the Cubs added four runs to their slim one-run lead. The second game was much more comfortable, with the Cubs scoring in the first, third, sixth, seventh, and eighth innings on their way to an 8–2 win behind the continued good pitching of Jack Pfiester.[7]

Still in third place, the Cubs made a quick overnight trip to Pittsburgh for a two-game series against the second-place Pirates. Mordecai Brown went against the veteran ace of the Pittsburgh pitching staff, Vic Willis. Neither man blinked. At the end of nine innings, each pitcher had allowed four hits, but no runs. Willis retired the Cubs in order in the top of the tenth. Clarke opened the Pirate tenth inning with a ground single to left. Leach bunted Clarke to second. Then the National League's leading hitter, Hans Wagner, came to the plate. Brown worked him carefully, but the right-handed-hitting Pirate shortstop hit a sharp grounder toward right field. Evers made a desperate lunge and managed to knock the ball down but Wagner reached first safely, although Evers's effort held Clarke at third, saving the game — at least temporarily. Brown hit the next batter, rookie first baseman Warren Gill, in the ribs with a curve ball, loading the bases with only one out. Second baseman Ed Abbaticchio struck out for the second out, but right fielder Owen Wilson, another rookie, hit Brown's first pitch past Evers into right center field for a single, scoring Clarke with the winning run. Everyone thought the game was finished and headed for the clubhouse, including Hank O'Day, the only umpire for the game, and Warren Gill, the rookie base runner on first. Gill never got within thirty feet of second base. Evers, seeing Gill head off the field instead of touching second, yelled to Slagle in center field to throw him the ball. Evers tagged second base and turned to claim a force out on Gill, only to see umpire O'Day making for an exit with his back turned completely to the play. Evers ran after O'Day and claimed the force out on Gill. As he continued toward the exit, O'Day replied, "Clarke was over the plate, so his run counted anyway."[8]

O'Day was incorrect. Baseball rules clearly stated a run could not score on a forced third out, regardless of when the runner crossed home plate. According to the rules, Gill's failure to touch second base produced a force out and negated the Pirates' winning run. Murphy fired off a telegram to National League president Harry Pulliam, protesting the game.[9]

The next day, O'Day admitted that he did not see whether or not first baseman Warren Gill touched second base. "He also stated he did not see Slagle and Evers make the play which they claim forced Gill out. The crowd

Leading the team with a .300 batting average in 1908, second baseman Johnny Evers was called "the Crab" both for his scuttling run after grounders and for his prickly temperament. A student of the game, he understood the subtleties of the rules better than most umpires.

which was on the field broke and ran across the diamond for the exits as soon as Clarke scored his run and O'Day asserts he could not have determined in that crowd whether or not Gill was forced out even if he had been looking for the play."[10] In essence, O'Day confessed he made a mistake by not watching the completion of the play. Sanborn claimed this incident presented "another argument for bigger baseball stands (to keep fans off the field) as well as the double umpire system."[11]

Reulbach and the Cubs avenged the disputed loss the next day, Saturday, September 5, whipping the Pirates 11 to 0. The Cubs tallied four runs in the fourth inning, five in the fifth, and a final two in the ninth. Tinker and Chance led the hitting attack with three and two hits respectively, each hitting a triple. Reulbach pitched a complete-game, four-hit shutout.[12]

The three-member National Commission consisted of the presidents of the National and American Leagues, Harry Pulliam and Ban Johnson, and a team owner selected to chair the Commission. Garry Herrmann of the Cincinnati Reds served as the current Commission chair. While the Cubs were pounding the Pirates, baseball's governing body announced the adoption of a system for umpire selection for the World Series. Each league would provide two men, and each game would have two umpires, one from each league, with the four men rotating game assignments.[13]

After two days in Pittsburgh, the Cubs and Pirates boarded separate trains heading for Chicago to play a Sunday doubleheader. Pittsburgh did not allow Sabbath baseball. Chicago was one of only three National League cities that did; St. Louis and Cincinnati were the other two. O'Day made the trip to continue serving as sole umpire for the two teams.[14]

A large crowd squeezed into the West Side Grounds to watch two games for the price of one. Fans overflowed from the stands to form a solid ring around the field with the players in the middle. Just before play started, a small black bear cub with a blue ribbon around its neck was staked out in front of the Cubs' bench, attended by the bat boy. A substitute bat boy sat with the bear; Red, the regular bat boy, remained at home. "A few days ago Red sat down on some scantling across a sewer some gentlemen were digging. The scantling broke, dumped Red into the sewer, and broke his shoulder."[15]

The Pirates took the first game, 3 to 0, behind right-hander Nick Maddox. The Cubs managed only four hits while the Pirates rapped out eight against Overall. The game remained a scoreless affair until the seventh inning when the Pirates bunched three runs on two hits, two throwing errors (Overall and Chance), and a wild pitch. Overall struck out eleven Pirates, but the disastrous seventh inning gave the game away.[16]

After scoring four runs in the first and fifth innings against Lefty Leifield, the Cubs held on to squeak out an 8–7 win in the second contest. Pfiester sailed through the first six innings, but the Pirates duplicated their efforts from the first game, scoring three runs in the seventh. Still, the Cubs maintained a comfortable five-run lead going into the ninth inning. Then, the first three Pirate hitters, Ed Abbaticchio, Owen Wilson, and Ed Phelps, the back-up catcher, all singled, loading the bases. George "Moon" Gibson, the regular Pirate catcher, pinch hit for Leifield and also singled, scoring Abbaticchio and Wilson to bring the Pirates closer at 8 to 5. Slagle's throw to the plate hit Wilson in the back and rolled toward the stands, allowing Phelps to advance to third and Gibson to second. Manager Chance yanked Pfiester and called on the reliable Mordecai Brown, who proceeded to strike out center fielder Shannon for the first out. Clarke grounded out, Tinker to Chance, for out number two, but Phelps scored on the play: score, 8 to 6. Tommy Leach rapped a shot back to the mound. Brown knocked it down, but Leach reached first safely while Gibson scored, making it an 8–7 game. Wagner strode to the plate. Brown worked carefully, but confidently. Wagner hit a ground ball to shortstop. Tinker fielded the ball cleanly and tossed it to Evers to force Leach out at second base, ending the game and leaving the Pirates one run short.[17]

It was a tough day for fans. In the first inning of the second game, Evers fouled off a pitch into the crowd standing behind home plate. The gentlemen in the front row ducked, allowing the ball to strike a female patron behind them squarely in the right eye. She received treatment, but remained at the game. After Wagner made the last out of the day, "a crowd of boneheads and multi-mutts started the cushion throwing business."[18] One of the "multi-mutts" received a gash across his face from a metal hook attached to a cushion. He did not receive attention, leaving the field bloodied but not bowed.[19]

The Cincinnati Reds arrived in Chicago on Monday, Labor Day, to play a doubleheader, making it four games in two days for the Cubs. The games were split into morning and afternoon sessions, and fans had to pay separately for each game. Fraser started the morning game, but he had a bad outing, giving up four runs in only five innings. Floyd Kroh made his debut with the Cubs, pitching the final four innings. The twenty-two-year-old youngster gave up two runs in his first inning of work, the sixth, but he pitched well after that. Charlie Dryden of the *Tribune* stated his favorable assessment of the left-handed Kroh: "He is a big man (6'2"), with plenty of speed, and a curve that wiffed four of the Reds."[20]

While Fraser and Kroh allowed six runs, the Reds rookie pitcher Jean "Chauncey" Dubuc, a week shy of his twentieth birthday, performed brilliantly. Dubuc pitched a complete-game, two-hit shutout (6 to 0) with only Tinker and Evers collecting singles. Chance developed a charley horse in his leg in the first inning of the first game and did not play the rest of the day. Sheckard also sat the bench with a knee injury, so Slagle returned to the lineup playing left field. A severe cold and sore throat rendered umpire O'Day almost speechless, his voice reduced to a thin whisper, but he worked both games flawlessly.[21]

Before fans were admitted for the second game, the players nourished themselves at one of two locations. "Between combats the athletes fed their stalwart frames, some at a grab and run joint across the street, while others inserted their legs beneath the tables at the Cafe de Cub under the grand staircase." The Cafe de Cub, a recent Charles Murphy addition to the West Side Grounds, served standard ballpark cuisine, specializing in hotdogs. Renewed, the Cubs woke up for the second game to score a 4–0 victory. Andy Coakley, recently purchased from the Reds, beat his former teammates, allowing only four hits. Schulte (two doubles) and Slagle (one double) provided the firepower the Cubs needed to score a run in the first inning, two more in the fourth, and a final tally in the sixth. Pitcher Coakley received acknowledgment from *Tribune* reporter Charlie Dryden as the innovator of the catcher's shin guards. "The urbane and gentlemanly Mr. Coakley enjoys wide vogue as the instigator of the shin guards, coco covers, and wrist protectors affected by Messrs. Bresnahan and McGann. Even Long Larry McLean has taken to the leg guards. He looks like a gentleman about to dig a can of worms in a swamp."[22] Neither Kling nor Moran wore the latest catching gear.

The headline after Tuesday's game read, "Slagle, Smallest Gent on Team, Largest in 3 to 2 Outcome." Slagle was not having a good year. The veteran thirty-five-year-old outfielder had patrolled center field for the Cubs since he joined the team in 1902. A left-handed hitter, Slagle hit .273 in the 1907 World Series against the Detroit Tigers, but his current .199 average forced Chance to bench him. Slagle was in the game only because Sheckard's knee injury prevented him from playing. But on this day Jimmy Slagle returned to form with three singles, a walk, and all three runs for the Cubs. In the first inning, after a single, Slagle came home on a double by Evers. In the third inning, Slagle singled, stole second, and advanced to third when the throw escaped second baseman Miller Huggins. Slagle scored the second run on another hit by Evers. After the Reds tied the game with single runs in the fourth and fifth innings, Slagle walked to begin the seventh and scored the winning run when pitcher Jack Rowan, with two outs, tried to pick him off first. The ball sailed away from first baseman Dick Hoblitzel, and Slagle raced around the bases before the ball could be retrieved and relayed to the plate. Reulbach held the Reds scoreless in the eighth and ninth innings to earn the victory, 3 to 2, giving the Cubs two of the three games. Another long time Cub outfielder, Jimmy Ryan (1885–1900) watched the Cubs and Slagle perform. Currently the forty-five-year-old player-manager of the Montgomery, Alabama, minor-league team, Ryan still made his home in Chicago. The minor-league season over, Ryan came to the West Side Grounds to watch his former team play.[23]

The last-place St. Louis Cardinals stopped in Chicago for one game on

September 10—Despite a nine-game winning streak to end the month of August and another four straight victories in early September, the Cubs remain in third place behind Pittsburgh and New York.

Wednesday, September 9, as they made their way home. O'Day regained his voice to make his calls as the Cubs contributed another loss to the Cardinal record, 5 to 3. Frank Schulte went three for four, all singles, scoring a teammate with each hit. After seven innings, the Cubs led 5 to 0. Cardinal first baseman Ed Konetchy belted an Overall pitch between Slagle and Howard in left center field for a home run in the eighth inning, and St. Louis scored two more runs in the ninth, but fell a little short. In the fast-paced game, (one hour, twenty minutes), Overall allowed only four hits — a single, double, triple, and home run — as the Cardinals, as a team, hit for the cycle.[24]

Twenty-four games remained on the Cubs' schedule, the next twenty-three on the road. Only the last game of the season against the Pittsburgh Pirates on Sunday, October 4, was scheduled at the West Side Grounds. The Cubs would follow the Cardinals to St. Louis for four more contests, then jump to Boston to begin their last East Coast tour of the season against the Doves (three games), Phillies (four games), Giants (four games), and Dodgers (three games). On their way home for the last game of the season against the Pirates, the Cubs' train would stop in Cincinnati for five games against the Reds.

Fraser, Lundgren, Durbin, and Sheckard remained in Chicago. In his attempt to regain first place, Chance decided to use pitchers Brown, Reulbach, Overall, Pfiester, Coakley, and Kroh. Sheckard would

September 10 — A confident and smirking New York Giant contemplates winning the pennant.

rejoin the team as soon as his knee allowed. In St. Louis, Chance returned to the lineup and led the Cubs' attack with three hits, all singles. Slagle continued to hit well, collecting two singles, as did St. Louis native Artie Hofman. The Cubs scored five runs in the first three innings, as Mordecai Brown breezed through the Cardinal lineup, winning easily 7 to 2.[25]

National League president Harry Pulliam announced his decision on the Cubs' protested Pirate game of September 4. Pulliam found against the Cubs, claimed umpire decisions supreme, and, in an amazing exercise in convoluted logic, issued the following statement: "This is a case simply of fact and judgment, and the ruling of the umpire is final. The question of whether there was a force play or not cannot be established by the evidence of players or spectators. It rests solely with the umpire. The umpire in this case, by allowing the winning run, ruled that there was no force at second, because if there had been the run would not have scored."[26] No mention was made of O'Day's incorrect remark to Evers that Clarke had crossed the plate anyway, thereby winning the game.

The Cubs continued their dominance over the Cardinals on Friday, September 11, again winning by five runs, this time 8 to 3. Chance duplicated his efforts of the previous day, hitting three singles. Kling, Steinfeldt, and Evers contributed two hits apiece to the Cubs twelve-hit attack, with every Cub except Schulte and Pfiester having at least one hit. The Cubs scored early, two runs in the first and another in the second, to give Pfiester a 3–0 lead. The Cardinals made it close for a while, with two runs in the fourth, to edge within a run at 3 to 2. But the Cubs put the game away with another three runs in the fifth and two more in the sixth. Pfiester allowed only a single run for the final five innings, cruising to the victory. In the ninth inning, umpire O'Day, still suffering mild symptoms from his recent cold, drew a handkerchief from his pocket to blow his nose. A Cardinal fan, frustrated with the game, let out a bellow, "blow your brains out, Hank."[27] This caused Evers to double over with laughter and even "the dignified umpire himself was seen to smile."[28]

Charles Murphy announced that the Cubs had signed Frank Chance to play and manage the Cubs for another four years. His salary was not published, but it was noted that Chance held $10,000 in Cubs stock. Dryden informed his readers that the previous evening the Cubs attended a play titled *Panhandle Pete*. Said Dryden, "the show was much better than 'Macbeth,' which they saw here last spring."[29]

On Saturday, the Cardinals finally gave the Cubs a fight, but Chance remained in his hotel bed with severe stomach problems from drinking St. Louis' legendary bad water. Brown served as manager. This time, the Cardinals scored first with runs in the first and second innings against Cub pitcher Andy Coakley. A double and triple scored a run in the first, and another double followed by a single plated another run in the second. Manager Brown wisely decided to replace Coakley with Reulbach in the second inning. The Cardinals' two-run lead lasted until the fifth inning when the Cubs tied the score with two runs against Cardinal pitcher Johnny Lush. St. Louis took the lead again with a single run in the sixth. With one out, Ed Konetchy singled. The next hitter, third baseman Bobby Byrne, sent a hot grounder close to the bag at first. Hofman, playing first for the ailing Chance, made a diving catch and retired Byrne with Konetchy advancing to second. Catcher Bill Ludwig sent a routine ground ball to the normally sure-handed Evers. But this time the ball rolled past him into right field, allowing Konetchy to score the go-ahead run. Lush blanked the Cubs in the sixth, seventh, and eighth innings to nurse his one-run lead into the ninth.[30]

Evers bunted safely to begin the ninth inning. Schulte sacrificed Evers to second, and Hofman followed with a single to center field, sending Evers to third. Steinfeldt hit a roller to second baseman Chappy Charles, who threw home in an attempt to nail Evers at the plate. His throw, a little high to Ludwig, allowed Evers to make a beautiful hook slide across a corner of the plate, avoiding Ludwig's sweeping tag, to score the tying run and make up for his sixth-inning error. Reulbach blanked the Cardinals in their half of the ninth to send the game into extra innings.[31]

Reulbach and Lush remained on the mound. Neither team scored in the tenth or eleventh innings, but the Cardinals came close to winning in the eleventh. Left fielder Wilbur Murdock hit his fourth single and advanced to third on a single by Byrne. Reulbach made an errant pitch that escaped a short distance from catcher Kling. Murdock and Reulbach simultaneously broke for home plate. Kling pounced on the ball and threw quickly to Reulbach, who tagged the sliding Murdock. O'Day made the out call, and the game proceeded to the twelfth inning.[32]

The first Cubs hitter, Steinfeldt, singled. Zimmerman, who pinch hit for center fielder Del Howard in the ninth inning, stayed in the game and walked in the twelfth, advancing Steinfeldt to second. Tinker laid down a sacrifice bunt attempt; Lush fielded the ball and made a throw to third, but Steinfeldt arrived before the ball, loading the bases. Kling came to the plate and promptly lined a drive over left fielder Murdock's head. Steinfeldt, Zimmerman, and Tinker scored as Murdock raced to retrieve the ball. Kling circled the bases, scoring the fourth run of the inning with his grand-slam home run. Reulbach retired the Cardinals in order in the bottom of the twelfth to secure the hard-fought 7–3 victory.[33]

The umpire baiting started as soon as O'Day arrived in St. Louis. Having few opportunities to cheer for the last-place home team, Cardinal fans took to roasting O'Day. On Friday, the normally stoic, stone-faced O'Day allowed his emotions to take control. When the result of the game between the American League St. Louis Browns and Cleveland was posted on the scoreboard, O'Day, seeking revenge on the St. Louis fans, in a loud voice called attention to another St. Louis loss. The message was clear. St. Louis represented losers. The next day, fan remarks and threats turned uglier, increasing in number and intensity. So much so that after the twelve-inning contest on Saturday, a squad of four policemen, two in front, two behind, escorted umpire O'Day from the field. The defiant O'Day made a point of brandishing his face mask in his right hand as a weapon as he walked off the field, lest any fan had thoughts of a physical assault. The menacing fans kept their distance and confined their demonstration to loud, insulting shouts and yells.[34]

Back at the hotel, winning manager Mordecai Brown pleaded with the ailing Chance to be relieved of his managerial duties. The shy, reserved pitcher found the job onerous. Chance assured Brown that he, Chance, would be on the field on Sunday for the last game in St. Louis. True to his word, the still-weak Chance not only managed, but played the next day as well. St. Louis fans continued their verbal harassment of O'Day. In the later innings, one especially boisterous fan hurled the ultimate personal 1908 umpire insult at O'Day, "Say, Hank, Rudderham was a star alongside of you."[35] O'Day did not respond directly, instead, "Hank got wise, however, and cut out the retort courteous. He kept his back turned to the insulting mourners and brushed the home plate every little while with a vigor that made the dust fly in clouds."[36]

Slagle raised his anemic batting average to .213 with three more singles, leading the team to a sweep of the four games in St. Louis, and giving the Cubs their seventh-consecutive victory, 3 to 0. The Cubs scored three times in the first inning, and Overall pitched a four-hit shutout to keep the Cardinals in last place. The Cubs' win and the Pirates' loss to the Reds in Cincinnati allowed Chicago to climb over Pittsburgh into second place.[37]

Departing St. Louis at midnight, the Cubs made themselves comfortable for their long train ride to Boston. At daylight, the northeast-bound train became engulfed in thick clouds of smoke caused by a huge forest fire to the north. "In some places the smoke was so thick it put the scenery on the blink and dimmed the eagle eyeballs of the athletes. Artie Hofman thought the gloom portended a storm, in which the train might be lost with all on board. At Cleveland he wrote a farewell message to his girl at Englewood, Ill., placed the note in a pop bottle, and tossed it into the lake. If the Cubs disappear and are not heard from again the pop bottle washed upon the romantic shores of Englewood will reveal a sad fate. Artie Hofman is nothing if not poetical in the time of peril."[38] Chance, guarding his health, brought distilled water with him to drink during the long journey. Heading east, the train gradually emerged from the smoke, putting Hofman at ease. The Cubs arrived in Buffalo at 8:00 P.M. Reulbach found a comfortable spot in the smoking room of the coach car and read until 4:00 A.M. "Then Edward reposed in his bunk until noon today, and got up and ate a breakfast of raw beef and ice tea."[39] The train rolled on toward Boston.

After the thirty-six hour train trip, the Cubs reached Boston at noon on Tuesday, September 15, in time for the afternoon contest with the Doves. The muggy ninety-degree heat of St. Louis gave way to cooler temperatures in New England. Boston reached only a chilly fifty degrees by game time. The fans watched in overcoats. Trainer Bert Semmens purchased a wool undershirt for manager Chance, who still felt woozie from the St. Louis water.[40]

Vivan "Vive" Lindaman, Boston's best pitcher, opposed Brown in the first game of the three-game series. The Doves scored first with two runs in the second inning, but the Cubs knotted the count in the top of the third. With one out, Slagle singled and went to second on a walk to Evers. Schulte singled to right field, sending Slagle across the plate. The throw to the plate escaped catcher Frank Bowerman, allowing Evers to third base. He scored the tying run on a passed ball, and Schulte advanced to third. Chance lifted a fly ball to medium-deep left field; Schulte tagged and tried to give the Cubs the lead, but Herbie Moran made a strong accurate throw to nail Schulte at the plate and end the inning.[41]

The Doves pushed across the go-ahead run in the fifth. Bowerman led off with a single and advanced to second on a sacrifice bunt. Lindaman struck out for the second out, but right fielder Beals Becker, a rookie, lined a single to center field. Hofman charged the ball and made a wide throw to the first-base side of home plate. Kling grabbed the ball and made a swing for Bowerman as he reached home. Umpire Bob Emslie was spared making a close call as the ball fell from Kling's glove when he tagged Bowerman. Neither pitcher allowed another run, and the Cubs managed only two more hits, four in total, off Lindaman as the Boston ace beat the Cubs and Brown, 3 to 2.[42]

Boston player-manager Joe Kelley used rookie Al Mattern on Wednesday. Chance countered with Jack Pfiester. Slightly built at one hundred sixty-five pounds, Mattern relied mostly on his spitball delivered from the left side. In this, his first major-league start, he performed magnificently. He allowed the Cubs only three hits in eight innings. Unfortunately, a walk and two of those hits occurred in the fifth inning, providing the Cubs' one run. And one run was all Pfiester needed as he pitched his own four-hit shutout. Trailing 1 to 0, Mattern left the game in the eighth inning for a pinch hitter. His replacement, rookie Bill Chappelle, had a more difficult time in his one inning of work. Before the dust settled, the Cubs bunched three singles and two walks to score another four runs, winning 5 to 0.[43]

That evening, some players from both teams gathered at a local bar. After a few drinks, an interesting rumor concerning New York Giants manager John McGraw began to circulate. Reporter Charlie Dryden informed his readers back in Chicago, "the tavern the Cubs infest was filled with rumors last night to the effect that McGraw had sent V. Lindaman a large check for beating the champions in the opening game of the Boston series. This is important if true. If McGraw is willing to pay alien pitchers $500 each for walloping the Cubs from now until the end of the season, the Giants should win the pennant with ease. Lindaman says he has not seen the check as yet."[44]

Evers sat out the last game in Boston, nursing a severe stiff neck due to a bad cold. The Cubs' leading hitter (.313) was replaced by Heinie Zimmerman. The utility man actually had the team's highest batting average (.317), but Zimmerman had played in only 41 of the Cubs 136 games.[45] Boston bats came alive against Reulbach as the Doves collected eleven hits. Reulbach also issued two walks, but the Dove batters could not deliver the timely hit. Only once, in the seventh inning, did the Doves send a runner across the plate. Shortstop Jack Hannifin doubled (the only extra base hit against Reulbach) and scored on a single by left fielder Herbie Moran. Substitute second baseman Zimmerman made a sparkling play to prevent Boston from scoring in the third inning. With one out and a runner on third, Zimmerman went high in the air to block a line drive with his glove, caught the ball in his throwing hand on his way down, and, as his feet touched the earth, rifled a throw to Steinfeldt at third base for an inning-ending double play. Zimmerman also plated the Cubs' first run in the first inning, sending the ball to the left field fence and scoring Slagle, who had walked. Reulbach stopped a Boston scoring threat, striking out Herbie Moran with the bases loaded in the Doves' second inning. Reulbach helped his own cause with a single in the sixth, scoring Steinfeldt and Tinker with two of the Cubs' three runs that inning on his way to a 4–1 win.[46]

Winning two of the three games in Boston, the Cubs headed for Philadelphia to play four games against the fourth-place Phillies. Jack Hayden, an outfielder with the Indianapolis team, joined the Cubs in Philadelphia. Murphy announced Hayden's signing on September 13 after Hayden finished the minor-league season with the champion Indianapolis Indians batting .330. The soon-to-be twenty-eight-year-old Hayden came to the major leagues with the Philadelphia Athletics in 1901, but he only lasted that season. He played in 51 games and hit .265. Five years later in 1906, Hayden played for the American League Boston club, hitting .280 in 85 games, but again only for one year. President Murphy felt the hard-hitting outfielder could bolster the Cubs outfield and contribute more offensively than Slagle (.213) or even Howard (.271). A native of Bryn Mawr, Pennsylvania, Hayden was presented a $100 gold watch, presented by home town friends in a ceremony at home plate prior to the Friday, September 18 game.[47]

Dressed in his Sunday suit, Evers sat in the stands to watch the game. His neck remained too stiff to play; he could barely turn his head without excruciating pain. Pfiester had developed a muscle cramp in his left arm after his shut-out performance in Boston. He received treatment from Semmens, but the knotted muscle remained.[48]

Kling doubled in the third inning against the Phillies' ace George McQuillen and scored when Slagle dropped a Texas leaguer into shallow center field. That was the end of the Cubs' scoring for the day. Overall matched McQuillen pitch for pitch, but Phillie John Titus pushed across a lone run in the eighth inning to tie the game. At the end of nine, the score remained tied at one. The Cubs loaded the bases with one out in the tenth, but McQuillen struck out Zimmerman, and Tinker, the runner on third, tried unsuccessfully to steal home with Schulte at bat. The Phillies won the game, 2 to 1 in the bottom of the tenth, when second baseman Otto Knabe tripled and scored on a sacrifice fly to left field, again by right fielder Titus.[49]

Reporter Charlie Dryden felt the tough extra-inning loss, in combination with the Giants' doubleheader win against the Pirates, dealt a serious blow to the Cubs' pennant aspirations, but the three teams remained very close in the standings and the Giants had played five fewer games than the second-place Cubs.[50]

NATIONAL LEAGUE STANDINGS
(FIRST THREE TEAMS)

	W	L	Pct.
Giants	87	46	.654
Cubs	85	53	.616
Pirates	85	54	.612

On Saturday, September 19, the Cubs and Phillies played a doubleheader. Chance moved Schulte to left field in place of Slagle, and placed the new arrival, Jack Hayden, in right field. Zimmerman, still playing second base, sustained a spike wound to his foot in the second inning from the sliding Frank Corridon, the Philadelphia pitcher, and was unable to continue; Hofman moved from center field to second base, and Howard played center field. Brown had gotten off to a slow start, surrendering six hits in the first three innings, including two triples and a double as the Phillies scored their two runs, but the reliable Cub pitcher settled down and shut out the Phillies for the final six. Titus knocked in both Phillie runs, just as he had the day before. Meanwhile, the Cubs scored a single run in the third inning, two more in the eight, and a final insurance run on a Tinker triple and Kling single in the ninth to win 4 to 2. Hayden had his first hit as a Cub, a single, during the two-run eighth inning.[51]

It was not uncommon for a single baseball to be used for an entire game in 1908. Fans were required to return foul balls hit into the stands to the field of play. It was literally against the law for any fan to keep a baseball. During the first game of the doubleheader, one man refused to return a ball and eventually was taken into custody by Philadelphia police.[52]

In the second game, Reulbach and Lew Richie hooked up in a classic pitcher's duel. Neither team could score, and, after ten innings, umpires Bob Emslie and Jim Johnstone declared the game a draw and suspended play due to darkness. Tinker tried to score twice, but he was thrown out at the plate both times. In the third inning, Tinker tried to tag and score from third on a fly ball to left field by Jack Hayden, and, in the eighth inning, with Hayden again at bat, Tinker tried to steal home. Chance saved the game in the sixth inning when he made a running catch of a foul fly off the bat of John Titus and threw a strike to catcher Kling, who applied the tag to the sliding Phillie pitcher, Richie, as he tried to score from third base. Both pitchers allowed eight hits, with Richie striking out five Cubs, while Reulbach struck out three Phillies. The Phillies management announced the tie game would be played over on Monday as part of a doubleheader.

Observing the Sabbath baseball ban, both teams rested on Sunday in the Quaker City. Unable to play because of the spike wound to his foot, Zimmerman made his way to New York City, his home, to recuperate and wait for his teammates to arrive for the pennant showdown series with the Giants. Jack Pfiester, with another day of rest and, especially, massage therapy on his muscle-knotted left arm, hoped to heal in time to pitch against the Giants, but he remained pessimistic. Another rumor circulated that "the New York players already have ordered coronation gowns of black velvet in which they always play for the world's pennant. There is something gloomy and mortuary about black robes that puts the other team on the blink, as witness the fate of the Philadelphia Athletics in the series with the Giants a few seasons back."⁵³ One of McGraw's intimidation tactics, the Giants wore black uniforms against the Athletics during the 1905 World Series, winning easily, four games to one.

On Monday morning, September 21, the Cubs trailed the first-place Giants by four games and faced a doubleheader against a tough Phillie team. In New York, Christy Mathewson pitched against the Pirates. Two new acquisitions, Floyd Kroh and Andy Coakley, pitched for the Cubs in Philadelphia, and, in the second game, George McQuillan, who had beaten the Cubs 2 to 1 on Friday, took the mound. The Cubs' prospects for inching closer to the Giants seemed dim.⁵⁴

"Kid" Kroh, so labeled by Dryden, started his first game as a Cub. He began well, striking out two batters in the first inning and putting five goose eggs in a row on the scoreboard for Philadelphia. The Phillies scored a lone unearned run in the sixth inning; with a runner on third and two outs, Steinfeldt fielded a routine ground ball and threw low to first base. Chance tried to make a scoop catch, but failed as the runner on third crossed the plate. Following this flurry, Kroh recovered and again hung zeros on the scoreboard for the next two innings. Phillie pitcher Tully Sparks pitched as well as Kroh and had better fielding support. For eight innings, Sparks blanked the Cubs, and he entered the ninth leading 1 to 0. Howard began the ninth inning by pinch-hitting for Kroh, knocking a single to center field. Hayden, batting in the lead-off slot, followed with another single, sending Howard to second. Back in the lineup Evers laid down a sacrifice bunt. Howard made third, but the Phillies were able to force Hayden at second base, placing Cub runners, Howard and Evers, on the corners with only one out. Schulte delivered a single to right that scored Howard and tied the game. Sparks retired Chance and Steinfeldt on fly balls to end the inning. Overall came on to pitch the ninth inning and retired the Phillies in order, sending the game into extra innings, the third extra-inning game in three days.⁵⁵

Hofman tripled to begin the tenth inning. Tinker grounded out, third to first, with Hofman holding at third base. Kling walked, and Overall sent a medium-deep fly ball to Fred Osborne in center field. Hofman tagged and raced for the plate; the ball arrived ahead of Hofman, but it was wide of the plate, allowing the go-ahead run to score. Kling scored the second run of the inning from second base when Knabe booted a ground ball off the bat of Hayden. Overall again retired the Phillies in order in the tenth to record the 3–1 victory. Assessing Kroh's performance, Dryden wrote, "Young 'Kid' Kroh made an excellent showing against the Phillies. He had a deceptive curve and good command of the ball and kept his nerve in the most trying situations."[56]

In the second game, with the score tied at two in the eighth, it looked like extra innings for the fourth time in three days. The Cubs scored a run against McQuillen in the first inning when Evers scored on a single by Chance, but the Phillies scored two in their half to take a 2–1 lead. In the third, another Chance single scored Hayden with the tying run, and, for the next five innings, Coakley and McQuillen battled, with neither team able to score.[57]

Disaster struck McQuillen in the ninth. He walked Chance, who advanced to second on Steinfeldt's sacrifice bunt. Chance took a big lead off second while Hofman batted. McQuillen suddenly made a quick throw to second in an attempt to pick off Chance. The ball sailed wide into center field as Chance retreated toward second base. When the ball eluded center fielder Osborne, Chance reversed direction and raced all the way home to score the winning run. Coakley retired the side in order in the ninth to give the Cubs a 3–2 victory and a sweep of the doubleheader. The two latest Cub pitchers, Kroh and Coakley, came through. Then the Cubs received the crowning news that the Pirates had beaten the Giants and Mathewson, 2 to 1. Suddenly, the morning gloom turned to evening elation as the Cubs gained a game and a half towards first place — just in time for their show-down four-game series with the Giants.[58]

On Tuesday, September 22, the Cubs played their third doubleheader in a row, with only a day of rest on Sunday in between, to begin the series with the Giants. Over 25,000 New Yorkers jammed the Polo Grounds and the surrounding environs, including Coogan's Bluff above the ballpark, to root for their heroes to vanquish the invading Chicagoans. In the first game, Overall pitched superbly for the first six innings, limiting the Giants to only three hits and zero runs. The Cubs took the lead in the third inning when Overall hit a double, took third on an infield out, and scored when shortstop Al Bridwell booted a ground ball off the bat of Frank Schulte. In the fourth, the Cubs continued their attack against pitcher Red Ames. Steinfeldt singled to center field, but was forced at second when Hofman bunted too hard to third baseman Art Devlin. Clutch hitter Joe Tinker moved Hofman to second with a single to center, and Hofman promptly stole third base. Kling rapped a ground ball to the hole between first baseman Fred Tenney and second baseman Buck Herzog; both Tenney and Herzog moved to make the play. Herzog got to the ball but threw wide to the pitcher, Ames, covering first base. Hofman scored, Tinker raced to third, and Kling reached first safely. Overall brought Tinker home with a sacrifice fly to center fielder Cy Seymour. Kling sprinted home on Jack Hayden's double with the third run of the inning. Either left fielder Mike Donlin or Cy Seymour in center could have caught Hayden's hit, but each deferred to the other, and the ball landed safely between them.[59]

Overall began the seventh inning leading 4 to 0, but Mike Donlin bounced a ball over Chance's head down the right field line and into the outfield crowd for a double. Donlin moved to third on Seymour's single. Devlin made the third consecutive hit off Overall with another double, scoring Donlin and placing Seymour on third. Chance yanked Overall and brought in his best, Mordecai Brown, to face left fielder Harry "Moose" McCormick. Brown grooved his first pitch, and the left-handed hitting McCormick pulled a shot over the first-base bag for the third Giant double in the inning. Both Seymour and Devlin scored, cutting the Cubs' lead to a single run, 4 to 3. The next hitter, Al Bridwell, bunted; Kling pounced on the ball and threw to Steinfeldt at third, heading off the runner, McCormick. A rundown between second and third ensued with Steinfeldt eventually tagging McCormick for the first out. Brown easily retired pinch-hitter Shad Barry (in for pitcher Red Ames) on an infield pop up to Tinker and Fred Tenney on a foul pop fly to Chance. "Iron Man" Joe McGinnity held the Cubs scoreless in the eighth and ninth innings. Brown sat the Giants down in order in the eighth and retired the first two hitters in the ninth. Only a run behind, the Giants had a chance when Moose McCormick hit his second double with two outs, but Brown induced Bridwell to pop out to Steinfeldt for the final out, giving the 4–3 decision to the Cubs.[60]

Brown remained on the mound to pitch the second game against Doc Crandall. The Giants scored first in the fourth inning on a Buck Herzog double that landed just inside the right-field foul line before bounding into the crowd, a wild pitch, and finally catcher Roger Bresnahan's double into the center-field crowd. The Cubs took the lead with two runs in the sixth. Crandall walked Evers and Chance, and Steinfeldt lined a ball into the outfield fans in left center. Evers scored the tying run, and Chance moved to third. Then Hofman drove a deep fly ball to center, allowing Chance to tag and score the Cubs' second run. Brown controlled the Giants through the fifth and sixth innings, but in the seventh the Giants loaded the bases with two outs. Into this do-or-die situation, against one of the best pitchers in baseball, John McGraw sent a nineteen-year-old first baseman to pinch-hit for the pitcher, Doc Crandall. Brown threw three quick strikes past the youngster, and Fred Merkle returned to the bench. The Cubs added a run in the ninth on a Johnny Kling single and Jack Hayden's third double of the day to expand their lead to 3 to 1. Brown retired the last six Giant hitters in a row in the eighth and ninth innings to complete the double victory and earn the following adulation from reporter Charlie Dryden: "MIGHTY MORDECAI SAVES CHAMPIONS."[61] Hard-hitting newcomer Jack Hayden had seven hits in four games in the past two days, including three doubles against the Giants. But he joined the Cubs too late in the season to be eligible for the World Series should the Cubs overtake the Giants and hold off the Pirates to win the National League pennant.[62]

The knotted left arm of Jack Pfiester, to the surprise of everyone, including the pitcher himself, returned to normal by Wednesday, September 23. Delighted with the news, Chance decided to use "Jack The Giant Killer" immediately. McGraw sent Mathewson to the mound with only one day of rest. Matty had pitched and lost the 2–1 decision to the Pirates just two days before.[63]

At Orchestra Hall in Chicago, thousands of fans paid twenty-five cents each to "watch" the Cubs in New York on the Electric Scoreboard. At the top of their form, both Pfiester and Mathewson lived up to everyone's expectations. A somber moment occurred in the second inning when Pfiester lost control of a fast ball that struck Moose McCormick in the head. The Giant left fielder crumpled to the dirt, unconscious. Teammates brought a bucket of water and a sponge to revive the fallen athlete. After a few minutes of sponging, McCormick revived and, amazingly, remained in the game. After four innings, neither team had scored.[64]

Even at his best, Mathewson always found Joe Tinker a difficult out. In the fifth inning, his nemesis did it again, hitting a low line drive to right that got by Mike Donlin and rolled to the far recesses of the Polo Grounds. Tinker easily circled the bases for a home run, the game's first and only Cubs' run. The Cubs made only four more hits in the game, all singles (Evers, Chance, Hofman, and Kling) against Matty.

The Giants tied the score in the sixth with an unearned run off Pfiester. Buck Herzog hit a hard ground ball to third that temporarily handcuffed Steinfeldt to start the inning. The Cubs' third baseman recovered and made a hurried throw to first, wide of the mark, and past Chance. Herzog went to second on the throwing error, and Bresnahan laid down a bunt to sacrifice Herzog to third. The Giant's leading hitter (.317), Mike Donlin shot a single to center field scoring Herzog to tie the game.[65]

And so it remained until the Giant ninth inning. With one out, Devlin singled. McCormick forced Devlin at second base for the second out, and it looked like extra innings. But the teenage first baseman, Fred Merkle, playing for the injured Fred Tenney, delivered a clutch single to right field,

7. Touching Second, Twice 161

sending McCormick to third. Still, there were two outs. Bridwell stepped to the plate; he had not had a hit all day against Pfiester. But in his fourth at bat, Bridwell hit Pfiester's first pitch into center field for a single. McCormick trotted home with the winning run. The Polo Grounds erupted in pandemonium. As soon as Bridwell's hit landed safely and even before McCormick crossed the plate, hordes of jubilant Giant fans engulfed the players on the field. As the outfield crowd surged toward the infield, Merkle stopped short of second base, turned, and jogged off the field and away from the mob. Umpire Bob Emslie, working the bases, also retreated and did not see if Merkle reached second base or not. But there were two umpires. Hank O'Day, working behind the plate, did not retreat; instead, he ran to the pitcher's mound on Bridwell's hit to watch second base. Evers and a number of other Cub players, seeing Merkle leave the field, screamed for center fielder Hofman, who fielded Bridwell's hit, to throw to second base to force Merkle out. If Evers touched second before Merkle for the force out and the third out of the inning, Bridwell could not be credited with a hit, and, most importantly, McCormick's winning run would not count.

Charlie Dryden described the subsequent events:

> Capt. Donlin realized the danger about to overtake the Giants, so he set off after the fat headed Merkle.... Hofman ... threw to Evers for a force play on the absent Merkle. But, McGinnity, who was not in the game (coaching at third base), cut in ahead and grabbed the ball before it reached the eager Trojan (Evers). Three Cubs landed on the iron man from as many directions at the same time and jolted the ball from his cruel grasp. It rolled among the spectators, who had swarmed upon the diamond like an army of starving potato bugs. At this thrilling juncture "Kid" Kroh, the demon southpaw, swarmed upon the human potato bugs and knocked six of them galley-west. The triumphant Kroh passed the ball to Steinfeldt after cleaning up the gang that had it. Tinker wedged in, and the ball was conveyed to Evers for the force out of Merkle, while Capt Donlin was still some distance off towing that brilliant young gent by the neck. Some say Merkle eventually touched second base, but not until he had been forced out by Hofman, to McGinnity, to six potato bugs, to "Kid" Kroh, to some more Cubs, and the shrieking, triumphant Mr. Evers.... There have been some complicated plays in baseball, but we do not recall one just like this in a career of years of monkeying with the national pastime.[66]

Police officers surrounded O'Day to escort him from the field as Chance, with help from Doc Marshall and Del Howard, fought his way through the crowd towards the umpire. The police fended off Giant fans and deposited O'Day safely in a room under the stands. Chance finally reached O'Day, asked for his decision, and was told Merkle was out, McCormick's run did not count, and the game was officially a tie.[67]

During an interview later that evening, umpire O'Day informed the gathered journalist that his partner, Bob Emslie, did not see the play at second base because of the hordes of spectators on the field, but from the pitcher's mound, O'Day had witnessed Evers touch second base. Further, O'Day ruled that since the third out occurred on a force play, the McCormick run did not count, and the game remained tied. O'Day stated the game should have continued with the Cubs coming to bat for the top of the tenth inning, but that was impossible due to the huge numbers of fans on the field. Therefore, he ruled the game a tie.[68]

Charles Murphy immediately filed a protest with National League president Harry Pulliam.

> President Murphy ... made a formal claim of today's game on behalf of the Chicago club on the ground that the New York club did not legally score a run in the last half of the ninth inning and that the interference of the crowd prevented continuing the contest, which therefore should have been forfeited to the visiting club, which was ready and willing to continue ... and cited in support of his contention the decision rendered in the game between the Cubs and Pittsburgh at Pittsburgh on Sept. 4 in which precisely the same contingency arose. The Chicago club protested that game, but the protest was not allowed because the single umpire in charge of that game did not see the play in dispute. In today's game the omission of Merkle of the New York club to touch second base in the last half of the ninth inning was noted by Umpire O'Day....[69]

Murphy further clarified his position: "we are asking for a forfeit, but at the same time the Cubs would play the game over."[70]

The next morning, umpires O'Day and Emslie submitted a written report to Harry Pulliam and met with the National League president in his New York office. In attendance at the Polo Grounds the previous day, Pulliam had personally witnessed the chaotic ninth inning. Pulliam met briefly with reporters in his outer office, "where he conversed on general topics in his usual affable manner. Then he retired to the inner sanctum (with O'Day and Emslie), and sent out a neatly typewritten ruling." The temporary ruling supported O'Day's decision. "Without entering, at this time, into the merits of the controversy or passing upon the legality of any decision, the game will be recorded as reported–namely: a tie score."[71]

Pulliam said nothing about replaying the game, which was required by the constitution of the National League. Headlines in the *Chicago Tribune* kept readers informed of the legal proceedings: "League Chief Rules Disputed Game 'a Tie' and Constitution Is Ignored."[72] For the rest of the day, the soft-spoken Pulliam remained secluded in his office, refusing to meet or even answer questions submitted in writing by the gentlemen of the press.

7. *Touching Second, Twice* 163

Umpires O'Day and Emslie were notified by Cubs secretary Charlie Williams that, even through Giant manager John McGraw announced the evening before that the tie game would not be played the next day as part of a doubleheader, the Cubs "would be at the Polo Grounds at 1:30 o'clock today, the regular hour for starting double headers." Frank Chance and "the Cubs swallowed a swift lunch and hiked to the scene of combat." A dozen or so Giants, in uniform, were already there as a steady stream of people began arriving for the scheduled three o'clock game. The Giants made no attempt to assemble to replay the tie game. Chance, however, decided to put a team on the field to demonstrate the Cubs were present and willing to play a doubleheader. "At 1:30 o'clock the Peerless Leader put a complete team on the field, with Coakley pitching and Kling behind the bat. Tom Needham, (a Giants' player) kindly stood at the plate with a pestle in his hand while Coakley pitched four balls, the last of which was wild. There were no umpires to tell Needham whether he struck out or got a pass."[73]

Howls of derision greeted Chance and the Cubs when they took the field. Most fans knew what Chance was up to, and they did not like it. If Pulliam refused to award the tie game to the Cubs due to fan interference, the Cubs could claim the game if the Giants refused to play a doubleheader

No-nonsense Hank O'Day, the "King of Umpires," made the courageous force-out call at the Polo Grounds in the infamous "Merkle Game."

September 24 — The day after the most famous game in baseball history, a dazed and doubly-wounded Giant (New York lost both games of doubleheader the day before) cannot believe the ruling handed down by National League president Harry Pulliam. Pulliam disallowed New York's winning run after Fred Merkle failed to touch second base.

the next day. As Chance saw it, this was the only opportunity to replay the game as required by the League Constitution. The Giants did not have any open home dates for the final two weeks of the season, which ended on Wednesday, October 7.[74] But, with no official umpires present, his tactic failed: no umpires, no game.

As three o'clock neared, tension enveloped the Polo Grounds. Hank O'Day, the villain who, in the eyes of Giant fans, stole yesterday's game from New York, endured vicious personal remarks and a thunderous chorus of catcalls and jeers as he made his appearance. New York catcher Roger Bresnahan suggested the umpire wear a letter "C" on his shirt. The dignified, stoic O'Day ignored fans and catcher alike. The fans were no less kind to the Cubs with a hail of boos, hisses, and name-calling from start to finish. "The crowd roasted the Cubs ... calling them yellow dogs, quitters, and bribers of umpires. One of the cruelest gibes hurled at the Cubs was heard in the early part of the game. A bug back of the press coop yelled, 'You fellows play like the Yankees.'" McGraw kept up a verbal battle with Evers throughout the game. Evers gave as good as he got. Most of the language exchanged could not be printed in the newspaper. "Evers and McGraw kept up a continual chewing match during the combat. McGraw called the Trojan a pin head and Johnny came back with 'fat head' and other pleasant names."[75]

Mordecai Brown drew the Cubs' pitching assignment before the hostile New York crowd. McGraw tabbed Wiltse as the Giant pitcher. The Giants scored two runs in the first to temporarily soothe the savage, revenge-minded spectators; they were further mollified when the Giants scored three more runs in the fifth inning and knocked Brown out of the game. Meanwhile, Wiltse held the Cubs scoreless through six innings as the Giants built a commanding 5–0 lead. But for Evers's spectacular play in the fifth, the Giants' lead would have been even larger. Devlin sent a looping fly ball into shallow center field. Evers raced to the outfield grass, made a flying leap for the ball, and caught it with his bare hand. Recognizing a spectacular play and temporarily forgetting their hatred of the Cubs, the fans came to their feet and cheered Evers.[76]

No cheering occurred in the seventh inning as the Cubs rallied. Steinfeldt singled, and Hofman reach safely on an error. Tinker lined a single to right, and Steinfeldt scored the Cubs first run of the day. Kling followed with a triple to right, scoring Hofman and Tinker. McGraw yanked Wiltse and brought on Mathewson yet again. Howard pinch hit for pitcher Andy Coakley, who had relieved Brown in the sixth inning. Howard stroked a single off Mathewson, and Kling scored to bring the Cubs within one run, 5 to 4. But Hayden grounded into a double play, and Evers made the last out of the inning.[77]

The Cubs continued their attack in the eighth. After one out, Chance reached on a Herzog throwing error. Steinfeldt singled, placing Cubs on first and second with only one out. Matty struck out Hofman for out number two, but that brought Tinker, Mathewson's great nemesis, to the plate. Tinker lofted a deep fly ball just short of the right field stands and into the waiting glove of Mike Donlin, just missing a three-run home run. After his eighth-inning scare, Mathewson retired three Cubs in order in the ninth to save the 5–4 win and give the Giants a victory in the final game of the series.[78]

Only a short distance away, Brooklyn was a million miles from the electric atmosphere of the Polo Grounds experienced by the Cubs for the past three days. Compared to the emotion-laden series in New York, the three-game series in Brooklyn offered a relaxing, almost idyllic climate for the Cubs. The "sylvan glades and bosky dells of Brooklyn were a grand relief after the riotous siege at the Polo Grounds. We could almost smell the new mown hay and hear the gentle hum of the bees." Unlike the Polo Grounds, alcohol was not served at Washington Park. This fact alone ensured more civil behavior among the bugs and, perhaps, the next-to-last league position of Brooklyn played a role as well.[79]

A new umpire greeted the Cubs in Brooklyn. Up from the American Association Clarence "Brick" Owens was John Rudderham's replacement. His nickname stemmed from an incident in the minor leagues when irate fans threw a brick, hitting him in the head.[80] Owens had already established a reputation as a good-natured fellow and a competent arbitrator among the public and players of other teams despite his brief three-weeks tenure in the National League. The rookie umpire teamed with Bob Emslie in Brooklyn.[81]

The Cubs won easily. After a first-inning home run by second baseman John Hummel gave the Dodgers a 1–0 lead, Overall allowed only two more hits and shut out Brooklyn for the final eight innings. Meanwhile, the Cubs scored a run in the second to tie, and they won the game, 5 to 1, with single runs in the seventh and eighth innings and a final pair of runs in the ninth. Tinker took hitting honors with three hits, including a double.[82]

If the Cubs enjoyed the day in Brooklyn, the Giants were miserable in New York. The Cincinnati Reds followed the Cubs to the Polo Grounds, and, while the Cubs waltzed over the Dodgers, the Giants lost a doubleheader to their new visitors. Their double loss and the Cubs' victory brought the Cubs to within a single percentage point of the first-place Giants (.629 to .628). Meanwhile, Pittsburgh split a doubleheader in Boston to remain in third place, but only a few more percentage points (.623) behind the Cubs.[83]

Barraged by telegrams and letters inquiring about the status of the notorious Giants-Cubs game of September 23, Harry Pulliam issued a statement on Friday, September 25.

> The umpires in charge of this contest filed their written reports at National League headquarters on September 24, stating that the New York-Chicago game of September 23 resulted in a tie score. This report of the umpires was accepted in the usual manner, without prejudice to the rights of either club.
>
> Under the constitution of the National League either club has a right to appeal from the decision of the umpires within five days of the date of the

Opposite: September 25 — Tattered, torn, but triumphant, the Cubs leave New York, crossing the Brooklyn Bridge to play the Trolley Dodgers. The briefcase shows how they took care of business in New York.

7. Touching Second, Twice

game. The New York club on this day has notified this office that it will appeal from the decision of the umpires.

In compliance with the provision of section 22 of the National League constitution the protest of the New York club, when received, will be submitted to the Chicago club and that club has five days in which to file an answer, if it so desires. The same procedure will prevail in the event that the Chicago club protests the decision of the umpires.

When the case is made up a decision on the facts and evidence will be rendered by the president of the league, which decision is subject to appeal within five days to the board of directors, whose decision is final.[84]

Pulliam made no mention in his statement of the protest correspondence he had received from the Cubs' Charles Murphy.

On Saturday, September 26, Reulbach had a great day. In the first game of the doubleheader against Brooklyn, with rookie umpire Clarence Owens calling balls and strikes, Reulbach struck out seven Dodgers, walked only one, scattered five hits, and, in an hour and forty-five minutes, pitched a complete-game shutout. Evers, Steinfeldt, and Kling led the Cubs' hitting attack with three hits apiece, including doubles by Evers and Kling, in the 5–0 victory. Reulbach, still feeling strong and energized, asked Chance if he could pitch the second game against the seventh-place Dodgers. Chance consented, and Reulbach duplicated his first-game performance, only better, again pitching a shutout but at an even quicker pace, one hour and fifteen minutes. He allowed only three hits, walked only one, and struck out four Dodgers. Kling led the Cubs with two hits, while Hayden, Evers, and Schulte each contributed a hit apiece in the 3–0 win. The Cubs remained a percentage point out of first place as the Giants won both games of their doubleheader against the Reds.[85]

Hayden had played well, patrolling right field while Schulte moved to the injured Jimmy Sheckard's left-field position. Joining the team on September 18 in Philadelphia, Hayden played in eleven games, making 19 put outs and contributing several clutch hits, including two doubles. But Chance did not invite Hayden to travel with the Cubs to Cincinnati for the next series against the Reds. Hayden would not be eligible for the World Series, should the Cubs win the pennant, and Sheckard, his knee healed, was waiting in Cincinnati to rejoin his teammates and reclaim his outfield position. Jack Hayden returned to his home in Bryn Mawr, Pennsylvania.[86]

Pulliam issued his second statement regarding the disputed September 23 game through a press release on Saturday, September 26, and explained, in a somewhat defensive manner, why he did not schedule umpires to replay the tied game the next day as required by the League Constitution.

7. Touching Second, Twice

Pitcher Ed Reulbach won 24 games with only 7 losses in 1908. Impressively, on September 26, he pitched both games of a doubleheader in Brooklyn, shutting out the Dodgers twice, 5 to 0 and 3 to 0.

Pending the final adjudication of the disputed game of Wednesday, September 23, I want you to know why I assigned umpires for but one game at the Polo Grounds on Thursday, September 24, and why the provisions of the National League constitution, governing the playing off of postponed and tie games was not enforced.

I was present at the game which, it is well known, ended in a scene of great confusion. With a desire to protect the interests of both clubs and carry out the provisions of our laws, I sent for the umpires in charge of the game that night. They informed me that the game resulted in a tie.

> While in conference with the umpires I received a formal protest from the Chicago club claiming the game by a score of 9 to 0 (forfeit), alleging a violation of rule 26, section 4, of the playing rules. The moment this claim of Chicago was received I was stopped from taking any steps to have the tie game played off the next day by the provisions of section 22 of the constitution, which provides that the claim, together with the accompanying proofs, must be furnished to the other club, which club has five days in which to reply.
> A second communication from the Chicago club was received at about 11o'clock the next morning, stating it did not desire to protest the decision of the umpires. It was then too late, in my judgment, to give the proper notice to both clubs that the game must be played over on that day, and therefore, I did not assign umpires for two games.
> The action of the Chicago club in filing its original claim for a forfeited game on the night of September 23 prevented the operation of section 45 of the constitution, providing for the playing off of postponed or tie games, and now that the action of the umpires in declaring a tie game has been protested by the New York club, the entire matter must be decided in accordance with the provisions of the constitution.[87]

The Cubs departed Brooklyn for Cincinnati and their last road series of the season after winning 14 games and losing only 3 on their East Coast trip. After falling behind the Giants by four and a half games on September 18, the Cubs had closed the gap to a single percentage point by the time they arrived in Cincinnati on Sunday, September 27. Only five games with the Reds and a single contest at home with the Pirates remained on the Cubs' schedule. Taking no chances with the weather, Murphy rented the infield tarpaulin from Pirate president Barney Dreyfuss to protect the field at West Side Park for the final home game with the Pirates. Murphy had the tarpaulin sent by special train to Chicago.[88]

After Pfiester had pitched the tie game in New York, his left arm again became useless. Trainer Bert Semmens treated the arm for the next several days, but without success. On the way to Cincinnati, Pfiester, desperate for relief, decided to visit John "Bonesetter" Reese in Youngstown, Ohio, the same renowned doctor that had so successfully treated Artie Hofman's knee earlier in the season. On Monday, an off day for the Cubs and Reds, Pfiester rejoined his teammates in Cincinnati.

> This morning the hotel porters removed the storm door from its hinges to admit Mr. Pfiester and his glad smile. He had just returned from Youngstown, O., with his pitching elbow entirely repaired. Bonesetter Reese made the astounding discovery that Pfiester had pitched the world renowned tie game at New York last Wednesday with the contents of his left arm dislocated. The large tendon running from the shoulder to the wrist had slipped off the point of the elbow and the arm was of no more use than an unstrung bow. Reese

fixed the busted wing in three minutes.... In relating his visit to the wonderful bonesetter the returned athlete said Reese felt around, located the distorted tendon, and snapped it back in place with his powerful fingers. The entire diagnosis and cure occupied less than ten minutes.... He (Pfiester) is as tickled as a boy with a tin locomotive to find his arm in good condition again, and Chance is more than glad to have the crack southpaw back on the job.[89]

The Cincinnati ballpark, Palace of the Fans, had a new look. Owner Garry Herrmann invested $4,000 to install three huge lighttowers to allow the Reds to play baseball after dark, but they would not be operable for another two weeks. Pitcher Chick Fraser, summoned from Chicago by Chance, and Jimmy Sheckard, his injured knee healed, rejoined their teammates in Cincinnati. Sheckard returned to his left-field position, and Schulte returned to his accustomed right-field position for the first game with the Reds on Tuesday, September 29. Pitcher Kirby "Red" White, a recruit from the Ohio State League, also joined the Cubs in Cincinnati and warmed up with Brown during practice. "The new man is a well built right hander and he looks like Hugh Jennings of ten years ago."[90]

Led by Tinker's two hits, including a two-run home run, the Cubs built a 6–0 lead after six and a half innings. Brown shut out the Reds for the first six innings, allowed two runs in the seventh, then blanked the Reds for the final two innings to record the 6–2 win. The Giants split a doubleheader with the Phillies in New York, so, with the Cubs' victory, the clubs reversed positions in the standings. The Cubs rotated to the top position and now led the Giants by a single percentage point. Meanwhile, the Pirates more than kept pace by winning a doubleheader against the St. Louis Cardinals in Pittsburgh. Only four percentage points separated the top three teams.[91]

Less than eight hundred fans turned out to watch the Cubs play the Reds on Wednesday, the last day of September. The few spectators present witnessed a fine, hard-fought contest, won by the home team in the bottom of the ninth inning. The Cubs and Overall led 5 to 3 as the Reds came to bat for the last time. Third baseman Mike Mowrey singled to begin the inning. Right fielder Mike Mitchell hit a slow roller toward Steinfeldt at third. Steinfeldt, hobbled by a leg-muscle strain from the day before, could not charge the ball with any speed. Mitchell reached first base safely without a throw from Steinfeldt. Then, right-handed hitting catcher Larry McLean cued a shot between Chance and the first-base bag, scoring Mowrey and sending Mitchell to third. John Kane, a reserve outfielder, went in to run for McLean at first base, and manager John Ganzel sent himself to pinch-hit for pitcher Dubuc, but he popped out to Steinfeldt at third. Another pop up to Evers retired second baseman Dick Egan for the second out. Needing a final out to win the game, Overall walked Dode Paskert to load the bases. After four pitches, the count stood two balls and two strikes on shortstop Hans Lobert. On the next pitch, Lobert sent a line drive over Tinker's head into left field. Mitchell and Kane both scored to win the game, 6 to 5. Paskert, the runner on first, advanced and stood on second base, avoiding any possible doubt that the winning run would be counted.[92]

It was a difficult day for the Cubs. In the first inning, Evers took a pitch to the head and lay unconscious for several minutes. Howard ran for Evers, but after being revived with some water, Evers returned the next inning and finished the game. Baseball rules did not require players to be removed from the game for pinch runners. What looked like certain victory faded into defeat, and the tough loss dropped the Cubs from first to third place. Both the Giants and Pirates had won their games. And, after thirteen years pitching in the major leagues, Chick Fraser announced his retirement from baseball after the current season.[93]

CHAPTER 8

Triumphs and Scandal

On the first day of October, Ed Reulbach pitched his fourth-straight shutout, allowing only two hits, both by Cincinnati second baseman Dick Egan. Artie Hofman (two singles) and Jimmy Sheckard (a double) shared hitting honors as the Cubs scored a single run in the second inning, bunched four more in the fourth, and added a for-good-measure run in the ninth on their way to the 6–0 victory over the Reds. Harry Steinfeldt sat out the game with his damaged leg, and Johnny Evers, after going to bed with a headache and a lump the size of an egg in front of his right ear, after his beaning from the day before, continued in the lineup. Hofman played third base for Steinfeldt, and Del Howard was stationed in center field. Charlie Dryden reported that Chick Fraser had begun training for his retirement days on an Idaho farm by having "a bell boy wake him every morning at 5 o'clock and moo like a cow."[1]

It did not seem possible, but the scramble of the three teams was even tighter. The Giants split another doubleheader with Philadelphia that day, and the Pirates did not play. The Giants, back in the lead, sported a winning percentage of .635 while both the Cubs and Pirates posted identical records of 95 wins against 55 losses, a .633 percentage.[2]

Charles Murphy took umbrage with Harry Pulliam blaming him for the delay in rendering a decision on the Chicago–New York tie game. In strong but rambling prose, Murphy wrote:

> It is unfortunate President Pulliam regards three communications from me within thirty-six hours in the matter as of vital importance to 80,000,000 people as interference with him. I also fail to see any complications, as he is quoted as saying. If Mr. Pulliam was clear on that portion of the constitution which gives the game to Chicago as he is in reference to that which governs me as a stockholder (not allowed to vote as team owner in self interest cases) it would not now be incumbent on him to issue what can only be justly termed an inane statement. His entire course in regard to the tie game has been weak and vacillating.

Personally I admire Mr. Pulliam, but officially he has been lamentably weak in this instance. To charge his procrastination to me is absurd.

I am working honorably to get a game that belongs to us by the constitution, and Mr. Pulliam, according to interviews credited to him, is trying to take that game away from us. He is hiding behind time, claiming enough hours would not elapse between the time his first belated statement to the public, which was about 10 A.M., and 1:30 P.M., when the other double headers in New York had been begun.

There is nothing in the constitution that gives Mr. Pulliam any such discretionary power. It is not for him to say how much time it is necessary to give the two clubs to play off a double header. Such an absurd position as he has taken in the matter is foreign to the real constitution.

After the game last Wednesday he locked himself away from all newspaper men in New York and the visiting correspondents who were clamoring for their reading clientele to know what he was going to do. Instead of coming out manfully that night, between 6 and 10 o'clock with the probable intention of claiming it now seems that time would prevent the New York club from playing the game over. That doubtless seemed to Mr. Pulliam to be the easiest way out of the matter. Both clubs were at the park in uniform, however, before 1 o'clock last Thursday and there is no real reason why the Giants did not play the Cubs.

If the Chicago club forces Mr. Pulliam to make a decision before the championship season ends we will feel amply repaid for the effort, even if it is adverse to us. What we want is a decision. We have waived everything presented by New York, as well as our five days to reply, and can imagine no reason for all the delay.

That afternoon, in New York, Harry Pulliam met with umpire Bob Emslie concerning the tie game. Pulliam made no statements.[3]

Mordecai Brown extended Cincinnati's scoreless-inning streak another nine innings on Friday, blanking the Reds on four hits. Hofman played third base for the still leg-injured Steinfeldt. Howard stood in Hofman's center-field position. Chance led the hitting attack with three singles as the Cubs scored three runs in the first inning and two more in the eighth to win, 5 to 0. After the game, Chance denied a report in a New York newspaper that the Cubs had offered the Giants $50,000 for Christy Mathewson. Murphy made no comment. The mad scramble for first place continued. The Pirates won two in St. Louis and tied the Giants, who beat Philadelphia, 7 to 2. The Cubs slipped to third place while winning, but they trailed the two leaders by only two percentage points.[4]

Pulliam issued his impatiently awaited decision on the tie game from his New York office on Friday evening, October 2. *Chicago Tribune* headlines told disappointed Chicago readers, "CHICAGO CLAIM NOT VALID" and "Official Says Question Hinges on Umpire, Who Must Be Upheld."

September 25 — After the disputed Merkle game, both teams filed protests and counter-protests. As Harry Pulliam delayed his decision, fans grew impatient. What did the presidential candidates have to say about it?

The National League president ruled against both of Chicago's claims for a forfeit: first, due to fan interference the day of the game, and the next day when the game was not replayed. Pulliam also ruled against the Giants' petition for a victory in the ninth inning, citing lack of evidence to prove Merkle touched second base before the force out. O'Day's tie-game decision was upheld. The final paragraph of Pulliam's strongly worded statement read, "Would it be good sportsmanship on my part as president of the league to repudiate my umpires simply to condone the undisputed blunder of a player? The playing rules say that the decision of the umpire on a question of fact is final. I rule that this game ended in a tie score and that for reasons stated above the Chicago club has no claim in equity for a forfeited game." Either or both teams had the right to appeal the decision to the National League Board of Directors, which scheduled a meeting for Monday.[5]

The Cubs easily won the last game of the series with the Reds on Saturday, 16 to 2. Howard led the Cubs' hitting parade with four of the team's eighteen hits, including a double. Hofman and Kling each had three hits with a double a piece. Chance had two hits, a double and a home run into the left-field bleacher seats. Tinker had only one hit, but it was a triple with the bases loaded. The Cubs scored early and often. Six Cubs crossed the plate in the first inning, four more in the second, and another four in the third. Only a single run scored in the fourth to bring the total to fifteen. One final run was added in the sixth. After five innings, Chance rested Reulbach and brought in Chick Fraser, giving the retiring pitcher one last opportunity to perform, pitching the final four innings.

Reulbach had held the Reds scoreless during his five innings of work to run his consecutive-scoreless inning streak to forty-four. The Boston Doves scored the last run off Reulbach in the seventh inning on September 17 in a 4–1 Cubs victory. Since then, Reulbach put together an amazing string of zeros: September 19, ten innings against Philadelphia; September 26, eighteen innings against Brooklyn, when he pitched both games of a doubleheader; October 1, nine innings against the Reds; and October 3, another five innings against the Reds.[6]

The Cubs arrived in Chicago on Sunday, October 4, to play the Pittsburgh Pirates in the final game of the regular season for both teams. The Pirates controlled their own fate. The day before, they beat the St. Louis Cardinals 3 to 2, edging into first place by half a game. With a win in Chicago, the Pirates would be champions of the National League, while a Cubs' victory would eliminate them. But the Giants still had three games to play against the Boston Doves. The combination of a Cubs' win and a sweep of sixth-place Boston by the Giants would mean a tie between the two clubs, both teams ending the regular season (154 games) with identical records: 98 wins, 55 losses, and 1 tie. While the Pirates and Cubs both won on Saturday, the Giants lost a heartbreaker to Philadelphia, 3 to 2, to set up Sunday's scenario. New York players and fans found themselves rooting for the Cubs against the Pirates. It was the only chance they had.[7]

NATIONAL LEAGUE STANDINGS
(FIRST THREE TEAMS)
OCTOBER 4, 1908

	W	L	Pct.
Pirates	98	55	.641
Cubs	97	55	.638
Giants	95	55	.633

The largest West Side Park crowd in history (30, 247) squeezed into the stands and overflowed onto the field of play.

8. Triumphs and Scandal

It is said the pack of human beings exceeded by 6,000 the largest crowd ever jammed into the West Side Park.... The reserve seats were sold out in advance, leaving the catch-as-catch-can folks to hustle for homesteads on the grass. The big run started at 11 o'clock, at which hour the portcullis was opened. Secretary Williams passed the park at 8:30 in the morning on his way home from Cincinnati, and found squads of early birds perched on the curb.

By noon the seating districts were filled and steady streams filed down the aisles and into the open, forming a fringe of society about the space in which the athletes were to perform. This fringe was modest at first, standing well back of the bulkheads, but as the hour approached the line grew restless. As far away as the press coop the snapping of rubber in eager necks was heard. Foot by foot the fringe drew closer.

The police halted the advance on the right flank by compelling the front row to squat. Those behind could only advance by stepping on the dead bodies in front, to which the said bodies objected. While the cops were busy planting this crop of bugs, the left and central districts broke loose. The Cubs were then at practice and the idea was to get still closer to the adored ones in white. The fringe extending across two-thirds of the outfield bent badly in places, but did not break. Squads of police hammered and punched the middle section back a few inches and while they were engaged in this noble and diverting work the left wing crawled up yards at a time. Less than ten minutes before play, bugs, male and female, were camped close to the shortstop position, leaving a vacant stretch behind the restless fringe. Ground rules with the crowd that close would give a player nothing more than a bunt for a smash into the overflow.

Seeing the cops were powerless to cope without expert assistance, Prof. (trainer) Semmens, ... hastened to the rescue. Arrayed in a baseball shirt, with a cap of the same, and an air of fierce determination, the professor bent the gaze of his hypnotic eye upon the multitude.... Mr. Semmens sprang a brand of oral salve along with the eye.

The combination worked fine. Sensible he bugs in the front clasped hands and formed a living rope. With the aid of the professor and the police the fringe was jammed back to the starting point. The cops plied their clubs gently and below the belt, rapping he bugs across the legs to make them move faster.

The inmates of the field boxes thought their light would be turned off by the overflow standing in front. Heretofore the crowd has not interfered with these sections, but the rush congested all spots. Cubs and Pirates were driven from their happy homes in the coops. The players camped on the grass near the base lines far from the water supply, which was cut off by the surging masses. At length the police guard yielded to the wails of box inmates and compelled the standing roomers to sit down.[8]

Umpires Hank O'Day and Cy Rigler appeared on the scene promptly to begin the three o'clock game. " Mr. O'Day appeared at 2:55 o'clock, trailed by Mr. Rigler. When any big doings are on they always send for the only Hank. He had his trousers creased fore and aft, and his haberdashery was real linen, fresh from the laundry. While Hank went from one team captain to the other for the line up Mr. Rigler stuck close to the premiere ump, so as to annex some of the glory. This is the first real big thing Mr. Rigler has been mixed up in and he didn't want to miss any of the emoluments thereunto appertaining."[9]

The pennant on the line, both teams started their best pitcher, Vic Willis for the Pirates and Mordecai Brown for the home team. Cubs third baseman Harry Steinfeldt still did not play due to his leg injury. Hofman played third, and Howard played center field. Schulte gave the Cubs a 1–0 lead in the first inning when he singled to left field after Sheckard's double and Evers's sacrifice bunt. Another single by Schulte in the fifth inning scored Evers with the Cubs' second run. Evers reached safely after shortstop Hans Wagner fielded his ground ball deep behind second base and, in a valiant attempt to throw Evers out, sailed the ball over the head of first baseman Alan Storke. Evers advanced to second base. Schulte hit a vicious line drive toward Willis. The Pirate pitcher got his glove on the ball, but he could only deflect it on its way to center field. The ball rolled far enough on the outfield grass to allow Evers to score. Meanwhile, Brown held the Pirates scoreless for the first five innings.[10]

But the Pirates fought back in the sixth and tied the score. Center fielder Roy Thomas began the inning with a single over Evers's head into right field. With Fred Clarke at the plate, Brown made a low throw past Chance at first trying to pick off Thomas, sending the runner to second base. Clarke popped out to Evers, and third baseman Tommy Leach grounded out, Evers to Chance; Thomas moved to third on the ground out. Wagner, the league's leading hitter, came to bat with two outs. Brown got two strikes on the Pirate shortstop, but Wagner shot a drive down the third-base line between Hofman and the base for a double, scoring Thomas with the first Pirate run. Brown made a wild pitch, sending Wagner to third. Finally, second baseman Ed Abbaticchio brought Wagner home with a bounding single into center field to tie the game at two. Catcher Kling then fired a strike to Evers at second to retire Abbaticchio trying to steal for the final out.[11]

The Cubs retook the lead in the bottom of the sixth inning. After Howard and Hofman flied out, Tinker hit a double. Willis walked Kling intentionally to pitch to Brown, normally a good strategy. But not on this day, as Brown poked a single to right field, scoring Tinker with the go-ahead run. Brown sat the Pirates down in order in the seventh. Another run in the bottom of the seventh increased the Cubs' lead to two, 4 to 2. Sheckard reached first safely when Wagner booted his ground ball, then Evers bunted Sheckard to second. Schulte drew a base on balls. At this point, the Cubs executed a hit-and-run bunt play. On the pitch, both runners broke for the next base, and Chance bunted the ball hard toward shortstop Wagner, the deepest infielder. Wagner charged hard, but Chance beat the throw to first, loading the bases with only one out. The next hitter, Howard, lofted a fly ball to center fielder Thomas. Sheckard tagged at third and raced for the plate. Thomas made a strong, but wide throw to catcher Gibson, and Sheckard crossed the plate standing up.[12]

The Pirates hit Brown hard in the eight inning. Jim Kane, a reserve first baseman, batted for Willis and sent a wicked ground ball to third, but Hofman made a fine play and threw Kane out. Thomas sent another hard one to Hofman, this time a line drive, which Hofman caught. Brown walked Clarke. Leach sent a screamer down the first-base line, "but Chance made a spread eagle leap, stuck out his mitted hand, and the ball stuck in the palm." Three hard hit balls, three fine plays, three outs, and no Pittsburgh runs.[13]

With two outs, the Cubs added another run to take a seemingly safe three-run lead. Brown singled off Leach's glove and advanced to second on a single by Sheckard. Evers followed with a ground-rule double into the crowd in left center field, scoring Brown with run number five for the Cubs. In their last at bat, the Pirates continued to hit the ball hard. Wagner singled to start the Pirate ninth. Abbaticchio lined a ball down the right-field line, but O'Day ruled the ball was foul. The Pirates thought the ball fair, strongly disputed O'Day's call, and appealed to Cy Rigler, the base umpire. Rigler upheld O'Day's call, and Abbaticchio returned to the plate and struck out. First baseman Alan Storke hit a sharp grounder to Hofman's left. The stand-in third baseman could only deflect the ball with his glove, but the ball took a Chicago hop right to Tinker; he made a quick throw to Evers covering second to force Wagner for out number two. Rookie right fielder Owen Wilson hit a routine ground ball to shortstop Tinker, who shoveled the ball to Evers at second base to force Storke and end the game. The Cubs' 5 to 2 victory eliminated the Pirates. A gracious Fred Clarke stated, "Of course we are disappointed. That decision in the ninth inning might have meant something to us, but I guess the Cubs were too strong for us today. We'll be back after them next year. We have no hard feelings and wish the Cubs luck if they play for the world's title." Pirate president Barney Dreyfuss's brief statement conveyed a greater sense of disappointment: "Somebody had to lose. It was Pittsburgh. We lost to a good team. We hope for better luck next time."[14]

The Giants received the glad news in New York. Chicago's win meant the Giants still had a chance for the crown. Both the Cubs and Giants had

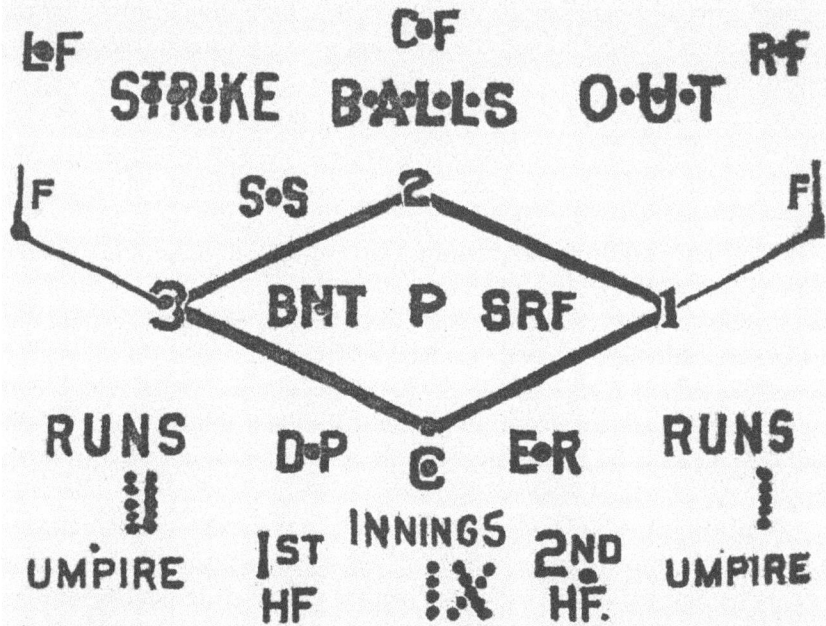

As the season drew to a close, the *Chicago Tribune* set up an electric scoreboard so fans could follow the games. The black dots are lights that display the action. In Detroit, the *Free Press* placed their own scoreboard at City Hall. On October 6, a large crowd watched as the Tigers defeated the White Sox to clinch the American League pennant.

55 losses, but the Giants had three games to play against Boston to finish the season. A single Boston win would give the championship to Chicago; a three-game sweep by the Giants would produce a Chicago-New York tie.[15]

The Detroit Tigers came to Chicago to play a season-ending three-game series with the White Sox to determine the American League champion. The Cubs developed a routine of practicing in the morning and watching the White Sox-Tigers game in the afternoon while waiting for the outcome of the New York-Boston game. New York won the first game on Monday.[16]

On Tuesday afternoon, October 6, after meeting for two days in Cincinnati, the three-member National League Board of Directors (Garry Herrmann, Cincinnati Reds owner; Harry Pulliam, National League president; and Charlie Ebbets, Brooklyn Dodgers owner) issued their ruling on the Cubs-Giants tie game. The Board upheld O'Day and Pulliam, ruled against both Chicago's forfeit claim and New York's victory claim, and declared the game a tie. But in a stunning addition, the Board ordered the game to be replayed in New York on Thursday, October 8. The mandate to replay the game after the regular season officially ended on Wednesday, October 7, was in violation of the League Constitution, which required all postponed and replayed games to be played before the end of the season. The Board acknowledged the violation, but justified their replay order as the only fair solution to the most important issue to ever be brought before the Board.[17] The decision of the Board made no reference to the possibility of a Giant loss to Boston; presumably the replayed game would take place regardless of the outcome of the final two Giant games. New York beat Boston on Tuesday.

Charles Murphy had presented the Cubs' position one more time before the Board of Directors in Cincinnati. When the Board made their announcement, a disappointed Murphy telephoned Frank Chance with the news and issued his statement.

> We will play them on Thursday, and we'll lick em too. We'll make it so decisive this time that no boneheaded base running can cast a shadow of doubt on the contest. We want to win the championship on the playing field and not in the legislative halls of baseball politics. The Cubs will take the Twentieth Century flyer tomorrow in Chicago and arrive in New York Thursday morning. Manager Chance and his players are all in good condition and will have no excuse if we fail to bring the third successive National League pennant to Chicago.
>
> The members of the board of directors of the National League, who handed down their decision today, did so only after long and careful consideration of the complicated matters before them, and I think that each acted to the best of his judgment and belief in the premises. Of course, the decision is a disappointment to the Chicago club, as we felt that it was ours under the constitu-

tion. We will take our medicine, however, and play the game; and I feel sure that the Cubs again will prove that they are the greatest team of ball players in the world.[18]

Chance took the decision much more personally and directed harsh criticism towards Charlie Ebbets, the Brooklyn Dodgers' president. Chance said, "Ebbets was not qualified to pass on the case. He is prejudiced and would always give us the worse of it." Further, Chance claimed that during the Cubs' last series in Brooklyn, Ebbets called a team meeting with his players "and told them he wanted the team to play its hardest against us and that he would see that any player playing 'soft ball' was barred from baseball for the rest of his career ... and added that he hoped the Giants would win the pennant...." Even worse, "On another occasion Mr. Ebbets went on to say to some friend that he was sorry he did not let the crowd kill me at the time of my troubles in Brooklyn last year when fans threw pop bottles at me and I was saved from serious injury or even death only by a police guard."[19]

Sixteen Cubs gathered at the Lake Shore Station on Wednesday afternoon to board the Twentieth Century Limited for New York. Railroad officials provided an additional two luxury coaches to the normal six-coach train carrying the Cubs and party to New York. Special arrangements were made to provide a relay of number "44" engines, "the most powerful in the service, to insure the prompt arrival of the team on schedule (9:30 A.M. Thursday morning), so as to give the ballplayers a few hours to catch their baseball legs." The "44" engines reduced the travel time between Chicago and New York by ten hours.[20]

Kling barely made it back to Chicago in time to board the train with his teammates. At home in Kansas City, Kling "knew nothing of this trip of the club until 10 o'clock last night (Tuesday), giving him barely one hour to catch the 11 o'clock train. Then that train was three hours late, reaching Chicago only about half an hour before the team left for the east. Chance heaved a sigh of relief when he saw the catcher come through the gate at the La Salle street station." Kling and his teammates (Chance, Evers, Tinker, Steinfeldt, Schulte, Hofman, Sheckard, Moran, Howard, Slagle, Brown, Reulbach, Overall, Pfiester, and Coakley) received a tremendous send off from a crowd of adoring fans at the station (Durbin, Campbell, Marshall, Fraser, Lundgren, and Kroh did not accompany the team). " As the hopes of local fandom climbed aboard ... they were given a rousing reception by the several hundred fanatics who had assembled to pay homage. As the train pulled out ... a final volley of cheers and good wishes sounded in the ears of the departing heroes." New Yorker Heinie Zimmerman had stayed in New York after the last Cubs-Giants series nursing his toe injury. His healed toe awaited the arrival of his teammates for another go at the Giants. Newspaper reporters, Cub officials (Murphy and Williams), and a small group of prominent Chicago supporters joined the team for the trip to New York. "With the Cubs on the Twentieth Century train were a number of west side fans, among them E.A. Hamill, president of the Corn Exchange Bank; John Farson Jr., Albert Weeghman, and others."[21]

The Twentieth Century Limited made its first stop on the way east at Elkhart, Indiana, where another two to three hundred fans greeted and cheered the Cubs, and especially Mordecai Brown, the pride of Indiana. "Elkhart fans cheered lustily for Brown, and refused to be appeased, until the great twirler show them the mangled mitt with which he downed Pittsburgh last Sunday." The Cubs also learned of the Giants' third win against Boston, giving both the Cubs and the Giants identical records, 98 wins and 55 losses. Tomorrow's game would decide the National League championship. The winner would advance to play the Detroit Tigers in the World Series. The American League championship had been decided the day before, on the last day of the season, when Detroit beat the White Sox in Chicago to win the pennant. For the loser of the Cubs-Giants replayed game, the season would simply end.[22]

To a player, the Cubs felt they were a better team than the Giants. Unconcerned about the long train ride and the probability of a hostile New York crowd, the Cubs were confident of victory. On board the train in Elkhart, Chance said it best: "Whoever heard of the Cubs losing a game they had to have? Chicago is going to win this flag. To do it we must beat New York, and we are going to do it."[23]

National League president Harry Pulliam selected Bill Klem and Jim Johnstone to umpire the emotion-laden game. On the morning of the game, Klem and Johnstone reported an attempted bribing incident to Pulliam, and both requested to be relieved of their umpire duties. The report stated that the day before Joseph Creamer, the New York Giants team physician, approached Klem and Johnstone and offered Klem $2,500 to bias his calls the next day toward the Giants. Klem declined the bribe offer and made his report. Pulliam accepted the report, but he kept his two honest umpires on the job. Johnstone confirmed the Creamer bribe attempt.[24]

Another bribery attempt of a more innocent nature occurred before the start of the game and met with greater success. "A gang of small boys broke through the fence back of the grand stand and met a special policeman. They were ordered back through the hole, but one of them held out a quarter in temptation ... and it worked. Every kid that could raise a quarter gave it over, and these were allowed to climb to the roof of the grand stand."

Other kids climbing the fences met with police fire hoses, but, " many of the youngsters preferred to stick and see the game through drowning eyes than to scurry for cover."[25]

The Cubs arrived at Grand Central Station Thursday morning, October 8, right on schedule. They were greeted by a large crowd, but not of well wishers this time. Indeed, the New York mob did not hide their animosity. Hostile and rude remarks met the Chicago team at the station. Uncivil and unruly crowd behavior continued at the Polo Grounds as the Cubs appeared to begin their pre-game practice. A steady stream of rude remarks and obscene language and a swelling crowd overflowing onto the field created a nasty, intense atmosphere. The two umpires, Klem and Johnstone, grew nervous. Tickets had been sold out since noon, and the entrance gates closed since 12:45. As the Giants took batting practice for the usual twenty minutes, the umpires decided to start the game fifteen minutes early. After the Giants finished, the Cubs, unaware of the early start decision, began their own twenty-minute batting-practice session. But after only five minutes, Joe McGinnity, with bat in hand, approached the plate to begin the Giants' pre-game infield practice. Chance, who was hitting, refused to leave. "As McGinnity stepped to the plate under orders to begin knocking grounders to the Giants for fielding practice Chance tried to brush him away and the 'iron man' raised his bat threateningly. For one instant it looked like the beginning of a riot, which would forever have disgraced the game, but the other players of both teams rushed in and surrounded the belligerents, smoothing out the incident quickly. When the thing was explained to Chance there was nothing for him to do but smile contemptuously at the trick and acquiesce."[26]

Recovered from his leg injury, Steinfeldt returned to the lineup and third base on Thursday. The same two pitchers from the tie game, Pfiester and Mathewson, faced each other again. Mathewson retired the Cubs in order in the first. Sheckard struck out swinging. Evers hit the ball hard, but second baseman Buck Herzog made a good play and threw Evers out. Schulte, called out on strikes, ended the inning. Jack "The Giant Killer" Pfiester, winner in three-straight starts against the Giants prior to his equally effective tie-game performance, ran into trouble in the first inning. Fred Tenney, the lead-off hitter, was back at his regular first-base position for the Giants; Fred Merkle watched from the bench. Pfiester's first pitch hit Tenney on the arm, putting him on first base. After getting two strikes, Pfiester walked Herzog, placing Giant runners on first and second. Bresnahan struck out, but Kling dropped the third strike. Bresnahan was out automatically because first base was occupied, but Kling made the throw to first and Herzog, forgetting he was not forced off first, left the bag. Chance tagged Herzog, completing a double play — another Giant baserunning error. Tenney remained at second base with two outs. The next hitter, right fielder Mike Donlin, pulled a line drive over first base close to the foul line. The Cubs thought the ball foul, but Johnstone ruled otherwise. Tenney scored from second, and Donlin reached second base with his double. The Cubs protested Johnstone's call, but to no avail, as Klem upheld Johnstone (New York reporters later confirmed the ball was foul). Losing the argument, Pfiester lost the plate yet again, walking Cy Seymour, the second walk of the inning. With one run in, runners on first and second, and Mathewson pitching for the Giants, Chance did not hesitate to remove Pfiester, summoning Mordecai Brown to the rescue. Brown made his way to the mound and promptly struck out Art Devlin to retire the side.[27]

Chance singled to begin the Cubs' second inning, but he wandered too far off base with his lead. Mathewson made a quick throw to Tenney. On a close play, Klem called Chance out; Chance and Hofman, coaching at first base, argued the call. Hofman vigorously objected to Klem's judgment, so much so that he was ejected from the game. Mathewson then struck out Steinfeldt and Howard, who came into the game to fill Hofman's vacancy. In the bottom of the inning, Brown sat the Giants down in order on two fly balls to Schulte and a ground out by Mathewson to Tinker at shortstop.[28]

Tinker hit the first pitch from Mathewson over Seymour's head in center field for a triple to begin the third inning. Kling sent a drive into left center field for a single, scoring Tinker and tying the score. Brown laid down a sacrifice bunt to Tenney at first to advance King to second base. After retiring Sheckard, Mathewson walked Evers intentionally, but the strategy backfired when Schulte hit a drive over third base into the crowd for a ground-rule double and Kling scored the second Cubs' run. Evers and Schulte both crossed the plate when Chance doubled to right field, but then Mathewson struck out Steinfeldt for the second time to end the Cub rally.[29]

In the third inning, Brown gave up two singles, but the Giants were unable to score. Mathewson regained command in the fourth — three up, three down for the Cubs. Brown returned the favor in the bottom of the inning — three Giants up, three down. The two great hurlers settled into a classic pitcher's duel. Mathewson shut out the Cubs in the fifth, sixth, and seventh innings before leaving the game for a pinch hitter in the bottom of the seventh. Brown blanked the Giants in the fifth and sixth innings, but in the bottom of the seventh the Giants mounted a rally, loading the bases with singles by Devlin and McCormick and a walk to Bridwell. With no one out, Doyle pinch hit for Mathewson and popped out in foul territory to catcher Kling. Tenney lofted a fly ball deep enough to Schulte in right field to score

Devlin, making the score 4 to 2. Schulte relayed his throw to Evers, holding McCormick at second base. Herzog came to the plate with the tying runs on base, but he grounded out, Tinker to Chance.[30]

Chicago threatened to score again in the eighth against Hooks Wiltse, Mathewson's replacement. Sheckard struck out, but Evers sent the ball to the left-field fence for two bases. Tenney fumbled Schulte's ground ball at first; Evers went to third, and Schulte reached safely on the error. Chance lifted a fly ball to left fielder McCormick; Evers tagged on the catch and raced for the plate, but McCormick threw him out to complete the double play and end the inning. Brown now needed only six more outs to win the National League pennant. Bresnahan sent a shot back to the mound to lead off the eighth. Brown knocked the hard-hit ball down, recovered, and threw Bresnahan out. Donlin flied out to Sheckard in left field and then Seymour grounded out, Tinker to Chance. Three outs to go. Wiltse retired the Cubs in order in the ninth, and Brown took the mound for the ninth inning. The season came down to the next three hitters for the Giants: Art Devlin, Moose McCormick, and Al Bridwell. Brown went to work. Devlin grounded to third, and Steinfeldt threw to Chance — one out. McCormick brought Giant fans to their feet with a long fly ball to left, but Sheckard ran the ball down and made the catch — two outs. Bridwell became the last Giants' hitter of the long season when he grounded out, Tinker to Chance. Three outs. The Cubs retained their National League title for the third consecutive year.[31] The New York fans were stunned.

A gloom settled over the Polo Grounds. "Forty thousand grief stricken fans, the greatest crowd of mourners that ever has attended baseball obsequies in this country, watched the Chicago Cubs administer the last sad rites to the New York Giants' 1908 pennant aspirations at the Polo Grounds this afternoon." Cubs manager Frank Chance pushed toward the clubhouse through the crowd on the field; some cursed at him, a few offered congratulations. Suddenly a man approached Chance from the rear and struck him, hard, in the neck. Before Chance could respond, the coward melted back into the sea of fans and disappeared. A few other angry Giant fans threw glass pop bottles at Cub players, but no one was hurt.[32]

Chicago Tribune reporter I. E. Sanborn wrote, "All honor will be given the Cubs as long as baseball is played for what they did this afternoon in the shadow of Coogan's Bluff." President Murphy stated, "The winning of the third successive National League pennant by the Cubs, we claim with pardonable pride. It is the most remarkable achievement ever accomplished in organized professional baseball. Manager Chance deserves a world of credit for his generalship, individual play, and incessant earnestness. Every member of the team is also deserving of unstinted praise. No gamer ball club has ever trod the diamond. The New York Giants have put up a great fight. They fought us to a finish, but in my judgment the better team won. I am glad our victory today was a decisive one, so that it cannot be charged to anything of a technical nature." Chance offered a gracious assessment of his team: "My boys were nervous at the start of the game. The circumstances naturally account for that. But then they braced up and you know the rest. The team is the finest in the history of the sport." Asked about his performance, the modest and reserved Mordecai Brown said, "I simply did the best I could and our boys did the rest with their bats." Brown's rival, mild-mannered Christy Mathewson, true to character, was equally laconic, "I did the best I could, but I guess fate was against us." The president of the Giants, John T. Brush, graciously stated, "We have been beaten by a good team in a fair game, and have no excuses to offer. I congratulate the Chicago club on its victory and hope it will win the world's championship." But the combative Giant manager John McGraw offered no such conciliatory remarks. Instead, McGraw expressed his still-seething anger: "I do not feel badly about this game. We merely lost something we had won before. This cannot be put too strongly." McGraw did offer praise for his pitcher, Mathewson. "As for Mathewson, he pitched winning ball. It was merely one of those lapses which the best pitchers experience under such terrific strain. The whole team showed the effects of it, but they fought to the end."[33]

The New York press lavished praise on Mordecai Brown for his performance and gave the shy pitcher a new moniker: "'Undertaker' Brown, the three fingered pitcher who helped lower the Pittsburgh remains into the grave at Chicago last Sunday, officiated at the burial. Above the newly made mound he planted this epitaph: 'Chicago, 4; New York, 2.' Then he went away, followed by his eight agile assistants...."[34]

Tragically, a real funeral shortly occurred for a New York fan. Anxious to see the game, but arriving too late to enter the jammed Polo Grounds, Henry T. McBride, a fireman attached to engine company number 71, climbed an elevated railroad pillar. He reached a point where he was able to see over the fence, but lost his grip and fell to the sidewalk, striking his head, and dying almost instantly.[35]

World Series

The three-member National Commission (Ban Johnson, Harry Pulliam, and Garry Herrmann), met in Cincinnati earlier in the week and made plans for the World Series. A coin toss determined that the first game would be held in the city of the American League champion Detroit Tigers on Saturday, October 10. The next two games, on Sunday and Monday, shifted to Chicago. The fourth, and, if-needed fifth would be in Detroit again, and a sixth in Chicago. If a seventh game became necessary, the site would be determined by another coin toss.[36]

The Cubs had swept Detroit in four straight games in 1907. But this year confident Tiger fans were eager for their World Series rematch, certain the outcome would be different. Tiger spirit flooded Detroit and the entire state of Michigan. "The business part of town is decorated more gayly than Chicago was for the visit of the two presidential candidates. Nearly every shop window has a Tiger in some form or other among its displays. Three-quarters of the young men and women flaunt Michigan colors on the street and frequent bursts of wee-e-ahs enliven the village quietue." Wee-e-ah was the famous and, to opposing teams, utterly irritating battle cry loosed by Tiger manager Hughie Jennings.[37]

Tiger management purchased "circus seats" (wooden bleachers) from a firm in Chicago and had them erected in center field for the World Series, expanding the seating capacity of Bennett Park from 10,500 to 18,000. Bennett Park, built in 1896, served as a minor-league park until the Tigers became charter members of the new American League in 1901. The park honored Charlie Bennett, a catcher who played fifteen years, eight with the National League Detroit Wolverines. Detroit lost its team in 1889, but Bennett played another five years in Boston before both his legs were amputated after a train accident in 1894. Charlie Bennett threw out the first ball for every season's opening day in Detroit, beginning in 1896 until his death in February 1927.[38]

Tickets for the first game went on sale at 10:00 o'clock Friday morning, and by noon all the reserved seats were sold out. Fans had begun forming a line for tickets shortly after midnight, and men who had been in line since daylight did not reach the ticket window.[39]

The Cubs' train departed New York Thursday evening at 8:00 P.M. and arrived in Detroit at noon on Friday. Offered free hotel accommodations for his team, superstitious Frank Chance declined; instead, he opted to have the Cubs check into the Tully Hotel, the same hotel they stayed in the year before when they became champions. Chance, his neck swollen and his voice hoarse and barely audible, immediately sought medical attention for his injured throat. An examination revealed a broken cartilage that temporarily damaged his vocal cords, but did not prevent him from playing.[40]

The three members of the National Commission arrived in Detroit late

Friday evening and checked into the Hotel Pontchartrain. The next morning the commissioners met with players of both teams "to give them final instructions regarding conduct becoming champions on a ball field. But as both teams are used to being champions, and have met once before for the world's title, they are not likely to learn much they do not already know."[41]

The lineups for the first game of the World Series:

Chicago Cubs		Detroit Tigers	
Sheckard	LF	McIntyre	LF
Evers	2B	O'Leary	SS
Schulte	RF	Crawford	CF
Chance	1B	Cobb	RF
Steinfeldt	3B	Rossman	1B
Hofman	CF	Schaefer	3B
Tinker	SS	Schmidt	C
Kling	C	Downs	2B
Reulbach	P	Killian	P

Two umpires from each league worked the World Series on a rotating schedule with one umpire from each league working each game. O'Day and Klem represented the National League, while the American League sent veterans John Sheridan and Tom Connolly. First-game honors went to O'Day and Sheridan.[42]

The game began "in the early stages of a rain storm which never ceased and it was finished on a field so soggy that footing was insecure and the base lines almost two inches deep in mud." The extra seats installed in center field were not necessary as only a small, hardy group of fans (10,812) braved the elements and showed up at Bennett Park. Those who did attend got a solid drenching and witnessed a slug fest.[43]

Managers Chance and Jennings tabbed Ed Reulbach and Ed Killian to pitch the first game. Jennings decided to go with Killian, a six-year veteran and a Tiger since 1904, primarily because he threw from the left side. Killian had pitched the fewest games (27) and the fewest innings (181) of the five-man Tiger pitching staff in 1908. He won 12 games and lost 9, with 1 save and an earned run average of 2.99. Killian was not the most effective Tiger pitcher, but he was left handed, and conventional wisdom believed Cub hitters were less effective against left-handed pitchers. Reulbach, clearly Chicago's second-best pitcher after Brown, possessed more impressive season statistics than Killian. Reulbach had pitched 298 innings in 46 games, winning 24, and losing only 7 with a 2.03 earned run average. Perhaps the sloppy weather conditions were a factor, for neither pitcher performed well, although Reulbach lasted until the seventh inning while Jennings removed Killian with only one out in the third.[44]

Sheckard lofted a fly ball to right field to begin the game. Right fielder Ty Cobb initially misjudged the ball and recovered too late as he made a dive for the ball at the last instant, but he could not make the catch. Sheckard raced to second base and received credit for a double. But Evers struck out after missing two bunt attempts. Sheckard reached third base when Schulte grounded out to second baseman Herman "Germany" Schaefer. Chance received an intentional walk and then stole second, placing Cubs on second and third with two outs, but Steinfeldt hit a lazy fly to Sam Crawford in center field for the final out.[45]

The Tigers took the lead against Reulbach in their half of the first inning. Left fielder Matty McIntyre singled sharply to left. Both shortstop Charley O'Leary and center fielder Sam Crawford struck out, but McIntyre stole second base on the third strike to Crawford. Cobb chopped a high bounding ball that hopped over Steinfeldt's head into left field. With two outs, McIntyre broke for third on contact and scored easily. Cobb tried to stretch his hit into a double, but Sheckard retrieved the ball in left field and threw the speedy Cobb out at second, Evers applying the tag.[46]

In the second inning, it began to rain hard. Crawford ignored the wet surface and made a sensational catch when Tinker hit a ball deep toward the gap in left center field. Crawford, running at full tilt, lunged at the last instant and caught the ball with his bare hand.[47] A short pause before the Cubs came to bat in the third inning allowed the Detroit groundskeepers to scatter large amounts of sawdust around the plate and the pitcher's mound to firm up some of the mud. The first hitter, Jimmy Sheckard, pulled a pitch down the first-base line. First baseman Claude Rossman got his glove on the ball, but he could not keep it from going into the outfield. Sheckard sprinted to second base with his second double of the day. Then Evers laid down a sacrifice bunt on the third-base line. Schaefer charged the ball, slipped in the mud, and fell flat; Evers reached first, and Sheckard went to third base. Schulte singled to right field, scoring Sheckard with the Cubs' first run while Evers held at second base on Schulte's hit. Chance attempted to sacrifice bunt, but he hit the ball too hard back to the pitcher Killian, who forced Evers out at third base. But Schulte crossed the plate when Steinfeldt rapped a single to left, giving the Cubs a 2–1 advantage. Chance reached third and Steinfeldt went to second when third baseman Schaefer muffed the throw in from McIntyre.

After Killian walked Hofman to load the bases with only one out, Tiger manager Hughie Jennings replaced Killian with Ed Summers. The six-foot, two-inch right-hander had been impressive in his first year in the majors. Summers led the Tigers' pitching staff with 24 victories (12 losses), most innings pitched (301) and the lowest earned run average (1.64). Tinker, the first to face Summers, tapped a ball to second baseman Red Downs, who flipped to shortstop O'Leary, covering second to force Hofman for the second out. But Chance scored on the play and Steinfeldt went to third. Tinker stole second base with Kling at bat; Kling then hit a grounder to Schaefer at third. Already having fallen down fielding a bunt and muffing a throw from the outfield, the tough inning continued for Schaefer, who misplayed Kling's ground ball, allowing Kling to reach first, Tinker third, and Steinfeldt to score the fourth run of the inning. Tinker and Kling unsuccessfully attempted a double steal. Catcher Schmidt threw through to second baseman Downs, who ran Kling back toward first base, tossing the ball to Rossman, who applied the tag before Tinker could cross the plate.[48]

Reulbach blanked the Tigers for the next four innings, thanks to a sparkling play by Tinker and Chance on a ball hit by Red Downs in the third inning. Tinker made a one-hand backhanded stop in the hole at deep short, planted his feet in the mud, and threw an arrow to Chance. The low throw skipped through the mud at first, but Chance scooped the ball and mud, on the short hop for the put out. Sheckard made his third consecutive hit, a single in the fourth inning, but Summers shutout the Cubs for the next three innings.[49]

At the end of six innings, the score remained Cubs 4, Tigers 1. When Steinfeldt's sacrifice fly scored Evers with another Cubs' run in the seventh inning, Detroit fans started to get nervous. But the Tigers rallied in the bottomed of the seventh to score three runs on four hits (singles by Cobb, Rossman, Summers, and a double by Downs) to chase Reulbach from the game. Overall put out the fire without any further damage, but as the eighth inning began, the Tigers trailed by only a single run, 5 to 4. Tinker singled to right field to begin the eighth and advanced to second on alert baserunning when Cobb lobbed his throw to the infield. Tinker made third base on Kling's sacrifice bunt, but he remained there as Overall struck out and Sheckard failed to get his fourth consecutive hit, grounding out to O'Leary at shortstop.[50]

Overall walked Crawford to begin the Tiger eighth, and, with a slim one-run lead, Chance replaced Overall with Brown, depending on his best pitcher to again save the day. But this day the Tigers would not be denied. Brown made a wild pitch, sending Crawford to second, and a throwing error to Chance on Cobb's hit back to the mound, placing Tiger runners on first and third with no one out. Crawford scored the tying run on a Rossman single to center field. When Hofman threw the ball to Evers at second, Cobb aggressively ran for third base. Evers, surprised, rushed and threw wildly passed Steinfeldt at third, and Cobb scored Detroit's go-ahead run. "Thinking that would put the Cubs down and out, the crowd (small and wet) went mad with glee and hats were thrown ruthlessly into the soaked air, while umbrellas were wrecked with greatest abandon. What mattered a little more soaking if the Tigers really were to win a game in a world's series after five futile efforts in a previous season (one tie game)."[51]

The crowd's delight continued into the ninth when Evers grounded out to Rossman unassisted, to begin the inning. Summers, the rookie phenomenon, needed only two more outs for a Tiger victory. But Schulte beat out an infield single deep in the hole between shortstop and third, and Chance and Steinfeldt lined singles to center and left field, loading the bases. After fouling off two pitches and letting three pitches out of the strike zone go by, Hofman silenced the Detroit crowd with a sharp single to left, scoring Schulte with the tying run and Chance with the go-ahead. Steinfeldt went to third and then scored when Tinker bunted safely. Hofman and Tinker worked a double steal, reaching third and second, and both scored on Kling's single to center field. Summers retired Brown and Sheckard for the final two outs, but not before the Cubs tallied five runs to take a commanding 10–6 lead. Brown gave up a walk and a single in the bottom of the ninth, but he struck out Davy Jones, a pinch hitter for Summers; retired Crawford on a fly ball to Hofman in center; and ended the game on a ground out by Ty Cobb.[52]

"ONE," announced the *Chicago Tribune* as the newspaper began the Cubs' World Series victory count. Frank Gries, a twenty-one-year-old Cubs fan, took to the streets of Chicago (Dearborn) to cheer the Cubs' first-game victory. A policeman thought Gries "was making too much noise on a public street and ordered him to stop." Gries "then shouted to a crowd of his friends who were with him that the Cubs had won, and he was going to cheer for them all he pleased." Promptly arrested, the boisterous Gries was escorted to the Central Police Station.[53]

Both teams and the three members of the National Commission boarded a special, nineteen-sleeper-car train Saturday evening for Chicago for games two and three on Sunday and Monday. Early Sunday morning, Chicago Police Chief Shippy dispatched an extra squad to maintain order among the throng of fans gathering outside West Side Park to purchase tickets for game two. But the gathering masses only made themselves as comfortable as they could and waited for the ticket windows to open.

Experienced and foxy fans brought shoe boxes filled with edibles and munched and smoked during the wait for the opening of the gates. Others secured sandwiches, hot and cold frankfurters, cakes, pies, and liquid refreshments from the vendors who sidled through the lines. Comfort on the sidewalks and ground was obtained by improvising beds after a fashion with newspapers and overcoats. The waiting fans amused themselves by gazing wistfully at the high board fences, gulping down incongruous foods, reading the account of the slugging victory in Detroit, and surmising the outcome of the series.

When the box offices were opened the mass of human beings surged frantically towards the gates. Pea green fedoras, various colored derbys, and other forms of headgear were trampled under feet, but throughout the jamming the disposition of the fans remained intact. When the box offices announced that no more seats could be obtained the hundreds of disappointed waiters threatened, pleaded, and coaxed for admission. Then began an excited hunt for points of vantage outside the grounds. Telegraph poles, porches of neighboring buildings, improvised seats on roofs and housetops served as a refuge for the disappointed ones.

Crowd civility ended when the gates were closed. "Long before the game heated verbal encounters cropped out between the unfortunate fans on the outside and their brothers in the stands. The latter jeered, scoffed, and hurled jests at the furious crowds on the sidewalks, and added to their humiliation by burying them under a shower of cigarette stumps, bottles, and newspapers." Denied tickets and abused by ticket holding fans, the final insult occurred when the outside crowd "learned there were several thousand seats unoccupied and the cheaper seats at that."[54]

Unlike the first game's slugging festival, game two developed into a pitcher's duel. After seven scoreless innings, Overall had surrendered only three hits to the Tigers. "Wild Bill" Donovan, the Tigers pitcher, performed even better, throwing a no-hitter for five innings. Overall broke up the no-hitter in the sixth with a single to center field, but he was erased when Sheckard hit into a double play, second baseman Downs to O'Leary to Rossman.[55]

Overall continued his mastery in the eighth inning, retiring the Tigers in order. It looked like only a single run would be needed for the victory, and Tinker provided two in the bottom of the eighth when, with one out and after an infield single by Hofman, he caught a Donovan fast ball, a little late, but square, and drove the ball high over the head of Cobb into the right-field bleachers for a two-run home run. "Instantly the crowd found the voice which had been kept to perfunctory tones by the brilliancy of the pitched battle it was watching. As the ball disappeared outside the enclosure to be snapped up by some lucky souvenir hunter, a terrific paroxysm of yelling shattered the air for miles around and continued unabated while

The largest Cub (6'2" and 214 lbs.), pitcher Orval Overall had a season pitching record of 15–11 and the team's second-best earned run average of 1.92.

Tinker glided around the bases at leisure, pushing the lanky 'Circus Solly' ahead of him across the plate ... there was a period when the most clamlike rooter lost all control of himself and turned loose into the air everything that was not nailed down or buttoned or sewed tight to something else." Cub hitters were not finished: Kling doubled; Sheckard singled, scoring Kling; Evers bunted for a hit; and Schulte tripled, scoring Sheckard and Evers. Schulte scored the final run of the inning when Donovan threw a wild pitch. Overall needed only three outs for the shut-out win, but the Tigers mounted a brief rally in the top of the ninth to avoid the shutout, 6 to 1. Davy Jones, batting for O'Leary, received a base on balls, advanced to second on a ground out, and scored Detroit's only run of the game when Cobb singled to center field. Rossman ended the game, hitting a grounder over second base. Tinker grabbed the ball, touched second, and threw to Chance at first for the game-ending double play.[56]

"TWO," continued the victory count. Chicago fans looked forward to a repeat of the previous year's four-game sweep of the Tigers. If they were bettors, they also had to look out for plain-clothes detectives scattered throughout the crowd. Arrests were made during game two. The *Chicago Tribune* warned their readers:

> DETECTIVES TAKE BETTORS AT GAME. Speculative Fans Exchange Seats in Grand Stand for Place in Cell. It was not generally known that, acting under orders from the National Commission, which is trying to stamp out betting on baseball results, a score of plain clothes men were scattered through grand stand and bleachers looking for the speculatively inclined.
>
> In one of the upper boxes a Detroit enthusiast was being twitted with offers to bet from a party in a neighboring section and finally agreed to accept a $5 wager. As he walked toward the box with a $5 bill in his hand he was seized by two of the plain clothes gentry. When he showed a disposition to argue, four regular policemen swept down on the scene and the enthusiastic Detroiter was removed from the grounds....
>
> In one of the lower boxes just north of the press stand a tall young fellow in a light suit began to flash some money which said the Cubs would be the next world's champions. The young man and his money were soon reposing in Lincoln street, assisted on their way by the lynx eyed guardians of the welfare of the national game.[57]

As detectives monitored fan behavior, a motion-picture camera crew recorded the players' performance on film for the first time in World Series history.[58]

Manager Jennings made a lineup change for game three. Second baseman Red Downs watched the game from the bench. Germany Schaefer moved back to his more natural position at second base and veteran Bill Coughlin returned to third base. The manager's move may have helped as

Detroit disappointed Chicago partisans on Monday, October 12, Columbus Day, winning their first-ever World Series game, 8 to 3. There would be no sweep this year. Pfiester gave up a run to Detroit in the first inning when Cobb singled O'Leary home from second base, but he shut down the Tigers for the next three innings, allowing only one more hit. Detroit's George Mullin, a twenty-eight-year-old portly right-hander, pitched superbly. The Cubs managed to score three unearned runs in the fourth inning to take the lead, 3 to 1, but through no fault of Mullin's, as his teammates made three throwing errors in that inning. Detroit scored five times against Pfiester in the sixth to recapture the lead, 6 to 3, and added two more runs in the eighth to put the game away. Mullin blanked the Cubs for the final five innings. Detroit's superstar, Ty Cobb, finally came into his own with three singles and a double in five at bats and two stolen bases. He provided the hitting sparks that ignited the Tigers' run scoring first, sixth, and eighth innings.[59]

The special train, chartered by the National Commission, departed Chicago at eleven o'clock Monday evening and returned the World Series' warriors to Detroit for games four and five. "President Murphy did not accompany the Cubs to Detroit.... He went home directly after the game at the orders of his doctor who told him he was close to an attack of pneumonia."[60]

Two words sum up game four: "Mighty Mordecai." After winning the last game of the season against Pittsburgh and the replayed game against the Giants to win the National League pennant, the Cubs' ace had 29 wins and only 9 losses, with 312 innings pitched and a minuscule 1.47 earned run average. Now, he capped off his stellar year by pitching a World Series shutout, 3 to 0, against the Tigers, to gain a commanding three-games-to-one advantage. Brown did not walk a single batter (one Tiger was hit by a pitch) and allowed only four Detroit hits, two by shortstop Charley O'Leary and two by center fielder Sam Crawford. He even handcuffed the great Ty Cobb. In the last three innings, Brown was perfect, retiring the final nine Tiger hitters in a row. Only once did Detroit come even close to scoring. In the fourth inning, O'Leary and Crawford hit back-to-back singles, placing Tigers on first and second. Detroit's best hitter, Cobb, came to the plate. He tried to bunt for a hit, placing the ball down the third-base line, but Brown pounced on the ball and threw a bullet to Steinfeldt at third. O'Leary slid into the bag in a cloud of dust just as the ball reached Steinfeldt. Umpire Bill Klem signaled his razor-thin decision, out. Still, Tigers stood on second and first with only one out. But then, catcher Kling and shortstop Tinker executed a beautiful pick-off play. As Crawford took his lead off second base with Rossman at bat, Tinker stealthily moved behind the runner. Kling called for a Brown fastball wide of the plate, moved toward the pitch, and rifled a throw to Tinker, who blocked the base with his leg and made a sweeping tag on Crawford for the second out. Brown ended the threat, and the inning, by striking out Rossman.[61]

Summers lost his second game of the Series when the Cubs tallied two runs in the third. Schulte walked, stole second base, and scored when Steinfeldt singled. A walk to Chance moved Steinfeldt to second, and Hofman brought him home with a single to left field. The Cubs added a final insurance run in the ninth inning, but Brown needed no such insurance.

Back in Chicago, the *Tribune* added to the victory count, "THREE," and Murphy rose from his sickbed to address a growing ticket scandal. Thousands of seats had remained vacant during both World Series games in Chicago while fans were told tickets were no longer available. Charges of collusion between ticket scalpers and Cub officials ran rampant. Murphy issued a feeble and insufficient explanation, but the club president did offer to send a personal check to the National Commission for all unsold seats for the two games. That solved the problem of the players receiving less money from ticket sales, but it did nothing to soothe the growing anger of disappointed fans. Murphy telephoned the *Tribune* from his home and read his statement, "Any major league club owner who would take advantage of a world's series to extort money from regular patrons by collusion with scalpers would be not only unworthy to associate with decent people but a disgrace to the baseball profession as well." The *Tribune* reported Murphy's explanation: "tickets had been reserved in advance by many persons who had been regular patrons throughout the season and who would have felt insulted had their reservations not been honored without the customary certified check. Many of these either through lack of knowledge of where to call for their tickets or for other reasons, did not call, and the club was left with them on its hands and without the money."[62]

Back in Detroit, on Wednesday, October 14, the Cubs needed only one more win to defeat the Tigers and continue their championship reign. In a repeat of game two, pitchers Overall and Donovan faced each other. Unlike game two, the Cubs scored a run in the first inning against Donovan; after one out, Evers and Schulte singled, and Evers scored on a single to center field by Frank Chance. The Cubs added another run in the fifth on a pair of walks, to Kling and Sheckard, and a double by Evers, Kling scoring; but two runs were all the Cubs managed to collect against Donovan.[63]

On top of his game, Overall struck out ten Tigers, including four in the first inning. After O'Leary and Cobb struck out, Claude Rossman fouled off two pitches from Overall, then swung and missed a "fast drop" pitch.

The ball hit the ground, eluded catcher Kling, and rolled to the stands behind the plate, allowing Rossman to reach first base. The next hitter, Germany Schaefer, took three swings without connecting for the final out and the fourth strikeout of the inning.[64]

The Tigers mounted a mild threat in the fifth inning. Bill Coughlin's ground ball to third took a bad hop away from Steinfeldt for a single to begin the inning. After Donovan struck out, McIntyre pulled a line drive between Chance and the first-base bag that shot into the crowd for a ground-rule double. O'Leary lifted a fly ball to Hofman in shallow center field, too shallow for Coughlin to attempt to tag and score. Then hard-hitting Sam Crawford came to bat with runners still on second and third and two outs. Crawford had singled in the first inning between Overall's four strike outs, but he did not connect this time. Instead, Crawford became another strikeout victim, swinging and missing the third strike. Coughlin's bad-hop single in the fifth was the last Tiger hit of the day, and only one runner, Cobb with a walk in the sixth, reached first base during the last four innings. Overall was perfect for the last three innings, retiring nine Tigers in a row to win his second World Series game, 2 to 0.[65]

"FOUR." The Cubs were champions again. "Jennings' men trotted over to the Cub bench and congratulated Chance and his men on their triumph and the two time world champions hurried away to their camp to dodge the wildly enthusiastic fans who tried to head them off and make them a feature of a parade down town."[66] No bottles or punches were thrown at the Cubs' players in Detroit.

Chicago Tribune reporter I. E. Sanborn wrote,

> What those grass clad modest young warriors have accomplished will be remembered longer than any of them live. Not in the memory of this generation of fans has any team ever won its honors with greater credit than that which belongs to Frank Chance's warriors. Not in a thousand years has a team been compelled to fight as hard for its titles as has the Chicago team, which won the National League pennant twice inside of five days under the most trying circumstances. But once assured of the National League's banner, the rest proved comparatively easy....
>
> That stonewall infield has never been better, and Chance, Evers, Tinker, and Steinfeldt have written their names above those of Anson, Pfeffer, Williamson, and Burns, Chicago's original and long famous stonewall defenders. That lightening fast outfield, Schulte, Hofman, and Sheckard, has nothing to ask or learn from the fastest that ever won three pennants before. And in the batteries there is nothing in stonewall history in Chicago or elsewhere to equal the gameness and cunning that have been exhibited by those Cub twirlers who have borne the severest burdens of the battle, Brown, Overall, and Reulbach, with the help of John Kling and Patsy Moran." Commenting directly on the

8. *Triumphs and Scandal* 199

World Series, Sanborn continued, "After the terrific battles for the two major league pennants the world's series was only a gentle skirmish by comparison, and probably will be known in history as the anti-climax series."[67]

Back in Chicago, the ticket scandal intensified. On Friday, October 16, Chicago citizens, represented by William F. Carns, demanded Murphy be held accountable for his implausible explanation with a letter published in *The Tribune* column "Voice Of The Fans." Carns wrote:

> After a great deal of discussion during the last few days in regard to the tickets sold for the world's series between the Chicago and Detroit baseball teams, I have been requested to dictate a letter to Mr. Murphy of the local club, of which the following is a copy: Dear Sir: This morning's "Tribune" ... states that you feel much grieved following the criticisms of the method of distributing tickets for the world's series, and the insinuations that officials or employees must have been in collusion with scalpers, etc.
>
> ...you are credited with a statement that you had reserved tickets in advance for a great many of the regular patrons. Now, Mr. Murphy, in justice to yourself, as well as to your club and the people of the city of Chicago who have made the Chicago National League team possible, I want to ask you three questions which I think are fair, and I might add, that this letter is written by request of something like twenty-five people who will be interested in your reply: First-Inasmuch as you reserved seats for the regular patrons, please give us the names, that the same may be verified. Second-Why were hundreds of people forced to stand in line one morning on Wabash avenue from about 7 o'clock until noon, before they received information that tickets would not be placed on sale? Third-Why was the same performance repeated next morning at the west side park? Enclosed please find self-addressed, stamped envelope for reply. I believe "The Tribune" is big enough and broad enough to handle a matter of this kind from the public standpoint and not from the standpoint of an organization seemingly that has acted contrary to public policy in the disposition of the sale of seats for the ball games recently held in Chicago.[68]

The same day the fans' letter was published, Cub officials offered more excuses for the ticket mess as Murphy remained at home, "reported to be recovering slowly from a threatened attack of pneumonia and to be suffering from a high fever." In Murphy's absence at Cubs' headquarters in the Corn Exchange Bank Building, an official "stated that the club was being unjustly blamed for the tangle over reserved seats. He stated that 100 seats were turned back by a Detroit newspaper which had arranged for a special train for Sunday's game and ordered 200 seats reserved, but on arriving at the park took only 100 of the tickets ordered. Another hundred was held for President Murphy, for his own personal use, and these were turned back too late to be disposed of because the demand for reserved seats was practically over an hour before the game started last Sunday."[69]

The next day, Murphy submitted a rambling, repetitive, and evasive letter for publication in *The Tribune*. He denied any responsibility for the ticket fiasco and branded all charges as "absurd," ignored the direct questions asked by the fans, and defensively claimed there was no evidence to support any allegations of wrongdoing. Murphy wrote:

> Invidious persons seem to be busily engaged in an attempt to dim the luster of the artistic triumph of the Cubs by making absurd charges against the management. Of course, it is too bad that paid agents of ticket speculators, or scalpers, as they are better known, had to stand in line for a long time and then go away empty handed. The same is true of disgruntled seekers after courtesies to the west side park during the regular National League championship season. In addition to these two classes were the absolutely innocent persons, who now have no ulterior motives, who tried to get tickets and failed.
>
> To all these classes the management tenders its most abject apology over any dissatisfaction about seats. Many seem to think that scalpers have stirred up all this agitation because the west side club has always fought them bitterly.... As I was out of the city I am not familiar with all that transpired regarding tickets. I am most unwilling, however, to convict loyal employees of the club of collusion with scalpers on mere rumors and without proof. No baseball club has ever fought scalpers any harder than we have in the past, or will in the future. Many general charges have been made and reiterated against the management, but as yet no proof has been adduced. Mysterious persons have whispered into the ears of Chicago and Detroit players, making serious charges against ticket sellers, which as yet remain unproved.
>
> The valiant battle of the Cubs for the baseball honor and glory came to an agreeable end in the National League last Thursday in New York, and precious little time was allowed us by the national commission to get ready many necessary details before we entered the world's series, in which we triumphed again, as in 1907.
>
> We deplore the fact that all were not taken care of satisfactorily, because our great team has been handsomely patronized, and that support is heartily appreciated, both by the management and by the ball players. Any mistakes that were made were honest ones, I am sure, and due largely to the small space of time allotted to us to get ready to supply the wants of the fans.
>
> I said the other day that any major league club owner who would take advantage of a world's series to extort money from the public by collusion with scalpers would be a disgrace to the baseball business, and I have not changed my mind upon that subject. We were simply deluged with letters containing checks last Friday and Saturday, and these will be returned as soon as our office force can open the envelopes and attend to the clerical work involved. Honest criticism of our hurried business methods is all right, but abuse from persons having an ulterior motive to carry out, is unfair and not warranted by the facts. Rome was not built in a day, and it takes time even in Chicago to get ready for a world's series.[70]

The three-member National Commission received petitions requesting an investigation into the matter and claimed they would consider the request. American League president Ban Johnson said, "he would be in favor of barring permanently from baseball any person found guilty of dealing with scalpers during the series, but it would require direct evidence of such dealing to justify action, and as yet nothing definite in the way of information had been furnished so far as he knew."[71] Nothing ever came of the investigation, and the issue just faded away.

The Cubs arrived back in Chicago early Thursday morning, October 15, and by afternoon the players began to congregate at the Cubs' headquarters in the Corn Exchange Bank Building. They came to collect "their final salary checks of the season as (it was) the 15th and their contracts expired."[72]

On Friday, the players gathered at President Murphy's office to collect their World Series checks. President Murphy, suffering a fever and ticketitis, was not present. Chance served as host. The team voted to divide the World Series pie into twenty-one slices, and agreed, unanimously, to include "Treasurer Williams for his efforts to ameliorate the rigors of travel during the season ... on the same basis as a regular player." Nineteen players and Williams received full shares, fourteen hundred dollars. One share was split three ways between trainer A. Bert Semmens, Blaine "Kid" Durbin, and the late-season addition Floyd Kroh. Frank Chance personally donated a hundred dollars to the divided share to make it easier to divide by three, five hundred dollars apiece. The other nineteen players received full shares.[73]

Baseball rules stipulated that players receive a percentage of gate receipts from only the first four games of the World Series. All income from any World Series games after the first four was divided between the owners of the two teams and the National Commission. This year's game-five revenue was not part of the fourteen-hundred-dollar World Series share received by each of the Cub players, but it did include revenue from the few exhibition games the Cubs played during the regular season.[74]

As a means to increase their baseball income, the Cubs and Tigers played an exhibition game on Sunday, October 18, at West Side Park. All gate receipts were split among the players of the two teams. Cubs management donated use of the field, and Hank O'Day volunteered to umpire. A baseball field event competition was held prior to the game. Ty Cobb, the winner of the bunt and sprint-to-first-base event (3⅕ seconds), also won the 100-yard dash (10⅖ seconds), and the circling-the-bases contest (13⅞ seconds). Overall won the fungo-hitting-for-distance event (273 feet), and Hofman won the distance throwing competition (338 feet). Detroit won the post–World Series game, 7 to 3.[75]

The baseball year finally ended for the Cubs and Tigers on Tuesday, October 20, in Terre Haute, Indiana. Mr. L.D. Smith, president of the Terre Haute Hottentots' Central League baseball team, arranged for the Cubs and Tigers to play one more game as part of the ceremonies honoring Indiana's favorite son, Mordecai Brown. "Mordecai Brown will pitch for the Cubs and there will be a big demonstration in his honor. A local committee has arranged the reception and all the mines in the vicinity will close down for the day. Rosedale, Brown's home town, will send a special train with 1,000 rooters."[76]

Indiana citizens turned out in droves. According to the *Terre Haute Star*, over 10,000 people showed up to honor Indiana's native son. A chest of silver, purchased with contributions from admirers, was presented to Brown by Terre Haute Mayor James Lyons, prior to the game. Brown pitched six innings and, to the delight of his fans, both the Cubs and Tigers returned to their World Series form — Cubs 7, Tigers 1.[77]

Chapter Notes

Introduction

1. John Betts, "Sporting Journalism in Nineteenth-Century America," *American Quarterly* 5, no. 1 (Spring 1953): 39–56.
2. "Meet the Sportswriters," www.baseball-fever.com.
3. Ibid.
4. David L. Porter, ed., *Biographical Dictionary of American Sports: 1989–1992 Supplement for Baseball, Football, Basketball, and Other Sports* (Westport, CT: Greenwood, 1992), 341–42.
5. "Charles Dryden Dies; Once Sports Writer," *New York Times*, February 13, 1931.
6. Ibid.

Chapter 1

1. *Chicago Tribune*, March 5, 1908.
2. *The Baseball Encyclopedia*, ed. Jeanine Bucek, 10th ed. (New York: Macmillan, 1996).
3. *Chicago Tribune*, March 4, 1908.
4. Ibid.
5. *Chicago Tribune*, March 5, 1908.
6. *Chicago Tribune*, March 6, 1908.
7. Ibid.
8. Ibid.
9. *Chicago Tribune*, March 8, 1908.
10. Ibid.
11. *Chicago Tribune*, March 7, 1908.
12. Ibid.
13. *Chicago Tribune*, March 10, 1908.
14. *Chicago Tribune*, March 11, 1908.
15. *Chicago Tribune*, March 12, 1908.
16. *Chicago Tribune*, March 14, 1908.
17. *Chicago Tribune*, March 15, 1908.
18. Ibid.
19. *Chicago Tribune*, March 16, 1908.
20. *Chicago Tribune*, March 17, 1908.
21. *Chicago Tribune*, March 18, 1908.
22. *Chicago Tribune*, March 19, 1908.
23. Ibid.
24. *Chicago Tribune*, March 20, 1908
25. Ibid.
26. *Chicago Tribune*, March 21, 1908.
27. *Chicago Tribune*, March 22, 1908
28. *Chicago Tribune*, March 23, 1908.
29. *Chicago Tribune*, March 24, 1908.
30. *Chicago Tribune*, March 25, 1908.
31. *Chicago Tribune*, March 26, 1908.
32. *The Baseball Encyclopedia*, ed. Jeanine Bucek, 10th ed. (New York: Macmillan, 1996).
33. *Chicago Tribune*, March 26, 1908.
34. Ibid.
35. Ibid.
36. *Chicago Tribune*, March 27, 1908.
37. Ibid.
38. *The Baseball Encyclopedia*, ed. Jeanine Bucek, 10th ed. (New York: Macmillan, 1996).
39. *Chicago Tribune*, March 27, 1908.
40. *Chicago Tribune*, March 28, 1908.
41. *Chicago Tribune*, March 29, 1908.
42. *Chicago Tribune*, March 30, 1908.
43. *Chicago Tribune*, March 31, 1908.
44. Ibid.
45. *Chicago Tribune*, April 1, 1908.
46. Ibid.
47. *Chicago Tribune*, April 2, 1908.
48. *Chicago Tribune*, April 3, 1908.
49. Ibid.
50. *Chicago Tribune*, April 4, 1908.
51. *Chicago Tribune*, April 5, 1908.
52. Ibid.
53. *Chicago Tribune*, April 6, 1908.
54. Ibid.
55. Ibid.
56. Ibid.
57. Ibid.

58. *Chicago Tribune*, April 7, 1908.
59. Ibid.
60. *Chicago Tribune*, April 8, 1908.
61. *Chicago Tribune*, April 9, 1908.
62. *Chicago Tribune*, April 10, 1908.
63. Ibid.
64. Ibid.
65. *Chicago Tribune*, April 12, 1908.
66. *Chicago Tribune*, April 13, 1908.
67. *Chicago Tribune*, April 14, 1908.
68. *The Baseball Encyclopedia*, ed. Jeanine Bucek, 10th ed. (New York: Macmillan, 1996).
69. *Chicago Tribune*, April 14, 1908.
70. Ibid.

Chapter 2

1. *Chicago Tribune*, April 15, 1908.
2. Ibid.
3. Ibid.
4. Ibid.
5. Stephen A. Riess, *Touching Base: Professional Baseball and American Culture in the Progressive Era* (Westport, CT: Greenwood, 1980), 54.
6. Alfred H. Spink, *The National Game*, 2nd ed. (Carbondale: Southern Illinois University Press, 2000), 296.
7. *Chicago Tribune*, April 15, 1908.
8. *The Baseball Encyclopedia*, ed. Jeanine Bucek, 10th ed. (New York: Macmillan, 1996).
9. Ibid.
10. *Chicago Tribune*, April 15, 1908.
11. Ibid.
12. Ibid.
13. Ibid.
14. *Chicago Tribune*, April 16, 1908.
15. Ibid.
16. Ibid.
17. Ibid.
18. *Chicago Tribune*, April 17, 1908.
19. Ibid.
20. *Chicago Tribune*, April 18, 1908.
21. Ibid.
22. Ibid.
23. Ibid.
24. Ibid.
25. Ibid.
26. *Chicago Tribune*, April 19, 1908.
27. Ibid.
28. *Chicago Tribune*, April 20, 1908.
29. Ibid.
30. Ibid.
31. *Chicago Tribune*, April 21, 1908.
32. Ibid.
33. *Chicago Tribune*, April 22, 1908.
34. Ibid.
35. *Chicago Tribune*, April 21, 1908.
36. *Chicago Tribune*, April 22, 1908.
37. Ibid.
38. *Chicago Tribune*, April 23, 1908.
39. Ibid.
40. Ibid.
41. Ibid.
42. *Chicago Tribune*, April 24, 1908.
43. Ibid.
44. Ibid.
45. Ibid.
46. *Chicago Tribune*, April 25, 1908.
47. *Chicago Tribune*, April 26, 1908.
48. Ibid.
49. Ibid.
50. Ibid.
51. Ibid.
52. Ibid.
53. *Chicago Tribune*, April 27, 1908.
54. *Chicago Tribune*, April 28, 1908.
55. *Chicago Tribune*, April 27, 1908.
56. *Chicago Tribune*, April 29, 1908.
57. *Chicago Tribune*, April 30, 1908.
58. Ibid.
59. Ibid.
60. Ibid.
61. *Chicago Tribune*, May 1, 1908.
62. Ibid.

Chapter 3

1. *Chicago Tribune*, May 2, 1908.
2. Ibid.
3. Ibid.
4. *Chicago Tribune*, May 3, 1908.
5. Ibid.
6. Ibid.
7. *Chicago Tribune*, May 4, 1908.
8. Ibid.
9. Ibid.
10. *Chicago Tribune*, May 5, 1908.
11. Ibid.
12. *Chicago Tribune*, May 6, 1908.
13. *Chicago Tribune*, May 7, 1908.
14. Ibid.
15. Ibid.
16. *The Baseball Encyclopedia*, ed. Jeanine Bucek, 10th ed. (New York: Macmillan, 1996).
17. *Chicago Tribune*, May 7, 1908.
18. *Chicago Tribune*, May 8, 1908.
19. Ibid.
20. Ibid.

21. Ibid.
22. *Chicago Tribune*, May 9, 1908.
23. *Chicago Tribune*, May 8, 1908.
24. *Chicago Tribune*, May 10, 1908.
25. Ibid.
26. *Chicago Tribune*, May 11, 1908.
27. Ibid.
28. Ibid.
29. Ibid.
30. Ibid.
31. Ibid.
32. *Chicago Tribune*, May 12, 1908.
33. Ibid.
34. *Chicago Tribune*, May 13, 1908.
35. Ibid.
36. Ibid.
37. *Chicago Tribune*, May 14, 1908.
38. *The Baseball Encyclopedia*, ed. Jeanine Bucek, 10th ed. (New York: Macmillan, 1996).
39. *Chicago Tribune,* May 14, 1908.
40. *Chicago Tribune*, May 15, 1908.
41. *Chicago Tribune*, May 16, 1908.
42. *Chicago Tribune*, May 17, 1908.
43. Ibid.
44. Ibid.
45. Ibid.
46. Ibid.
47. Ibid.
48. Ibid.
49. Ibid.
50. *Chicago Tribune*, May 18, 1908.
51. *Chicago Tribune*, May 19, 1908.
52. *Chicago Tribune*, May 21, 1908.
53. Stephen A. Riess, *Touching Base: Professional Baseball and American Culture in the Progressive Era* (Westport, CT: Greenwood, 1980).
54. Ibid.
55. *Chicago Tribune*, May 21, 1908.
56. Ibid.
57. Ibid.
58. Ibid.
59. Ibid.
60. *Chicago Tribune*, May 22, 1908.
61. Ibid.
62. Ibid.
63. Ibid.
64. Ibid.
65. *Chicago Tribune*, May 23, 1908.
66. *Chicago Tribune*, May 24, 1908.
67. Ibid.
68. Chicago Tribune May 25, 1908.
69. David W. Anderson, *More Than Merkle: A History of the Best and Most Exciting Baseball Season in Human History* (Lincoln: University of Nebraska Press, 2000).
70. *Chicago Tribune*, May 25, 1908.
71. Ibid.
72. Ibid
73. Ibid.
74. *Chicago Tribune*, May 26, 1908.
75. Ibid.
76. Ibid.
77. Ibid.
78. *Chicago Tribune*, May 27, 1908.
79. *Chicago Tribune*, May 28, 1908.
80. Ibid.
81. Ibid.
82. *Chicago Tribune*, May 29, 1908.
83. Ibid.
84. *Chicago Tribune*, May 30, 1908.
85. Ibid.
86. Ibid.
87. *Chicago Tribune*, May 31, 1908.
88. Ibid.
89. Ibid.

Chapter 4

1. *Chicago Tribune*, June 1, 1908.
2. Ibid.
3. Ibid.
4. Ibid.
5. Ibid.
6. *Sporting Life*, August 1, 1908.
7. *Chicago Tribune*, June 2, 1908.
8. Ibid.
9. Ibid.
10. *Chicago Tribune*, June 3, 1908.
11. Ibid.
12. Ibid.
13. *Chicago Tribune*, June 4, 1908.
14. Ibid.
15. *Chicago Tribune*, June 5, 1908.
16. Ibid.
17. *Chicago Tribune*, June 6, 1908.
18. *Chicago Tribune*, June 7, 1908.
19. *Chicago Tribune*, June 9, 1908.
20. *Chicago Tribune*, June 7, 1908.
21. Ibid.
22. Ibid.
23. *Chicago Tribune*, June 9, 1908.
24. Ibid.
25. Ibid.
26. *Chicago Tribune*, June 10, 1908.
27. *Chicago Tribune*, June 11, 1908.
28. *Chicago Tribune*, June, 12, 1908.
29. Ibid.
30. Ibid.
31. *Chicago Tribune*, June 13, 1908.
32. Ibid.
33. Ibid.

34. *Chicago Tribune,* June 14, 1908.
35. Ibid.
36. Ibid.
37. *Chicago Tribune,* June 15, 1908.
38. Ibid.
39. *Chicago Tribune,* June 16, 1908.
40. *Chicago Tribune,* June 17, 1908.
41. Ibid.
42. Ibid.
43. Ibid.
44. *Chicago Tribune,* June 18, 1908.
45. *Chicago Tribune,* June 19, 1908.
46. Ibid.
47. Ibid.
48. Ibid.
49. *Chicago Tribune,* June 20, 1908.
50. Ibid.
51. *Chicago Tribune,* June 21, 1908.
52. Ibid.
53. *Chicago Tribune,* June 22, 1908.
54. *Chicago Tribune,* June 23, 1908.
55. Ibid.
56. *Chicago Tribune,* June 25, 1908.
57. Ibid.
58. Ibid.
59. Ibid.
60. Ibid.
61. *Chicago Tribune,* June 26, 1908.
62. *Chicago Tribune,* June 27, 1908.
63. *Chicago Tribune,* June 28, 1908.
64. *Chicago Tribune,* June 29, 1908.
65. *Chicago Tribune,* June 28, 1908.
66. *Chicago Tribune,* June 29, 1908.
67. *Chicago Tribune,* June 30, 1908.
68. *The Baseball Encyclopedia,* ed. Jeanine Bucek, 10th ed. (New York: Macmillan, 1996).
69. *Chicago Tribune,* June 30, 1908.
70. *Chicago Tribune,* July 1, 1908.

Chapter 5

1. *Chicago Tribune,* July 2, 1908.
2. Ibid.
3. Ibid.
4. *Chicago Tribune,* July 3, 1908.
5. Ibid.
6. *Chicago Tribune,* July 4, 1908.
7. Ibid.
8. *Chicago Tribune,* July 5, 1908.
9. Ibid.
10. *Chicago Tribune,* July 6, 1908.
11. Ibid.
12. Ibid.
13. *Chicago Tribune,* July 7, 1908.
14. Ibid.
15. *Baseball: The First 100 Years* (New York: Poretz-Ross, 1969).
16. *Chicago Tribune,* July 8, 1908.
17. *Chicago Tribune,* July 9, 1908.
18. Ibid.
19. Ibid.
20. *Chicago Tribune,* July 10, 1908.
21. Ibid.
22. *Chicago Tribune,* July 11, 1908.
23. Ibid.
24. Ibid.
25. *Chicago Tribune,* July 12, 1908.
26. Ibid.
27. *Chicago Tribune,* July 13, 1908.
28. Ibid.
29. Ibid.
30. Ibid.
31. Ibid.
32. *Chicago Tribune,* July 14, 1908.
33. Ibid.
34. *Chicago Tribune,* July 15, 1908.
35. Ibid.
36. *Chicago Tribune,* July 16, 1908.
37. *Chicago Tribune,* July 17, 1908.
38. Ibid.
39. Ibid.
40. Ibid.
41. Ibid.
42. *Chicago Tribune,* July 18, 1908.
43. Ibid.
44. Ibid.
45. *Chicago Tribune,* July 19, 1908.
46. Ibid.
47. Ibid.
48. *Chicago Tribune,* July 20, 1908.
49. Ibid.
50. *Chicago Tribune,* July 21, 1908.
51. *Chicago Tribune,* July 22, 1908.
52. Ibid.
53. Ibid.
54. Ibid.
55. Ibid.
56. *Chicago Tribune,* July 23, 1908.
57. Ibid.
58. Ibid.
59. Ibid.
60. Ibid.
61. Ibid
62. Ibid.
63. *Chicago Tribune,* July 24, 1908.
64. Ibid.
65. Ibid.
66. Ibid.
67. *Chicago Tribune,* July 25, 1908.
68. Ibid.
69. Ibid.
70. Ibid.

Notes—Chapter 6 207

71. *Chicago Tribune*, July 26, 1908.
72. Ibid.
73. Ibid.
74. Ibid.
75. Ibid.
76. *Chicago Tribune*, July 27, 1908.
77. *Chicago Tribune*, July 28, 1908.
78. Ibid.
79. Ibid.
80. Ibid.
81. Ibid.
82. Ibid.
83. *Chicago Tribune*, July 29, 1908.
84. Ibid.
85. Ibid.
86. Ibid.
87. *Chicago Tribune*, July 30, 1908.
88. *Chicago Tribune*, July 31, 1908.
89. Ibid.
90. *Chicago Tribune*, August 1, 1908.
91. Ibid.
92. Ibid.

Chapter 6

1. *Chicago Tribune*, August 2, 1908.
2. Ibid.
3. *Chicago Tribune*, August 3, 1908.
4. *Chicago Tribune*, August 4, 1908.
5. Ibid.
6. *Chicago Tribune*, August 5, 1908.
7. Ibid.
8. Ibid.
9. Ibid.
10. Ibid.
11. Ibid.
12. Ibid.
13. *Chicago Tribune*, August 6, 1908.
14. Ibid.
15. Ibid.
16. *Chicago Tribune*, August 7, 1908.
17. Ibid.
18. *Chicago Tribune*, August 8, 1908.
19. Ibid.
20. *Chicago Tribune*, August 9, 1908.
21. Ibid.
22. Ibid.
23. Ibid.
24. Ibid.
25. *Chicago Tribune*, August 10, 1908.
26. Ibid.
27. Ibid.
28. *Chicago Tribune*, August 11, 1908.
29. Ibid.
30. Ibid.
31. Ibid.
32. Ibid.
33. *Chicago Tribune*, August 12, 1908.
34. Ibid.
35. Ibid.
36. Ibid.
37. *Chicago Tribune*, August 13, 1908.
38. Ibid.
39. *Chicago Tribune*, August 14, 1908.
40. *Chicago Tribune*, August 15, 1908.
41. *Chicago Tribune*, August 14, 1908.
42. *Chicago Tribune*, August 16, 1908.
43. *Chicago Tribune*, August 17, 1908.
44. *Chicago Tribune*, August 18, 1908.
45. Ibid.
46. *Chicago Tribune*, August 19, 1908.
47. Ibid.
48. Ibid.
49. Ibid.
50. *Chicago Tribune*, August 20, 1908.
51. Ibid.
52. *Chicago Tribune*, August 21, 1908.
53. Ibid.
54. Ibid.
55. *Chicago Tribune*, August 22, 1908.
56. Ibid.
57. Ibid.
58. Ibid.
59. Ibid.
60. Ibid.
61. Ibid.
62. Ibid.
63. *Chicago Tribune*, August 24, 1980.
64. *Chicago Tribune*, August 25, 1908.
65. Ibid.
66. Ibid.
67. Ibid.
68. *Chicago Tribune*, August 26, 1908.
69. Ibid.
70. Ibid.
71. Ibid.
72. *Chicago Tribune*, August 27, 1908.
73. Ibid.
74. Ibid.
75. *Chicago Tribune*, August 28, 1908.
76. Ibid.
77. Ibid.
78. Ibid.
79. Ibid.
80. Ibid.
81. Ibid.
82. *Chicago Tribune*, August 29, 1908.
83. *Chicago Tribune*, August 28, 1908.
84. *Chicago Tribune*, August 29, 1908.
85. Ibid.
86. *Chicago Tribune*, August 30, 1908.
87. Ibid.
88. Ibid.

89. Ibid.
90. Ibid.
91. Ibid.
92. Ibid.
93. *Chicago Tribune*, August 31, 1908.
94. Ibid.
95. Ibid.

Chapter 7

1. *Chicago Tribune*, September 1, 1908.
2. *Chicago Tribune*, September 2, 1908.
3. Ibid.
4. Ibid.
5. *Chicago Tribune*, September 3, 1908.
6. Ibid.
7. *Chicago Tribune*, September 4, 1908.
8. *Chicago Tribune*, September 5, 1908.
9. Ibid.
10. *Chicago Tribune*, September 6, 1908.
11. Ibid.
12. Ibid.
13. Ibid.
14. *Chicago Tribune*, September 7, 1908.
15. Ibid.
16. Ibid.
17. Ibid.
18. Ibid.
19. Ibid.
20. *Chicago Tribune*, September 8, 1908.
21. Ibid.
22. Ibid.
23. *Chicago Tribune*, September 9, 1908.
24. *Chicago Tribune*, September 10, 1908.
25. *Chicago Tribune*, September 11, 1908.
26. Ibid.
27. *Chicago Tribune*, September 12, 1908.
28. Ibid.
29. Ibid.
30. *Chicago Tribune*, September 13, 1908.
31. Ibid.
32. Ibid.
33. Ibid.
34. Ibid.
35. *Chicago Tribune*, September 14, 1908.
36. Ibid.
37. Ibid.
38. *Chicago Tribune*, September 15, 1908.
39. Ibid.
40. *Chicago Tribune*, September 16, 1908.
41. Ibid.
42. Ibid.
43. *Chicago Tribune*, September 17, 1908.
44. Ibid.
45. *Chicago Tribune*, September 18, 1908.
46. Ibid.
47. *Chicago Tribune*, September 19, 1908.
48. Ibid.
49. Ibid.
50. Ibid.
51. *Chicago Tribune*, September 20, 1908.
52. Ibid.
53. *Chicago Tribune*, September 21, 1908.
54. *Chicago Tribune*, September 22, 1908.
55. Ibid.
56. Ibid.
57. Ibid.
58. Ibid.
59. *Chicago Tribune*, September 23, 1908.
60. Ibid.
61. Ibid.
62. Ibid.
63. *Chicago Tribune*, September 24, 1908.
64. Ibid.
65. Ibid.
66. Ibid.
67. Ibid.
68. Ibid.
69. Ibid.
70. Ibid.
71. Ibid.
72. *Chicago Tribune*, September 25, 1908.
73. Ibid.
74. Ibid.
75. Ibid.
76. Ibid.
77. Ibid.
78. Ibid.
79. *Chicago Tribune*, September 26, 1908.
80. David W. Anderson, *More Than Merkle* (Lincoln: University of Nebraska Press, 2000), 100.
81. *Chicago Tribune*, September 26, 1908.
82. Ibid.
83. Ibid.
84. Ibid.
85. *Chicago Tribune*, September 27, 1908.
86. Ibid.
87. Ibid.
88. *Chicago Tribune*, September 28, 1908.
89. *Chicago Tribune*, September 29, 1908.
90. *Chicago Tribune*, September 30, 1908.
91. Ibid.
92. *Chicago Tribune*, October 1, 1908.
93. Ibid.

Chapter 8

1. *Chicago Tribune*, October 2, 1908.
2. Ibid.
3. Ibid.
4. *Chicago Tribune*, October 3, 1908.

Notes — Chapter 8

5. Ibid.
6. *Chicago Tribune*, October 4, 1908.
7. Ibid.
8. *Chicago Tribune*, October 5, 1908.
9. Ibid.
10. Ibid.
11. Ibid.
12. Ibid.
13. Ibid.
14. Ibid.
15. Ibid.
16. Ibid.
17. *Chicago Tribune*, October 7, 1908.
18. Ibid.
19. Ibid.
20. *Chicago Tribune*, October 8, 1908.
21. Ibid.
22. Ibid.
23. Ibid.
24. Cait Murphy, *Crazy '08: How A Cast Of Cranks, Rogues, Boneheads, and Magnates Created the Greatest Year In Baseball History* (New York: HarperCollins, 2007), 261–62.
25. *Chicago Tribune*, October 9, 1908.
26. Ibid.
27. Ibid.
28. Ibid.
29. Ibid.
30. Ibid.
31. Ibid.
32. Ibid.
33. Ibid.
34. Ibid.
35. Ibid.
36. Ibid
37. *Chicago Tribune*, October 10,1908.
38. Philip J. Lowry, *Green Cathedrals* (New York: Walker Publishing, 2006), 83.
39. *Chicago Tribune,* October 10, 1908.
40. Ibid.
41. Ibid.
42. Ibid.
43. *Chicago Tribune*, October 11, 1908.
44. Ibid.
45. Ibid.
46. Ibid.
47. Ibid.
48. Ibid.
49. Ibid.
50. Ibid.
51. Ibid.
52. Ibid.
53. Ibid.
54. *Chicago Tribune*, October 12, 1908.
55. Ibid.
56. Ibid.
57. Ibid.
58. *Chicago Tribune*, October 17, 1908.
59. *Chicago Tribune*, October 13, 1908.
60. Ibid.
61. *Chicago Tribune*, October 14, 1908.
62. Ibid.
63. *Chicago Tribune*, October 15, 1908.
64. Ibid.
65. Ibid.
66. Ibid.
67. Ibid.
68. *Chicago Tribune*, October 16, 1908.
69. Ibid.
70. *Chicago Tribune*, October 17, 1908.
71. Ibid.
72. *Chicago Tribune*, October 16, 1908.
73. *Chicago Tribune*, October 17, 1908.
74. Ibid.
75. *New York Times*, October 19, 1908.
76. *Chicago Tribune*, October 17, 1908.
77. Cindy Thomson and Scott Brown. *Three Finger: The Mordecai Brown Story* (Lincoln: University of Nebraska Press, 2006), 83–84.

Bibliography

Anderson, David W. *More Than Merkle: A History of the Best and Most Exciting Baseball Season in Human History*. Lincoln: University of Nebraska Press, 2000.
Baseball: The First 100 Years. New York: Poretz-Ross, 1969.
Bogen, Gil. *Tinker, Evers, and Chance: A Triple Biography*. Jefferson, NC: McFarland, 2003.
Brown, Warren. *The Chicago Cubs*. Carbondale: Southern Illinois University Press, 2001.
Bucek, Jeanine, ed. *The Baseball Encyclopedia*. 10th ed. New York: Macmillan, 1996.
Chicago Tribune, February 1 to October 31, 1908.
Deford, Frank. *The Old Ballgame*. New York: Atlantic Monthly Press, 2005.
Evers, Johnny, with Hugh Fullerton. *Touching Second*. Chicago: Reilly and Britton, 1910.
Fleming, G. H. *The Unforgettable Season*. New York: Simon and Schuster, 1981.
Gentile, Derek. *The Complete Chicago Cubs*. New York: Black Dog and Leventhal Publishers, 2004.
Hageman, William. *Honus: The Life and Times of a Baseball Hero*. Champaign, IL: Sagamore, 1996.
Liberman, Noah. *Glove Affairs: The Romance, History, and Tradition of the Baseball Glove*. Chicago: Triumph Books, 2003.
Light, Jonathan Fraser. *The Cultural Encyclopedia of Baseball*. Jefferson, NC: McFarland, 1997.
Lowry, Philip J. *Green Cathedrals*. New York: Walker, 2006.
Murphy, Cait. *Crazy '08: How a Cast of Cranks, Rouges, Boneheads, and Magnates Created the Greatest Year in Baseball History*. New York: HarperCollins, 2007.
New York Times, September 21 to October 10, 1908.
Rielly, Edward J. *Baseball: An Encyclopedia of Popular Culture*. Santa Barbara, CA: ABC-CLIO, 2000.
Reiss, Steven A. *Touching Base: Professional Baseball and American Culture in the Progressive Era*. Westport, CT: Greenwood Press, 1980.
Smith, Curt. *Storied Stadiums: Baseball's History Through Its Ballparks*. New York: Carroll & Graf, 2001.
Spink, Alfred H. *The National Game*. Carbondale: Southern Illinois University Press, 2000.
Sporting Life, August 1, 1908.
Sullivan, Dean A., ed. *Early Innings: A Documentary History of Baseball, 1825–1908*. Lincoln: University of Nebraska Press, 1995.
Thomson, Cindy, and Scott Brown. *Three Finger: The Mordecai Brown Story*. Lincoln: University of Nebraska Press, 2006.

Voigt, David Quentin. *American Baseball: From the Gentleman's Sport to the Commissioner System.* Volume I. University Park: Pennsylvania State University Press, 1983.
Weisberger, Bernard A. *When Chicago Ruled Baseball: The Cubs-White Sox World Series of 1906.* New York: HarperCollins, 2006.

Index

Numbers in ***bold italics*** indicate pages with photographs.

Abbaticchio, Ed 53, 143, 145, 178–79
Alperman, Whitey 112, 131
American League 19
Ames, Fred 158–59
Anson, Adrian "Cap" 19, 39, 57, 136
assault: on fans by players 34; on reporters by players 18
Atlanta, GA 19–21
Atlanta Crackers 19
Atlantic City, NJ 79
attendance, ways to increase 54
automobiles, thefts from 102

Baker Bowl 119
ballplayers: assaulting fans 34; families of 8, 10, 13, 25, 31, 79, 98, 108; and fashion 17, 36, 54, 104; and free time 11; income of 200; teasing and practical jokes 15
Baltimore Orioles 13
Barry, John "Shad" 67, 79, 132–33, 136–37, 159
Baseball Writer's Association of America 3, 122
Bates, Johnny 107, 129
Baum (Birmingham Coal Barons president) 24
Beaumont, Clarence "Ginger" 61, 73, 105, 108, 129
Becker, Beals 44, 51, 153
Beebe, Fred 47–48, 142
Bell, George "Farmer" 131
Bennett, Charlie 188
Bennett Park 188
Bergen, Bill 56–57, 111, 113
Bernhard, Bill 80
betting 68, 70, 127, 195
Beville, Monte 95
Birmingham, AL 22–24; umpire incident 23–24
Birmingham Coal Barons 22
Birmingham umpire incident 23–24

Blackburn, George "Smiling George" 12–13, 15–17
Boston Americans 57
Boston Doves: and August 19 series 127–29; and July 19 series 104–8; and July 29 series 113–16; and June 4 series 73–75; and May 20 series 57–61; and September 15 series 153–54
Boultes, Jack 105
Bowerman, Frank 58, ***59***, 73–74, 106, 153
Bransfield, Bill "Kitty" 80–81, 97
Bresnahan, Roger 62–64, 82, 104, 121–22, 136–37, 159–60; and Cubs-Giants replay game 184, 186; and Merkle controversy 164
bribery attempt 183
Bridwell, Al 65, 82, 99, 132–33, 136–37, 158–59, 161; and Cubs-Giants replay game 185–86
Briggs, Clare E. 5
Brooklyn Bridegrooms *see* Brooklyn Dodgers
Brooklyn Dodgers 165; and August 23 series 130–32; and July 6 series 94–96; and July 24 series 109–13; and June 9 series 75–78; and May 15 series 55–57; and September 25 series 166–68
Brooklyn Superbas *see* Brooklyn Dodgers
Brooklyn Trolley Dodgers *see* Brooklyn Dodgers
Brown, Mordecai 8, 87, 135–36, ***138***; as acting manager 150–52; attacked by mosquitoes 113; and Boston series (August 19) 127–29; and Boston series (July 19) 105; and Boston series (July 29) 113–16; and Boston series (June 4) 74–75; and Boston series (May 20) 61; and Boston series (September 15) 153; and Brooklyn series (August 23) 131; and Brooklyn series (July 6) 95–96; and Brooklyn series (May 15) 57; and Cincinnati series (April 14) 32; and Cincinnati

series (September 29) 171, 174; and Cubs-Giants replay game 185–86; on Cubs' National League championship 187; death of sister 108, 111; and fans 183; and game honoring Brown 202; injuries of 39; mother's illness and death 79, 88, 91; and New York series (August 8) 120; and New York series (August 27) 136–37; and New York series (July 15) 99, 101; and New York series (May 24) 64; and New York series (September 22) 159–60, 165; nicknames of 9; and Philadelphia series (August 3) 117; and Philadelphia series (August 15) 125–26; and Philadelphia series (July 10) 96–97, 99; and Philadelphia series (June 13) 78–79; and Philadelphia series (May 11) 53; and Philadelphia series (September 18) 156; and Pittsburgh series (August 12) 124; and Pittsburgh series (July 2) 91–94; and Pittsburgh series (June 1) 71; and Pittsburgh series (May 6) 52; and Pittsburgh series (October 4) 178–79; and Pittsburgh series (September 4) 143, 146; and St. Louis series (April 30) 47; and St. Louis series (June 24) 86; and St. Louis series (May 28) 66–67; and St. Louis series (September 9) 150–51; and St. Patrick's Day game 14; and Spongberg 117–18; and spring training 27–28; statistics of 61–62, 104, 138, 140; and World Series 192, 196–97

Brush, John T. 31; on Cubs' National League championship 187

Buffalo Bisons 108–9

bugs *see* fans

Burch, Al 75–76, 78, 94–95, 113

Burns, James 121

Burns, Tom 121

Byrne, Bobby 151

Cafe de Cub 147

Camnitz, Howie 44

Campbell, Billy 40

Campbell, Vincent 67; and Boston series (June 4) 74; clothing of 36; illness of 77; makes the team 25–26; moved to Springfield 78; and St. Louis series (April 18) 35–36; and spring training 9, 12, 20, 26

Cardinals *see* St. Louis Cardinals

Carns, William F. 199

Catterson, Tom 119–20

Chadwick, Henry 37–38, 43; *see also* Father Chadwick Penny Memorial Fund

Championship pennant 86

Chance, Frank, 8, *20*, 35–37, **83**, 200; and Boston series (August 19) 127–29; and Boston series (July 19) 104–5, 108; and Boston series (July 29) 114–16; and Boston series (June 4) 73, 75; and Boston series (May 20) 58; and Boston series (September 15) 153; and Brooklyn series (August 23) 130–31; and Brooklyn series (July 6) 95; and Brooklyn series (July 24) 109, 111–13; and Brooklyn series (June 9) 76, 78; and Brooklyn series (May 15) 55–57; and Brooklyn series (September 25) 168; and Cincinnati series (April 14) 31, 33–34; and Cincinnati series (April 23) 40; and Cincinnati series (September 7) 146; and Cincinnati series (September 29) 174–76; and clubhouse fistfight 71; congratulates Taft 84; contract of 150; and Cubs-Giants replay game 184–86; and Cubs-giants rivalry 123; on Cubs' National League championship 187; and deal with Evers 115; on Ebbets 182; and gambling 12; illness of 68, 150, 153; injuries of 14–16, 20–21, 46, 71, 92–94, 188; and Merkle controversy 161, 163–64; and new automobile 96; and New York series (August 27) 132–33, 136–37, 140; and New York series (August 8) 121–22; and New York series (July 15) 99, 103–4; and New York series (June 18) 82, 85; and New York series (May 24) 62; and New York series (September 22) 159–60; nickname 3; and Philadelphia series (August 3) 118–19; and Philadelphia series (August 15) 125–27; and Philadelphia series (July 10) 97–99; and Philadelphia series (June 13) 79, 82; and Philadelphia series (May 11) 53; and Philadelphia series (September 18) 156–58; and Pittsburgh series (April 29) 43–44; and Pittsburgh series (July 2) 91–93; and Pittsburgh series (June 1) 68, 71; and Pittsburgh series (May 6) 49, 51–53; and Pittsburgh series (October 4) 178–79; and Pittsburgh series (September 4) 145–46; and player changes 54–55; and St. Louis series (August 31) 141–42; and St. Louis series (June 24) 86–89; and St. Louis series (May 28) 65–66; and St. Louis series (September 9) 150, 152; and spitballs 106, 110; and Spongberg 117–18; and spring training 7–10, 12, 14, 16, 18, 24; and Springfield game 37; statistics of 31, 38, 42, 52, 61, 75, 138; suspended 130; and team cuts 25; and two-baseball incident 81; and World Series 189–92, 195, 197–98

Chappelle, Bill 154

Charles, Raymond "Chappy" 86–87, 151

Chattanooga, TN 21

Chicago Cubs *167*; and clubhouse fistfight 70–71, 80, 120; and game honoring Brown 202; and injuries 75, 77, 79, 93, 124; 1906 season 4, 7; 1907 season 4–5, 7; origin of name 57–58; player changes 54–55; and post–World Series exhibition game 200–1; rivalry with New York Giants 62, 82, 123; stranded in Buffalo 108–9; team statistics 42, 52, 61, 74–75, 104; win National League championship 186; and World Series 188–98

Index

Chicago Sunday Times 4
Chicago Tribune 3, 19, 24, 32, 37, 54, 56; on betting in stadiums 195; and clubhouse fistfight cover-up 71; on Cubs winning the World Series 198–99; on Merkle controversy 162, 174–75; on Pfiester 140; on Philadelphia series (August 15) 126; on Pittsburgh series (July 2) 93; on Reulbach 97; on Rudderham's bad calls 119; on Schulte 84; on ticket scandal 197; on trade rumors 73; on West Side crowds 177; on World Series 192
Chicago White Sox 54, 80; nickname 3; series with Detroit Tigers 181
Chicago White Stockings 19, 38
Church, Archibald 15
Cincinnati, OH 8, 30–35
Cincinnati Inquirer 31
Cincinnati Reds 87–89, 146–47, 170–76; and April 14 series 30–35; and April 23 series 38–42; beat Giants 166; and June 25 series 87–91; and September 7 series 146–47; and September 29 series 170–76
Cincinnati Times-Star 31
Clarke, Fred 43–44, 51–53, 68, 93, 124, 143, 146, 178–79
Cleveland, Grover 87
Cleveland Naps 93
clubhouse fistfight 70–71, 80, 120
Coakley, Andy 33–34, 88, 142; and Cincinnati series (September 7) 147; and Merkle controversy 163; and New York series (September 22) 165; and Philadelphia series (September 18) 157–58; and St. Louis series (September 9) 151
Cobb, Ty 19, 195–96, 198; 1907 season 5; and post–World Series exhibition game 200–1; and World Series 190–93
Collier, Willie 49
Comisky, Charles 3, 54
Connolly, Tom 189
contract negotiations: and Kling 15; and Murphy 18; and Pfiester 18, 27–28
Coogan's Bluff 158
Corn Exchange Building 42, 199–200
Corridon, Frank 98, 156
Cotton States League 8, 16–17
Coughlin, Bill 195, 198
Crandall, Doc 99–100, 159
Crane, Sam 20
Crawford, Sam 190–92, 196–98
Creamer, Joseph 183
Cub (puppy) 123–24
Cubs-Giants replay game 184
"Cubs Notes" (Dryden) 5

Dahlen, Bill 105, 107, 129
Dayton Veterans 28
Delahanty, Joe 66, 142
detectives, and betting 127

Detroit Tigers 14, 19, 29; and game honoring Brown 202; 1907 season 5, 7; and post–World Series exhibition game 200–1; series with Chicago White Sox 181; win American League championship 183; and World Series 188–98
Devlin, Art 84–85, 104, 122, 158–60, 165; and Cubs-Giants replay game 185–86
Dodgers *see* Brooklyn Dodgers
doctors in stadium 87–88
Donahue, Joe 8, 39, 128; and spring training 12, 14–15, 19, 23
Donahue, Tim 121
Donlin, Mike 63, 82, 104, 121–22, 136, 140, 159–60, 165; and Cubs-Giants replay game 185–86; and Merkle controversy 161; and New York series (June 18) 84
Donovan, Patsy 112
Donovan, "Wild Bill" 193, 195, 197–98
Dooin, Red 98, 126
Doolan, Mickey 126
Dorner, Gus 107, 114
Doscher, Jack 89
Dovey, George 57, 60
Downs, Red 191, 193, 195
Doyle, Larry 63, 82, 84–85, 101, 133, 136–37; and Cubs-Giants replay game 185
Dreyfuss, Barney 49, 53, 92, 170, 179
Drill, Lew 27
Dryden, Charles 3–4; on Brown 160; on Chance 21, 23; on Chattanooga hotel 21; on Coakley 147; on Cubs pitching staff 106; on Evans 15 96; on Fraser 173; on free time 22; on Johnstone 97; on Kroh 146, 158; on mad dog scare 24; on McGraw rumors 154; on Merkle controversy 161; on Merry Widow hats 40; on Nashville field 26; and New York Giants 4; on O'Day 36; on Pfiester's bowling 11; and *Philadelphia North American* 4; on pitching machine 46–47; on player's sox 40; on playing in the streets of Vicksburg 17; and racism 21; on railroad travel 26; and Semmens interview 11; on spitballs 106; on Steinfeldt's playing 52–53; on weather in West Baden 10; on West Side clubhouse 42; on West Side park 38
Dubuc, Jean "Chauncey" 87–88, 146, 171
Durbin, Danny Blaine "Kid" 7, 200; and Brooklyn series (July 6) 94, 96; and father 97–98; and New York series (July 15) 100; and Philadelphia series (June 13) 78; and Pittsburgh series (June 1) 71; and Rochester exhibition game 72; and St. Louis series (June 24) 88; and spring training 12, 14–15; and uniform 30

Eagan, Dick 171
Eastern League 54, 109
Ebbets, Charles 55, 110; and Merkle controversy 181–82

Egan, Dick 173
electric score boards 133–35, 160, *180*
Elkhart, IN 183
Elston, Curt 20, 25, 27, 120
Elysian Fields 37
Emslie, Bob 62, 77, 125, 131–32, 153, 156, 166; and Merkle controversy 161–63, 174
equipment: Evans' molting mitt 15; hotel registers as 95; left in Chicago 8; one-ball policy 80–81, 156; shin guards 147; and two-baseball incident 81; and umpires 95
Evans, Arthur 16, 25–26, 96; and lost pipe 15–16; and ownership confusion 48, 51, 55, 72; and St. Patrick's Day game 15; signs with South Carolina 65; and spring training 12–13, 20
Evansville, IN 27
Evers, Johnny "Crab" 8, 116, *144*; and Boston series (August 19) 127–29; and Boston series (July 19) 107; and Boston series (June 4) 73–74; and Boston series (May 20) *59*, 61; and Boston series (September 15) 153; and Brooklyn series (August 23) 130; and Brooklyn series (July 6) 96; and Brooklyn series (July 24) 109–12; and Brooklyn series (June 9) 76–77; and Brooklyn series (May 15) 55–57; and Brooklyn series (September 25) 168; and Cincinnati series (April 14) 31–32; and Cincinnati series (September 7) 146–47; and Cincinnati series (September 29) 172–73; and Cubs-Giants replay game 184, 186; deal with Chance 115; illness of 21, 47, 154–55; injuries of 67, 71, 88, 94, 96; and Merkle controversy 161–62, 165; and migraine headaches 21; and New York series (August 8) 120, 122; and New York series (August 27) 132–34, 136–37, 140; and New York series (July 15) 99–100, 104; and New York series (June 18) 84, 86; and New York series (May 24) 63; and New York series (September 22) 159–60, 165; nickname 10; and O'Day 120; and Philadelphia series (August 3) 117–19; and Philadelphia series (August 15) 126; and Philadelphia series (July 10) 98–99; and Philadelphia series (June 13) 80–81; and Philadelphia series (September 18) 157–58; and Pittsburgh series (April 29) 43–44; and Pittsburgh series (June 1) 68, 71; and Pittsburgh series (May 6) 49, 52; and Pittsburgh series (October 4) 178–79; and Pittsburgh series (September 4) 143; and St. Louis series (April 18) 35–36; and St. Louis series (August 31) 141; and St. Louis series (June 24) 88; and St. Louis series (May 28) 67; and St. Louis series (September 9) 150–51; and St. Patrick's Day game 14–15; and spring training 10, 19; statistics of 42, 52, 61, 75, 104, 138; suspended 85–86,
112–13; and Troy, NY, exhibition game 85; and Waterbury, CN, exhibition game 121; and World Series 190, 192, 195, 197
Ewing, Bob 31, 39–40
exhibition game, post–World Series 200–1
Exposition Park 49–50

fans 30; appreciative of good play 84, 165; arrested 192, 195; and betting 68, 195; and Brown 183; in Chicago 135; and Cubs 183; and Cubs-Giants replay game 184; distractions by 71; fatal falls of 102, 108, 187; and fistfights 68; and gambling 127; and heckling 34, 120, 126; and Merkle controversy 161–63; raucous behavior of 63, 104, 118, 140, 193; rudeness of 138; and sense of fair play 58–59; and spring training 27; and ticket sales 192–93; and ticket scandal 197; vocalizing of 55; young boys 183–84
Farson, John, Jr. 183
Father Chadwick Penny Memorial Fund 43–45, 48, 53, 57
Ferguson, Cecil 116
fistfights: between Cub players 70–71; between fans 68, 70
Flahery (Boston pitcher) 106
food: field's resemblance to 10; in hotels 16, 22; and injuries 13; as missiles 63; at stadiums 92, 147, 193; as weapon 18
Ft. Wayne, IN 28
foul balls 80, 121, 126, 133, 156; and Cubs-Giants replay game 185
Foxen, Billy 96–97, 99
Fraser, Chick 7, 68, 172; and Boston series (July 29) 116; and Boston series (June 4) 74; and Boston series (May 20) 58; and Brooklyn series (August 23) 130; and Brooklyn series (July 6) 94; and Brooklyn series (June 9) 76; and Brooklyn series (May 15) 55; and Cincinnati series (April 14) 33–35; and Cincinnati series (April 23) 39; and Cincinnati series (September 7) 146; and Cincinnati series (September 29) 171, 176; and New York series (June 18) 85; and New York series (May 24) 62–63; and Philadelphia series (August 15) 126–27; and Philadelphia series (May 11) 53; and Pittsburgh series (June 1) 68, 71; and Pittsburgh series (May 6) 51–52; and St. Louis series (April 30) 45; and St. Louis series (August 31) 142; and St. Louis series (June 24) 88; and St. Louis series (May 28) 65; and St. Patrick's Day game 14; and spring training 8, 16, 18; statistics of 61–62, 104, 140; and Waterbury, CN, exhibition game 120–21
free time: and Atlantic City 79, 116; in Buffalo 109; in Cincinnati 32; Dryden on 22; in Philadelphia 80; in Pittsburgh 43, 49–51; in St. Louis 36; and spring training 11–12, 14, 16–17, 27

French Lick, IN 10
Fromme, Art 35–36, 86

Ganzel, John Hackenschmidt 32–34, 39, 87, 89, 171; and West Side clubhouse 41–42
Giants *see* New York Giants
Gibson, George "Moon" 124–25, 145–46, 179
Gilbert, Billy 35, 48, 66, 87
Gill, Warren 143
Graham, George "Peaches" 74, 105, 108, 128
grandstand fire incident 20
Grant, Eddie 79, 98, 117
Greenwood Cemetery 43
Gries, Frank 192
ground-rule double 132, 137
Gunning, Delancy 95–96, 101

Hagerman, Zeriah Zequiel 128
Hamill, E.A. 183
Hanifan, Jack 105
Hanlon, Ned 94
Hanlon's Superbas 94
Hannifin, Jack 154
Harris, Charles 22–23
Hart, James 31
Hayden, Jack 154–55, 165, 168; and Brooklyn series (September 25) 168; and New York series (September 22) 159–60; and Philadelphia series (September 18) 156–58
heckling 34, 120, 126
Herrmann, Garry 145, 171; and Merkle controversy 181; and West Side clubhouse 42, 44, 48
Herzog, Charles "Buck" 65, 82, 121, 158–60, 165; and Cubs-Giants replay game 184, 186
Hillebrand, Homer 49
Hoblitzel, Dick 147
Hoboken, NJ 37
Hoelskoetter, Art 35–36, 48, 87
Hofman, Artie "Circus Solly" 7–8, 66, 136–37, **139**; and Boston series (August 19) 127–29; and Boston series (July 19) 104–7; and Boston series (July 29) 114–15; and Boston series (June 4) 73, 75; and Boston series (September 15) 153; and Brooklyn series (August 23) 130–31; and Brooklyn series (July 6) 94, 96; and Brooklyn series (July 24) 113; and Brooklyn series (June 9) 75–76, 78; and Brooklyn series (May 15) 55–57; and bus incident 28; and Cincinnati series (September 29) 173–75; and Cubs-Giants replay game 185; injuries of 32, 57, 65, 68, 108, 110; and Merkle controversy 161; and New York series (August 8) 120; and New York series (August 27) 133, 140; and New York series (July 15) 99, 104; and New York series (June 18) 84; and New York series (September 22) 158–60, 165; and Philadelphia series (August 3) 118; and Philadelphia series (August 15) 125–26;

and Philadelphia series (July 10) 97–98; and Philadelphia series (June 13) 78, 80–81; and Philadelphia series (September 18) 156–58; and Pittsburgh series (April 29) 44; and Pittsburgh series (July 2) 93; and Pittsburgh series (June 1) 68, 71; and Pittsburgh series (May 6) 52–53; and Pittsburgh series (October 4) 178–79; and player changes 54; and post–World Series exhibition game 200–1; and railroad travel 152–53; and Rochester exhibition game 72; and St. Louis series (April 30) 47; and St. Louis series (August 31) 141–42; and St. Louis series (June 24) 86, 88; and St. Louis series (September 9) 150–51; and St. Patrick's Day game 15; and spring training 15, 25; statistics of 75, 138; as utility player 109; and Waterbury, CN, exhibition game 120; and World Series 191–93, 195, 197–98
hotels: in Chattanooga 21; and defective elevators 33; food in 16, 22; Piedmont Hotel 19; Tully Hotel 188
Howard, Del 7, 74; and Birmingham umpire incident 23, 91; and Boston series (August 19) 127, 129; and Boston series (July 29) 115; and Boston series (June 4) 73, 75; and Brooklyn series (August 23) 130; and Brooklyn series (July 24) 109–13; and Brooklyn series (July 6) 94, 96; and Brooklyn series (May 15) 56; and Cincinnati series (September 29) 172–75; and Cubs-Giants replay game 185; and grandstand fire 20; and Merkle controversy 161; and New York series (August 8) 120, 122; and New York series (August 27) 132–33, 136–37; and New York series (July 15) 101; and New York series (May 24) 63; and Philadelphia series (August 15) 125–26; and Philadelphia series (August 3) 118; and Philadelphia series (July 10) 98–99; and Philadelphia series (September 18) 156–57; and Pittsburgh series (August 12) 124; and Pittsburgh series (July 2) 91, 93; and Pittsburgh series (June 1) 68; and Pittsburgh series (October 4) 178–79; and Rochester exhibition game 72; and St. Louis series (April 30) 45, 48; and St. Louis series (August 31) 142; and St. Louis series (June 24) 86–89, 91; and St. Louis series (May 28) 65–67; and St. Louis series (September 9) 149, 151; and St. Patrick's Day game 14; and spring training 11, 14–15, 17, 25; and Springfield game 37; statistics of 74, 138; and Waterbury, CN, exhibition game 120–21
Hudson, Willie 102, 108
Huggins, Miller 33–34, 39, 52, 147
Hummel, John 76, 94, 96, 112, 131, 166

Indianapolis Indians 28
injuries: during ballgame 67–68, 72, 82,

Index

87–88, 96; during practice 10, 16; to fans 146; inflicted by fans 186; inflicted by fellow players 70–72; mosquito inflicted 113; and seat cushions 146; self-inflicted 13, 32; trainer inflicted 11
Isbell, Frank 48, 51

Jackson, MS 16
Jackson Senators 16
Jennings, Hughie 13, 171, 195; battle cry of 188; and World Series 189–91
J.G. Taylor Spink Award 4
Johnson, Ban 145; and ticket scandal 200
Johnstone, Jim 65, 97, 101, 125, 156; and Cubs-Giants replay game 183–85
Jones, Davy 192, 195
Jordan, Tim 56, 76–77, 95, 110–12, 131

Kane, John 171–72, 179
Karger, Ed 66, 73, 106
Kelley, Joe 58, 73, 153
Killian, Ed 189–90
Klawitter, Al 14
Klem, Bill 65, 78, 82, 84–85, 87–88, 105, 107–8; and bad calls 85; and Cubs-Giants replay game 183–85; and two-baseball incident 81; and World Series 189, 196
Kling, Johnny 7, **50**; and billiards 9, 51, 98; and Boston series (August 19) 128–29; and Boston series (July 19) 105; and Boston series (July 29) 115–16; and Boston series (June 4) 73–75; and Boston series (September 15) 153; and Brooklyn series (August 23) 130; and Brooklyn series (July 24) 112–13; and Brooklyn series (June 9) 75–77; and Brooklyn series (May 15) 56; and Brooklyn series (September 25) 168; and Cincinnati series (April 14) 31–33; and Cincinnati series (September 29) 175; and contract negotiations 15; and Cubs-Giants replay game 184; illness of 47; injuries of 92, 98, 109; and Merkle controversy 163; and New York series (August 8) 120–22; and New York series (August 27) 132, 135, 137, 140; and New York series (July 15) 103–4; and New York series (June 18) 85; and New York series (May 24) 63; and New York series (September 22) 158–60, 165; and Philadelphia series (August 3) 117; and Philadelphia series (August 15) 125; and Philadelphia series (June 13) 80; and Philadelphia series (September 18) 155–57; and Pittsburgh series (April 29) 44; and Pittsburgh series (July 2) 91–92; and Pittsburgh series (June 1) 68; and Pittsburgh series (May 6) 51; and Pittsburgh series (October 4) 178; and St. Louis series (June 24) 88–89, 91; and St. Louis series (May 28) 65; and St. Louis series (September 9) 150–51; and spring training 12, 15, 18, 20, 22, 26, 28; statistics of 42, 52, 75, 138; and World Series 191, 195–98
Kling, Mrs. (wife of J. Kling) 25
Knabe, Otto "Dutch" 80–81, 117–18, 155, 157
A Knight for a Day (musical) 36
Konetchy, Ed 66–67, 142, 149, 151
Kroh, Floyd "Kid" 119, 127, 131, 200; and Cincinnati series (September 7) 146; and Merkle controversy 161; and Philadelphia series (September 18), 157–58
Kuhn, Charlie 8, 38, 57; and ducks 41; and World Championship Banner 65, 71–72
Kuhn, Lenora 43

LaChance, George "Candy" 121
Ladies Day 53–54, 74, 105
Lajoie, Larry 97
Lardner, Ring 3
Leach, Tommy 43–44, 49, 51, 53, 71, 124, 143, 146, 178–79
league standings 62, 90, **100**, **114**, 130, 142, 152, 155, 166, 171, 173, 176
Leech, Tommy 92
Leher, Franz 25
Leifield, Lefty 44, 49, 124, 145
Lewis, Phil 56–57, 76–77, 94, 96
Lindaman, Vive 73, 105, 153
Lobert, Hans 33–34, 89, 172
Ludwig, Bill 66–67, 151
Lumley, Harry 96, 109, 112, 131
Lundgren, Carl "Lundy" 8; and Boston series (July 19) 105; and Boston series (July 29) 116; and Brooklyn series (July 24) 111–12; and Brooklyn series (June 9) 77; and Cincinnati series (April 14) 33–34; and Cincinnati series (April 23) 40; and New York series (June 18) 82, 84; and Philadelphia series (August 15) 126–27; and Philadelphia series (July 10) 98; and Philadelphia series (May 11) 53; and Pittsburgh series (July 2) 92; and St. Louis series (April 18) 37; and St. Louis series (June 24) 88; and St. Louis series (May 28) 65–67; and spring training 17, 22, 26, 28; statistics of 104, 140
Lush, Johnny 142, 151
Lynchburg, VA 51
Lyons, James 202

Mack, Bill 76, 85, 99, 117
mad dog scare 24–25
Maddox, Nick 145
Magee, Sherry 80, 118
Malarkey, Bill 64
Maloney, Billy 56, 76–77, 95
Marietta, OH 25
Markbreit, Leopold 31
Marshall, Bill "Doc" 66–67, 78, 94; and Brooklyn series (July 6) 94; and Brooklyn series (July 24) 109; and Brooklyn series

(June 9) 77; and Merkle controversy 161; and New York series (June 18) 84–85; and Pittsburgh series (July 2) 92–94; and Pittsburgh series (June 1) 68; and Rochester exhibition game 72; and St. Louis series (August 31) 141; as scout 115; and Troy, NY, exhibition game 85; and Waterbury, CN, exhibition game 120
Mathewson, Christy 62, 64, 84–85, 121–22, 136–37, 157, 160, 165; called from clubhouse 100–1; and Cubs-Giants replay game 184–85; on Cubs' National League championship 187; rumors about 174; statistics of 104
Mattern, Al 153–54
McBride, Henry T. 187
McCarthy, Tom 105, 115
McCloskey, John 46, 66; and West Side clubhouse 44
McConnell, George 109
McCormick, Harry "Moose" 159–61; and Cubs-Giants replay game 185–86; and Merkle controversy 162
McCormick, Jack 11
McGann, Dan 58, 73, 129
McGinnity, Joe "Iron Man" 63, 101, 159, 184; and Merkle controversy 161
McGraw, John 13, 62–63, 100–1, 121, 165; and Cubs-giants rivalry 123; on Cubs' National League championship 187; and illegal maneuvers 85; intimidation tactics 157; and Merkle controversy 163, 165; rumors about 154; and September 22 series 159
McIntire, Harry 75–76, 113
McIntyre, Matty 190, 198
McKinloch, George A. 94
McLean, Larry 33–35, 171
McPartlin, Frank 121
McQuillen, George 54, 78–79, 82, 97, 117, 125, 155, 157–58
Memphis Turtles 24–25
Meridian, MS 8, 17–18
Meridian White Ribbons 17–18
Merkle, Fred 84, 159–60; and Cubs-Giants replay game 184; and Merkle controversy 161; nickname 3
Merkle controversy 5, 161–62, *164*, *175*; and Cubs-Giants replay game 184; tie game replay ordered 181
Merry Widow hats 25, 36, *41*, 48, 70–71, 138
Mitchell, Mike 33, 171–72
Molesworth (Birmingham player) 22
Montgomery, AL 18–19
Montgomery Climbers 18–19
Moran, Herbie 153–54
Moran, Pat 7, 11, 72, 99–100; and Boston series (August 19) 129; and Boston series (July 19) 105, 107; and Boston series (July 29) 114–15; and Boston series (June 4) 75; and Brooklyn series (August 23) 131; and Brooklyn series (July 6) 95–96; and Brooklyn series (July 24) 110; and Brooklyn series (June 9) 76–77; gives puppy to Schulte 123; and New York series (July 15) 99, 101, 104; and Pittsburgh series (August 12) 124; and Pittsburgh series (July 2) 93; and Pittsburgh series (June 1) 68; and Pittsburgh series (May 6) 53; and St. Louis series (April 30) 47–48; and St. Louis series (August 31) 141; and spring training 8, 17, 20; and Springfield game 37; statistics of 138; and Troy, NY, exhibition game 85; and Waterbury, CN, exhibition game 120
More, Forrest 128
Morris, Walter 141
mosquitoes 111
motion pictures 195
Mowrey, Mike 171
Mullin, George 196
Murdock, Wilbur 151
Murphy, Charles 8; as bad luck 123–24; and Birmingham umpire incident 24; and Cincinnati series (April 14) 30–31; and contract negotiations 18; denies trade rumors 66, 73; and Evans' ownership confusion 51, 55; and field tarps 50, 53, 55, 170; files Merkle controversy protest 162; and Hayden 155; illness of 196; and Merkle controversy 168, 173–74, 181–82; and Pittsburgh series (July 2) 92; and player deals 54–55, 106, 108, 110–11, 119–20, 127–28, 142; protests O'Day call 143–44; responds to cushion throwing 63; and St. Louis series (April 18) 35; and salary dispute 120; and spring training 16; supports Taft 57; and team cuts 25; and ticket scandal 197, 199–201; and West Side clubhouse 42–44, 47–48; and World Championship Banner 72; and World Championship Banner Ceremony 60–61
Murray, Billy 54, 82, 142
Murray, John "Red" 47, 87
Myers, "Sham" 13

Nashville, TN 26–27
Nashville Volunteers 26
National Commission 51, 145, 187–88, 200
National League 19, 57; rules of 37, 52; and Spalding 38
National League Board of Directors, and Merkle controversy 181
National League constitution, and Merkle controversy 162
National League Rules Committee, and spitballs 110
Needham, Tom "Deerfoot" 64, 163
Neuer, John "Tacks" 123–24, 127
New York Evening Herald 4
New York Giants 14, *164*; and August 8 series 119–23; and August 27 series 132–40; and

220 Index

Dryden 4; and July 15 series 99–104; and June 18 series 82–86; and May 24 series 62–65; rivalry with Chicago Cubs 62, 82, 123; and September 22 series 158–65; and West Side clubhouse 42
New York Highlanders 19, 109; *see also* New York Yankees
New York Times 37
New York Yankees: comparison to as an insult 165; *see also* New York Highlanders
Nichols, Art 121
nicknames 3, 9, 54

O'Brien, Mike 23
O'Conner, Patrick 44
O'Day, Hank, *163*; and Boston series (June 4) 73; and Cincinnati series (April 14) 31–32, 34; and Cincinnati series (April 23) 39–40; and Cincinnati series (September 7) 146; and Evers 120; and Merkle controversy 161–64, 175; and New York series (August 8) 120, 123; and New York series (August 27) 132–33, 135; and New York series (July 15) 101; and New York series (June 18) 82, 84; and New York series (May 24) 62, 64; and Philadelphia series (August 3) 118–19; and Philadelphia series (August 15) 126; and Pirates second base call 150; and Pittsburgh series (May 6) 49, 52; and Pittsburgh series (October 4) 177–79; and Pittsburgh series (September 4) 143–44; and post–World Series exhibition game 200–1; and St. Louis series (April 18) 35–36; and St. Louis series (April 30) 44–45; and St. Louis series (September 9) 149–51; and World Series 189
Official Baseball Guide 37
Ohio River 50
O'Leary, Charley 190–91, 193, 195–96, 198
Olsen, Osborne T. 30–31
Olympic Games 98
Orchestra Hall 160
O'Rourke, Patsy 35, 48, 66
Osborne, Fred 80, 157–58
Overall, Orval 8, *194*; and Boston series (August 19) 127–28; and Boston series (July 19) 105–8; and Boston series (July 29) 115; and Boston series (May 20) 61; and Brooklyn series (August 23) 130–31; and Brooklyn series (July 24) 113; and Brooklyn series (September 25) 166; and Cincinnati series (April 14) 31–32; and Cincinnati series (April 23) 39–40; and Cincinnati series (September 29) 171–72; injuries of 67, 78–79; and new automobile 98, 104; and New York series (August 8) 121–22; and New York series (July 15) 99, 104; and New York series (September 22) 158–59; and Philadelphia series (August 3) 118; and Philadelphia series (July 10) 97–98; and Philadelphia series (June 13) 81; and Philadelphia series (May 11) 53–54; and Philadelphia series (September 18) 155, 157; and Pittsburgh series (July 2) 92; and Pittsburgh series (September 4) 145; and post–World Series exhibition game 200–1; and St. Louis series (April 18) 36–37; and St. Louis series (April 30) 47; and St. Louis series (August 31) 141; and St. Louis series (June 24) 89; and St. Louis series (May 28) 67; and St. Louis series (September 9) 149, 152; and St. Patrick's Day game 14; and spring training 18, 24; statistics of 62, 104, 140; wife's illness 122, 126–27; and World Series 191, 193, 195, 197–98
overturned bus incident 28
Owens, Clarence "Brick" 166, 168
owners, cheapness of 82; *see also* Murphy, Charles

Palace of the Fans 30, 171
Panhandle Pete (play) 150
Parker, T.B. 23
Paskert, George "Dode" 33–34, 89, 172
Pastorious, Jim 78, 111
Pattee, Harry 56, 76–77, 95
pennant race *107*, *148–49*, 176
Pfiester, Jack "Jack the Giant Killer" 8, 103, *139*; and bet with Chance 84; and Boston series (August 19) 127; and Boston series (July 29) 115; and Boston series (June 4) 73; and Boston series (May 20) 61; and Boston series (September 15) 153–54; and bowling injury 11; and Brooklyn series (August 23) 130; and Brooklyn series (July 6) 96; and Brooklyn series (July 24) 109; and Brooklyn series (June 9) 75–76; and Brooklyn series (May 15) 56; and contract negotiations 18, 27–28; and Cubs-Giants replay game 184–85; family of 10; injuries of 155, 170–71; and New York series (August 8) 123; and New York series (August 27) 132–33, 140; and New York series (July 15) 99; and New York series (June 18) 84; and New York series (May 24) 62–65; and New York series (September 22) 160–61; nickname 133, 140; and Philadelphia series (August 15) 125; and Philadelphia series (July 10) 97; and Philadelphia series (June 13) 80–81; and Philadelphia series (May 11) 53; and Pittsburgh series (April 29) 44; and Pittsburgh series (July 2) 92–93; and Pittsburgh series (June 1) 68; and Pittsburgh series (May 6) 53; and Pittsburgh series (September 4) 145–46; and St. Louis series (April 18) 35; and St. Louis series (August 31) 143; and St. Louis series (June 24) 89; and St. Louis series (September 9) 150; and signal stealing 62; and spring training 9–10; statistics

of 104, 140; wife's illness 13, 18; and World Series 196
Phelps, Ed 145–46
Philadelphia North American 4
Philadelphia Phillies: and August 15 series 125–27; and August 3 series 116–19; and July 10 series 96–99; and June 13 series 78–82; and May 11 series 53–55; and September 18 series 154–58
Phillies *see* Philadelphia Phillies
Piedmont Hotel 19
Pirates *see* Pittsburgh Pirates
pitching machine 46
Pittsburgh Pirates: beat Giants 158; eliminated from pennant race 179; Pittsburgh series (April 29) 43–44; Pittsburgh series (August 12) 124–27; Pittsburgh series (July 2) 91–94; Pittsburgh series (June 1) 68–72; Pittsburgh series (May 6) 48–53; Pittsburgh series (October 4) 176–79; Pittsburgh series (September 4) 143–46; and West Side clubhouse 42
policemen, as Murphy's guests 137–38
Polo Grounds 119, 158; alcohol served at 166; Dryden barred from 4
presidential politics 135
Providence, RI, exhibition game 78
Pulliam, Harry 30, 95; and Baseball Writer's Association of America 122; and Boston series (August 19) 127; and Merkle controversy 162–63, 166, 168–70, 173–75, 181; and Pirates second base call 145, 150; and salary dispute 120; suspends Chance 130; and West Side clubhouse 42, 44, 47; and World Championship Banner Ceremony 60

racism 24; and Dryden 21
railroad travel, 12, 18, 26, 152–53, 182–83, 196; Dryden on 26; and game-time limits 106; and theft 37; and Williams 93, 108–9, 125
Raymond, Charles "Bugs" 37, 66, 106, 141
Red (Cub's batboy) 145
Reese, John "Bonesetter" 108, 110, 170–71
reporters 7; assaulted by Tinker 18; *see also* Dryden, Charles; Sanborn, Ellis
Reulbach, Ed "Big Ed" 8, **169**; and Boston series (August 19) 128; and Boston series (July 19) 105; and Boston series (July 29) 115; and Boston series (June 4) 74; and Boston series (May 20) 58, 61; and Boston series (September 15) 154; and Brooklyn series (August 23) 130–31; and Brooklyn series (July 6) 95; and Brooklyn series (July 24) 109–11; and Brooklyn series (June 9) 78; and Brooklyn series (May 15) 56; and Brooklyn series (September 25) 168; and Cincinnati series (April 14) 33; and Cincinnati series (April 23) 40; and Cincinnati series (September 7) 147; and Cincinnati series (September 29) 173, 176; and New York series (August 27) 140; and New York series (July 15) 99–100, 103; and New York series (June 18) 82; and New York series (May 24) 64; and Philadelphia series (August 3) 118–19; and Philadelphia series (August 15) 126; and Philadelphia series (July 10) 97–98; and Philadelphia series (May 11) 53; and Philadelphia series (September 18) 156; and pitching control problems 10, 78, 82; and Pittsburgh series (August 12) 124; and Pittsburgh series (July 2) 93; and Pittsburgh series (June 1) 68, 71; and Pittsburgh series (September 4) 144; and railroad travel 93, 153; and Rochester exhibition game 72; and St. Louis series (April 18) 35; and St. Louis series (April 30) 47–48; and St. Louis series (August 31) 142; and St. Louis series (June 24) 86, 88, 91; and St. Louis series (May 28) 67; and St. Louis series (September 9) 151; and St. Patrick's Day game 15; and spring training 9–10, 12, 16, 21; and Springfield game 37; statistics of 104, 138, 140; and Troy, NY, exhibition game 85; and World Series 189–91
Richie, Lew 156
Richter, Francis C. 94
Rigler, Charles "Cy" 43–44, 56, 58, 95, 110–12, 121, 127, 141;and Pittsburgh series (October 4) 177–79
Ritchey, Claude 58, 73, 105, 129
Ritter, Lew 75
Robison, Stanley 36, 106, 108; and West Side clubhouse 44, 48
Robison Field 36
Rochester, NY 72
Rosedale, IN 9, 27, 202
Rossman, Claude 190–93, 195–98
Rowan, Jack 147
Rucker, George "Napoleon" or "Nap" 76, 95–96, 112
Rudderham, John 89, 117–19, 127, 129; and Chance suspension 130; released 141
Rudderham, John E. 43–44, 58–59
Russell, Lillian 14
Ryan, Jimmy 18–19, 147

St. Louis, MO 35
St. Louis Cardinals: and April 18 series 35–37; and April 30 series 44–48; and August 31 series 141–43; and June 24 series 86–87; and May 28 series 65–67; and September 9 series 147, 149–52; team statistics 52
St. Patrick's Day game 14
San Francisco Examiner 4
Sanborn, Ellis (E.I.) "Cy" 3, 54; and clubhouse fistfight cover-up 71–72, 120; on Cubs-Dodgers games 55–56; on Cubs-Giants rivalry 123; on Cubs' National League championship 186–87; on Cubs

winning the World Series 198–99; on doctors 87; on Kroh 131; on one-umpire system 81–82; on Pfiester 140; on Pirates second base call 144; on Schulte 82; on trade rumors 73; on weather 119; on World Championship Banner Ceremony 60–61
Schaefer, Herman "Germany" 190, 195, 198
Schlei, George "Admiral" 33–34, 40
Schmidt (Detroit Tigers catcher) 191
Schmit, Frederick "Germany" or "Crazy" 17–18
Schulte, Frank "Wildfire" 7, 75, 91, 109; attire of 17; and Boston series (July 19) 105; and Boston series (September 15) 153; and Brooklyn series (August 23) 130–31; and Brooklyn series (June 9) 75; and Brooklyn series (May 15) 56; and Brooklyn series (September 25) 168; and Cincinnati series (April 14) 31, 33–34; and Cincinnati series (September 7) 147; and Cincinnati series (September 29) 171; and Cubs-Giants replay game 184–86; and horse racing 11; and New York series (June 18) 82, 84; and New York series (May 24) 63–64; and New York series (September 22) 158; nickname 14; and Philadelphia series (August 15) 127; and Philadelphia series (July 10) 98–99; and Philadelphia series (June 13) 79–81; and Philadelphia series (September 18) 156–57; and Pittsburgh series (May 6) 51, 53; and Pittsburgh series (October 4) 178; and Rochester exhibition game 72; and St. Louis series (April 18) 35–37; and St. Louis series (April 30) 48; and St. Louis series (August 31) 142; and St. Louis series (June 24) 87; and St. Louis series (May 28) 67; and St. Louis series (September 9) 149–51; and spring training 9, 14, 25; statistics of 42, 52, 75, 138; and World Series 190, 192, 195, 197
seat cushions, as missiles 104, 133, **134**, 140, 146
second base, touching 143–44
Selee, Frank 8, 58
Semmens, A. Bert "Soldier" 98, 200; and Birmingham umpire incident 23–24; and cannon ball injury 11; and Cincinnati series (April 14) 31; and Cincinnati series (April 23) 39; and clubhouse fistfight 71; interview with Dryden 11; and railroad travel 93; and roller-skating 15; and spring training 8; treating players 16, 74, 94, 113, 153, 170; and West Side clubhouse 48
Seymour, Jim "Cy" 63–64, 82, 85, 104, 122, 136–37, 140, 159; and Cubs-Giants replay game 185–86
Shannon, Bill "Spike" 63, 146
Shaw, Al 141
Sheckard, Jimmy "Sheck" 7, **69**; and Boston series (August 19) 127; and Boston series (July 19) 108; and Boston series (July 29) 114; and Brooklyn series (August 23) 131; and Brooklyn series (July 6) 94, 96; and Brooklyn series (July 24) 111; and Brooklyn series (May 15) 56; and Cincinnati series (April 14) 31, 33–34; and Cincinnati series (September 7) 146; and Cincinnati series (September 29) 171, 173; and clubhouse fistfight 70–72, 74; and Cubs-Giants replay game 184, 186; injuries of 65, 68; and New York series (August 8) 122; and New York series (August 27) 133, 136–37, 140; and New York series (July 15) 101, 103–4; and Philadelphia series (August 3) 119; and Philadelphia series (August 15) 125; and Pittsburgh series (August 12) 124; and Pittsburgh series (June 1) 68, 71; and Pittsburgh series (May 6) 53; and Pittsburgh series (October 4) 178–79; and St. Louis series (April 30) 48; and St. Louis series (August 31) 142; and St. Louis series (June 24) 88; and St. Patrick's Day game 15; and spring training 12, 17, 25; statistics of 42, 75, 138; as temporary manager 14; and World Series 190–93, 195, 197
Sheehan, Tommy 76–77, 95, 111–13
Sheridan, John 189
Shippy (Chicago police chief) 192
"Sigma Outfield" 7
signal stealing 62
Slagle, Jimmy "Rabbit" 7, 54, 87, 93; and Boston series (July 19) 108; and Boston series (July 29) 113–16; and Boston series (June 4) 74; and Boston series (May 20) 58–59, **60**; and Boston series (September 15) 153–54; and Brooklyn series (August 23) 130; and Brooklyn series (July 6) 94; and Brooklyn series (July 24) 111–12; and Brooklyn series (June 9) 76–78; and Brooklyn series (May 15) 55; and Cincinnati series (April 14) 31; and Cincinnati series (April 23) 40; and Cincinnati series (September 7) 146–47; and New York series (August 8) 121–22; and New York series (July 15) 99, 101, 103; and New York series (May 24) 63–64; and Philadelphia series (August 3) 117, 119; and Philadelphia series (August 15) 125–26; and Philadelphia series (July 10) 98–99; and Philadelphia series (June 13) 80, 82; and Philadelphia series (September 18) 155–56; and Pittsburgh series (June 1) 71; and Pittsburgh series (May 6) 49; and Pittsburgh series (September 4) 143, 145; and Rochester exhibition game 72; and St. Louis series (April 30) 48; and St. Louis series (August 31) 142; and St. Louis series (June 24) 86, 89; and St. Louis series (September 9) 149–50, 152; and St. Patrick's Day game 15; and spring training 8–10, 24–25; statistics

of 42, 52, 75, 138; and trade rumors 73; and Troy, NY, exhibition game 85
Smith, L.D. 202
South End Grounds 116
Southern League 19
Spade, Bob 88–89
Spalding, Albert G. 38, 43
Sparks, Tully 80, 98, 126, 157
Spirit of the Times 37
spitballs 106, 110
Spongberg, Carl 111, 117–18; and Boston series (July 29) 113, 115–16
spring training 7–29; and conditioning 10–11; and free time 12, 14, 16–17; game results 29; schedule 9; and weather 9–12, 16; and West Baden, IN 7–12
Springfield, IL 37
Springfield Senators 37
stadium culture 24–25, 30, 132; and Sunday baseball 28; and West Side Park 38–39
stadiums: first field tarp 49–50; and unusual landscaping 49; *see also* names of stadiums
Steinfeldt, Harry "Steiny" 8, 85, 99, 109, 119; and Birmingham umpire incident 23–24, 91; and Boston series (August 19) 128–29; and Boston series (July 19) 105–6; and Boston series (July 29) 114; and Boston series (June 4) 73; and Boston series (September 15) 154; and Brooklyn series (August 23) 130; and Brooklyn series (July 6) 96; and Brooklyn series (July 24) 109–12; and Brooklyn series (June 9) 75–76; and Brooklyn series (May 15) 55–57; and Brooklyn series (September 25) 168; and Cincinnati series (April 14) 31, 33–34; and Cincinnati series (April 23) 40; and Cincinnati series (September 29) 171, 173; and Cubs-Giants replay game 184–86; and Merkle controversy 161; and New York series (August 8) 121–22; and New York series (August 27) 132–34, 136–37; and New York series (May 24) 63, 65; and New York series (September 22) 158–60, 165; and Philadelphia series (August 3) 117–19; and Philadelphia series (August 15) 125, 127; and Philadelphia series (July 10) 98; and Philadelphia series (June 13) 79, 82; and Philadelphia series (September 18) 157–58; and Pittsburgh series (April 29) 44; and Pittsburgh series (August 12) 124; and Pittsburgh series (July 2) 91–92; and Pittsburgh series (May 6) 51–53; and Pittsburgh series (October 4) 178; and Rochester exhibition game 72; and St. Louis series (April 18) 37; and St. Louis series (April 30) 45; and St. Louis series (August 31) 141; and St. Louis series (June 24) 88–89; and St. Louis series (May 28) 66; and St. Louis series (September 9) 150–51; and spring training 9, 12, 18; statistics of 42, 52, 74–75, 138; and Troy, NY, exhibition game 85; and World Series 190–92, 196–98
Storke, Allan 178–79
Streator Reds (semi-pro team) 95
Summers, Ed 191–92, 197
Sunday baseball 19, 28, 36, 75, 79, 85, 88, 110, 116, 145, 156
Sweeney, Bill 107, 129

Taft, Charles P. 31
Taft, William Howard 57, 84
Taylor, Jack 7
Taylor, Luther "Dummy" 63
Tenney, Fred 63, 82, 85, 99, 101, 104, 133, 136–37, 158–59; and Cubs-Giants replay game 184–86
Terre Haute, IN 27, 202
Terre Haute Hottentots 27
Terre Haute Star 202
Thomas, Roy 92, 124, 178–79
Three Eyes League 78, 128
ticket scandal 197, 199–201
Tinker, Joe 8, *102–3*; assaults reporter 18; and Boston series (August 19) 127–29; and Boston series (July 19) 107–8; and Boston series (July 29) 113–16; and Boston series (May 20) 61; and Boston series (September 15) 154; and Brooklyn series (August 23) 131; and Brooklyn series (July 6) 94, 96; and Brooklyn series (July 24) 109–11, 113; and Brooklyn series (June 9) 77; and Brooklyn series (May 15) 56–57; and Brooklyn series (September 25) 166; and Cincinnati series (April 14) 31–32; and Cincinnati series (April 23) 40; and Cincinnati series (September 7) 146; and Cincinnati series (September 29) 171, 176; and Cubs-Giants replay game 185–86; injuries of 13, 21, 142; and lawsuit 130; and Merkle controversy 161; and New York series (August 8) 120, 122; and New York series (August 27) 132–33, 135–37, 140; and New York series (July 15) 100–1, 103–4; and New York series (June 18) 85; and New York series (May 24) 63–64; and New York series (September 22) 158–60, 165; and Philadelphia series (August 3) 117–19; and Philadelphia series (August 15) 125–27; and Philadelphia series (July 10) 97; and Philadelphia series (June 13) 80; and Philadelphia series (September 18) 155–56; and Pittsburgh series (April 29) 43; and Pittsburgh series (August 12) 124–25; and Pittsburgh series (July 2) 93; and Pittsburgh series (May 6) 49; and Pittsburgh series (October 4) 179; and Pittsburgh series (September 4) 144, 146; and Rochester exhibition game 72; and St. Louis series (April 18) 35; and St. Louis series (April 30) 48; and St. Louis series

(June 24) 88–89, 91; and St. Louis series (May 28) 67; and St. Louis series (September 9) 151; and St. Patrick's Day game 15; and spring training 13, 16, 24; statistics of 42, 52, 75, 104; and Troy, NY, exhibition game 85; and World Series 191–93, 195–97
Titus, John "Silent John" 54, 98, 117–18, 126, 155–56
Toledo Mud Hens 21
Troy, NY, exhibition game 85
Troy Trojans 85
Tuckey, Tom 128–29
Tully Hotel 188
two-baseball incident 81

umpires: abuse of 22, 151–52, 166; and bad calls 85, 118–19, 141, 143–44; and Birmingham umpire incident 23–24; and bribery attempt 183; and Cubs-Giants rivalry 132; and equipment 95; injuries of 131–32; losing track of count 105; and Merkle controversy 164; numbers per game 62; and one-umpire policy 80–81; and Pittsburgh series (April 29) 44; and questionable calls 17–18, 22, 56, 58–59, 61, 81, 89, 117, 129; and team rivalries 82; and two-baseball incident 80–81; and World Series 189; World Series umpiring system 145; *see also* O'Day, Hank
uniforms 30, 40; and New York Giants 123, 156–57; shoes 18

Vaughn, Harry 91
Vicksburg, MS 8, 12–16
Vicksburg Hill Billies 12
Virginia League 10

Wagner, Honus "Hans" 43–44, 51–53, 71, 91–92, 124, 142–43, 146, 178–79; statistics of 138
Walsh, Martin 11, 25, 51; and spring training 10–11, 13–15, 19–20
Washington Nationals 19, 27
Washington Park 75, 111, 166; repairs to 110
Washington Senators 3
Waterbury, CN, exhibition game 120–21
weather: and Brooklyn series (July 24) 110; and Cincinnati series (April 14) 32; and New York series (August 8) 123; and Philadelphia series (August 3) 119; and Philadelphia series (June 13) 79; and Philadelphia series (May 11) 53–55; and Pittsburgh series (April 29) 43; and Pittsburgh series (May 6) 50–53; and St. Louis series (April 30) 46–47; and spring training 9–12, 16, 27–28; and World Series 189–90
Weeghman, Albert 183
Weimer, "Tornado Jake" 32; and West Side clubhouse 42
West Baden, IN 7–8
West Baden Mineral Springs Resort 8

West Side Park 3, 38–39, 59–61, 101; attendance 132–33, **135**, 176–77; and Chance statue 31; clubhouse 40–42, 44–45, 106; improvements to 8, 38, 86; rooftops of nearby buildings closed 108
West Side Rooters Club 43
Western Association 128
White, Kirby "Red" 171
Wildfire (play) 14
Wilhelm, Irvin "Kaiser" 77, 109–10
Williams, Charlie 28, 30, 200; and Birmingham umpire incident 24; and lost dog 48; and Merkle controversy 163; and railroad travel 93, 108–9, 125; and St. Patrick's Day game 15; and spring training 7, 12, 21; and Tinker lawsuit 130; and West Side Park 38
Willis, Vic 52–53, 68, 92, 143, 178–79
Wilson, Owen 53, 92, 145
Wiltse, George "Hooks" 64–65, 82, 99, 103, 132–33, 165; and Cubs-Giants replay game 186
Wilson, Owen 143, 179
women: as distractions 71; *see also* Ladies Day; Merry Widow hats; Russell, Lillian
World Championship Banner 65, 71–72
World Championship Banner Ceremony 57, 59–61
World Series 188–98; first game lineup 189; in 1906 4; in 1907 4–5; ticket sales 188, 192–93

Yingling, Francois Earl de Montmorency 28
Young, "Cy" 122
Young, Denton True "Cy" 57
Young, Irv 105

Zimmerman, Henry "Heinie" or "Big City" 7, **70**; and Boston series (August 19) 129; and Boston series (July 19) 105, 108; and Boston series (May 20) 61; and Boston series (September 15) 154; and Brooklyn series (August 23) 130; and Brooklyn series (July 6) 94, 96; and Brooklyn series (July 24) 112; and Cincinnati series (April 14) 32; and clubhouse fistfight 70–72, 74, 80; injuries of 11, 13, 71, 156, 182–83; and New York series (August 8) 120; and New York series (July 15) 103–4; and Philadelphia series (July 10) 97–99; and Philadelphia series (September 18) 155–56; and Pittsburgh series (July 2) 92–93; and Pittsburgh series (June 1) 68, 71; and St. Louis series (August 31) 142; and St. Louis series (June 24) 88–89; and St. Louis series (May 28) 65, 67; and St. Louis series (September 9) 151; and St. Patrick's Day game 15; and spring training 8, 17–20; and Springfield game 37; statistics of 75, 138; and trade rumors 73; and Waterbury, CN, exhibition game 120

www.ingramcontent.com/pod-product-compliance
Ingram Content Group UK Ltd.
Pitfield, Milton Keynes, MK11 3LW, UK
UKHW041949140426
5217IPUK00014B/719